WEST
of the
REVOLUTION

WEST

of the

REVOLUTION

An Uncommon History

of 1776

CLAUDIO SAUNT

W. W. Norton and Company

NEW YORK   LONDON

For information about permission to reproduce selections from
this book, write to Permissions, W. W. Norton & Company, Inc.,
500 Fifth Avenue, New York, NY 10110

For information about special discounts for bulk purchases, please contact
W. W. Norton Special Sales at specialsales@wwnorton.com or 800-233-4830

Manufacturing by Courier Westford
Book design by JAM Design
Production manager: Julia Druskin

Library of Congress Cataloging-in-Publication Data

Saunt, Claudio.
West of the Revolution : an uncommon history of 1776 / Claudio Saunt. — First edition.
    pages cm
Includes bibliographical references and index.
ISBN 978-0-393-24020-7 (hardcover)
1. United States—History—18th century. 2. America—Colonization—History.
3. America—Discovery and exploration—Spanish. 4. Europe—Colonies—America.
5. Indians of North America—History—Revolution, 1775–1783.
6. Europeans—America—History. 7. North America—Description and travel.
8. West (U.S.)—Discovery and exploration. 9. West (U.S.)—History—18th century.
I. Title. II. Title: Uncommon history of 1776.
E303.S28 2014
973.3'13—dc23

                                                         2014011360

W. W. Norton & Company, Inc.,
500 Fifth Avenue, New York, N.Y. 10110
www.wwnorton.com

W. W. Norton & Company Ltd.
Castle House, 75/76 Wells Street, London W1T 3QT

1 2 3 4 5 6 7 8 9 0

❦ CONTENTS ❧

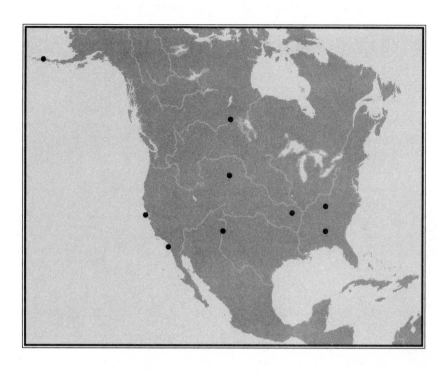

WEST
of the
REVOLUTION

"There is something very absurd, in supposing a continent to be perpetually governed by an island," declared Thomas Paine in *Common Sense*, his famous pamphlet that galvanized American revolutionaries in 1776. The war was "not the affair of a city, a county, a province, or a kingdom," he claimed, "but of a continent—of at least one eighth-part of the habitable globe." That eighth became, in the words of patriot David Ramsay, fully "a quarter of the globe," waiting to be redeemed from "tyranny and oppression." We know how the story of that redemption unfolded, even if we are sometimes hazy about the particulars. The American Revolution so dominates our understanding of the continent's early history that only four digits—1776—are enough to evoke images of periwigs, quill pens, and yellowing copies of the Declaration of Independence. Yet the colonies that formed the Continental Congress and filled the ranks of the Continental Army (paying men in Continental currency) made up only a tiny fraction of the actual continent—just under 4 percent of North America, to be more precise.[1]

In 1776, formative events were occurring not just along the Eastern Seaboard but across all of North America. In Alaska's Aleutian Islands, Russians were destroying Aleut villages. In San Francisco, native residents and Europeans made contact for the first time ever. Down the coast in San Diego, Kumeyaay Indians rose up against the Spanish, and participants spent months afterward dealing with the consequences of the failed revolt. That same year, the Sioux discovered the Black Hills. To many Americans, these stories are almost entirely unknown, as surprising and unpredictable as events that we watch transpiring in the present moment. They are the subject of *West of the Revolution*.

I grew up in San Francisco, twenty-five hundred miles from Boston and the seat of the American Revolution. San Francisco did not exist when British soldiers and American Minutemen met in battle at

Lexington and Concord in April 1775. In late June 1776, a week before Congress approved the Declaration of Independence, José Joaquín Moraga built a small shelter of branches on the banks of a lagoon that the Spanish called Arroyo de los Dolores. The site became Mission Dolores, the first colonial settlement in San Francisco. While the young republic took shape on the opposite side of the continent, San Francisco moved in its own direction. In 1808, shortly before James Madison became the fourth president of the United States, Ivan Kuskov, an employee of the Russian-American Company, secretly buried a copper plate in San Francisco that read, "Land belonging to Russia." Four years later, he would found the Russian outpost of Fort Ross less than one hundred miles to the north.[2]

As a child who was more interested in music than in the past, I remained ignorant of the history of my birthplace for many years. My summer music camp was located on the Russian River, which drains into the Pacific Ocean a few miles south of Fort Ross. For too long, I puzzled over the name: was it the Rushing River or the Russian River? The "Rushing River" seemed more plausible. As far as I understood, the Russians had nothing to do with California, and dropping the final "g" made perfect sense to a would-be jazz musician. After all, my favorite Miles Davis albums at the time were the classic LPs *Workin'*, *Steamin'*, *Relaxin'*, and *Cookin'*. Of course the river must have been "Rushin'."

There is further evidence of my historical ignorance. When I was eight and the Bicentennial of the United States rolled around, I was delighted to go on a field trip to see the world's largest birthday cake, which was illustrated with scenes from the American Revolution and had been trucked across the continent to San Francisco. At least, that is how I remember it. Reading through the historical record, I find a slightly different account of the festivities. The three-tiered, six-sided, revolving cake was indeed enormous, rising thirty feet (not counting the five-foot phoenix mounted on the top), and weighing in at 17.5 tons. But the monstrosity never crossed the continent, and its eighteen panels did not illustrate the Revolution, as I had remembered. The cake, made by a local pastry chef to celebrate San Francisco's own bicentennial, instead commemorated events from the city's history, beginning with Francis Drake's discovery of the bay and including the arrival of the Spanish. San Francisco's history was at such odds with the narrative being celebrated for the national Bicentennial that my fourth-grade imagination turned the cake into a tribute to events in Boston, Philadelphia, and elsewhere along the East Coast.[3]

My misconceptions about the Russian River and San Francisco's bicentennial surely suggest that I did not pay enough attention in elementary school, but they are also symptomatic of a broader phenomenon. Americans are generally unacquainted with the early history of their continent beyond the thirteen British colonies that formed the United States. Like the foreshortened continent in Saul Steinberg's famous *New Yorker* cover "View of the World from 9th Avenue" (Figure 1), early America recedes rapidly from our historical consciousness as we look west, vanishing at a horizon only a few hundred miles from the Atlantic Coast.

In contrast to that provincial perspective, it is possible to envision early America as stretching from one coast to the other and encompassing all the people who lived there. This exciting prospect reveals vast lands and multitudes of North Americans whose stories are unfamiliar to us. We have an intimate connection to those lands; we live on them, yet know little about their early history.[4]

West of the Revolution explores nine American places in 1776. The settings are diverse, stretching from the Aleutian Islands to San Diego, and from the Florida Gulf Coast to the Saskatchewan River. (I have chosen to ignore present-day national borders by including Cumberland House, located in what is now the Canadian prairies, and by venturing with a party of eighteenth-century Indians across the Straits of Florida to Havana.) Yet there are surprising connections between these places, sometimes through trade networks that intersected in distant warehouses, at other times through imperial administrators who plotted far-flung colonies on maps that contained more fiction than fact.

Of the many points of connection, two in particular stand out and serve to organize the chapters that follow. The first is a remote

FIGURE 1 Saul Steinberg, "View of the World from 9th Avenue" (1976).
© The Saul Steinberg Foundation/Artists Rights Society (ARS), New York.

locale called Kyakhta, which sits today on the border between Russia and Mongolia. The city is now an amalgamation of wooden houses, Soviet-era apartment buildings, Bolshevik monuments, and crumbling Russian Orthodox churches. Two hundred fifty years ago, it was a center of international commerce that transformed North America's Pacific Coast.

The second point of connection is the Hôtel de Grinberghen on Paris's left bank, across the river from the Louvre. There, in February 1763, ministers from France, Britain, and Spain signed the Treaty of Paris, formally concluding the Seven Years' War. North American populations a thousand miles apart, occupying distinct regions and facing vastly different challenges, all felt the repercussions of the imperial negotiations in the French capital. Unrelated in so many ways, they were nonetheless linked like spokes on a wheel to the treaty signed at the Hôtel de Grinberghen.[5]

The Aleuts of the Aleutian archipelago, the Miwoks and Costanoans of northern California, the Creek Indians of the Deep South, and the other peoples who figure in this book do not have the immediate resonance of musket-bearing Boston Minutemen, but in surprising ways their stories are as pertinent to the twenty-first century as the better-known history of the American Revolution. North Americans across the continent found themselves deeply entangled in a web of environmental, political, and economic relationships that they could neither fully control nor completely understand. Long-distance trade linked the Aleuts to the Chinese nobility, though neither party knew anything about the other or grasped the impact of the exchange at the opposite end of the chain; the arrival of the Spanish in Miwok and Costanoan lands initiated a cascade of devastating ecological consequences, unintentional and largely unrecognized at the time; imperial wars halfway around the world upended the regional economy of the Creek Indians, who struggled as best they could to navigate shifting commodity flows that were unpredictable to everyone involved. Today, in an era of global trade, emerging infectious diseases, biodiversity loss, and rapid climate change—all in one way or another set off by us but beyond our complete control or comprehension—we are perhaps better prepared than ever before to understand and relate to the experiences of eighteenth-century North Americans.

In our historical imagination, we usually spend 1776 confined to the mainland British colonies. We frequent Boston's taverns and churches, follow the Continental Army down New Jersey's rutted dirt roads, and take up residence in revolutionary Williamsburg, rarely straying more than a few hundred miles from the Atlantic Coast. We scrutinize consumer practices and cultural expression; explore the lives of elites and commoners, women and men, the free and enslaved; and analyze military strategy and political rhetoric—subjects unnecessarily restricted to the Eastern Seaboard. At the same time, from the Aleutian Islands to the Arkansas River, from the Black Hills to the Deep South interior, other extraordinary stories were unfolding across North America. This book invites readers to extend their bounds and discover the continent west of the Revolution.

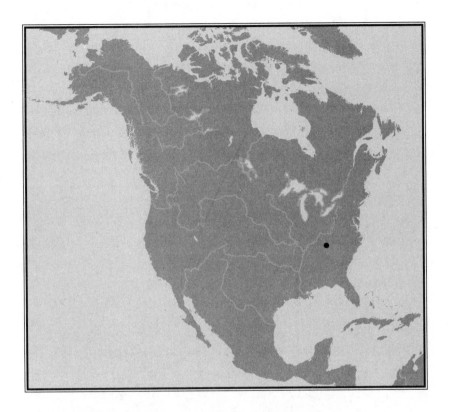

Western Speculation:
Henderson's Transylvania Colony

Three days after buying twenty-two million acres of land from the Cherokees, Richard Henderson set off to take possession of his prize. The forty-year-old North Carolinian had grandiose plans for the immense purchase, which lay "on the west side of the Mountains" and extended over most of Kentucky and part of Tennessee. He dreamed of establishing a fourteenth colony, of erecting a "palladium," whose "height and magnificence" lay "in the womb of futurity." "Equal in extent to a kingdom," said one awed admirer, it was acquired for a few wagonloads of "cheap goods." The enterprise promised to make Henderson one of the wealthiest men in all of America.[1]

Two long ridges, part of the Appalachian range that extends from Nova Scotia to Alabama, stood between Henderson and his purchase, as Figure 2 shows. Known as Pine and Cumberland Mountains, the ridges run parallel to each other for 120 miles, like the rails of a train track, separating the Piedmont and coastal plain from the vast interior. Long before Old World colonists arrived in the region, humans and animals alike crossed the range by making use of the Cumberland

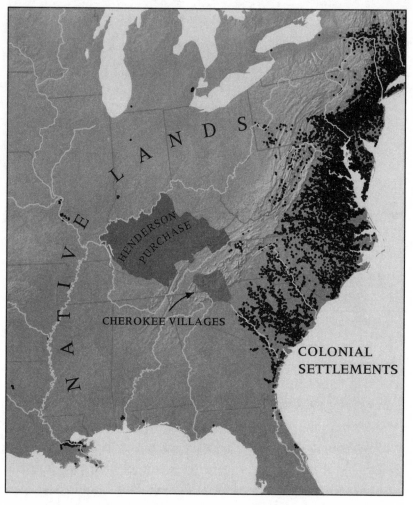

FIGURE 2 The Henderson purchase, with state boundaries superimposed.

Gap, a relatively gentle passage through the steep ridges. At its summit, travelers marked the way by carving figures on the mountain laurels, a practice that newcomers from Europe later adopted. Heading west, they exited the gap into the Middlesboro Basin, which separates Cumberland and Pine Mountains. There they met the Cumberland River and followed it down the narrow gorge that cuts through Pine Mountain and opens up to the continent's immense interior.[2]

In March 1775, Henderson put together a team of free and enslaved men and set out for the gap. They cut a seventy-mile wagon road west to Martin's Station, a small stockade with a few crude log cabins that was the last fortified British settlement in southwestern Virginia. Clearing brush and uprooting trees, the laborers carved a path over rugged mountains and forded icy rivers. The weather was frigid during the weeklong ordeal, and in the mornings they awoke to hard frost and ice. At last, they reached Powell Valley and followed it south across more "bad hils" before arriving at Martin's Station at the end of the month. There, Henderson decided to abandon the wagons. "We could not possibly clear the road any further," he concluded.[3]

They pushed on to Cumberland Gap, where Henderson received alarming news. Indians had ambushed and killed several people "on the road to the Cantuckee," setting off a general panic that spread "like wild-fire." In tears, Henderson contemplated the collapse of his momentous project to colonize the "western waters"—not the distant Columbia or Colorado, the great waterways on the opposite side of the continent that enter the Pacific Ocean and the Gulf of California, but the nearby Cumberland and Kentucky Rivers. At the crest of the Appalachians, he stood a mere 350 miles from the East Coast. In the nearly 170 years since the establishment of Jamestown, with enormous toil and sacrifice, the British had come as far as could be covered in a three-week journey.[4]

Henderson's ambitious scheme was born of ignorance and avarice, a fertile combination that gave life to many a colonial venture west of the Appalachians. Conceived on the eve of the War of Independence, it was nourished by the radical rhetoric of the era and ultimately extinguished by better-connected revolutionaries such as Patrick Henry, Virginia's governor and firebrand orator, who championed rival investments in the region. As Richard Henderson stood on the crest of the Blue Ridge and looked west, his expansive and fantastical project came into focus: a realm of landed gentry and hereditary rule, stretching as far as the eye could see across "new land," a part of the world with no history of its own and no people of any consequence. The view—one that still haunts our historical narratives—is provincial yet imperial, and it exposes just how little the continental colonists knew about the continent in 1776.[5]

. . .

Though he was born in Hanover County, Virginia (north of Richmond), and raised in Granville County, North Carolina (less than 150 miles from the Atlantic Ocean), Henderson was by the terms of British colonists a westerner. Granville County was part of the undeveloped backcountry, as the British liked to call it. The western population was "so sparse and scattered," recalled one of Henderson's descendants, that Richard's father had to hire a private tutor to educate his children. Hillsborough, the most important town in the area, was a "metropolis" in the eyes of one early resident and boasted a jail, courthouse, and two or three taverns. Yet it had only thirty or forty residents in the early 1760s.[6]

Ambitious colonists from more settled areas spotted opportunity in western Carolina. "Those lands were in their natural state," one resident recalled. "Not a tree had been cut." If land was not quite free for the taking, a few well-placed connections and the willingness to chase profits made it an easy acquisition. Henderson himself had an early introduction to the business of land jobbing. As a young man, he had often fulfilled his father's duties as sheriff of Granville County. In that role, he had witnessed the surveys that divided up the county's million acres, available to anyone who filed a claim and paid the requisite fees. Even the most tireless speculators, however, were small fry compared with the absentee proprietor, John Carteret, Earl Granville, who possessed original title (as far as the British were concerned) to the entire northern half of North Carolina, a strip of land 68 miles wide that presumptuously stretched from the Outer Banks straight across to the "south seas." Precisely where the continent came to end, no Englishman quite knew, though he could be sure that the Pacific Ocean lapped its shores.[7]

In the 1760s, word arrived of new opportunities west of the Appalachians, where the country was said to be fertile and abounding with game. Even better, speculators could run roughshod over the local residents, Cherokees, who, unlike white North Carolinians, had no rights as British subjects. The distinction was essential. Backcountry farmers had recently formed the Regulator movement to protest embezzlement, fraud, and extortion—the mainstay of Henderson's avaricious associates.[8]

One barrier remained. According to the Royal Proclamation of 1763, British subjects could not purchase territory directly from Native Americans, nor could they settle west of the Appalachians. The proclamation was "a temporary expedient to quiet the minds of the Indians," surmised George Washington, who had his eyes on western lands too. Nonetheless, it left white Americans with no way of securing title to lands they deeply coveted and already envisaged as theirs.[9]

Such frustrations made revolutionaries out of Henderson and his associates. The colonies "are striding fast to independence, and ere long will build an empire upon the ruins of Great Britain," wrote Henderson's friend William Hooper, five months before the First Continental Congress met in Philadelphia. Henderson seized the moment. While North Carolina representatives selected delegates to the Continental Congress, Henderson gathered five members of the local elite in Hillsborough to form the Louisa Company, named for the Louisa or, as it is now called, Kentucky River. (In early January 1775, Henderson's organization would be renamed the Transylvania Company.) The association proposed to "rent or purchase a certain Territory or Tract of Land lying on the west side of the Mountains."[10]

A scheme was set in motion. Henderson and Louisa investor Nathaniel Hart headed for Cherokee country in the fall, where they negotiated a preliminary agreement with the Indians. Moving quickly,

Henderson and Hart returned home in late November, bringing with them the aged Cherokee leader Attakullakulla and two other Indians, whose names were not recorded. The delegation spent one night in Bethabara, the Moravian settlement near present-day Winston-Salem. "It can hardly be believed," wrote the church diarist on hearing of the land transaction. Whether he was amazed by Henderson's audacious violation of the Proclamation of 1763, the extent of the purchase (which was, in fact, over one hundred times larger than he thought), or the magnitude of the payment (reportedly £4,000), is uncertain. During the evening worship, the Indian guests were "quiet and attentive" but "wondered much" at the church organ. With its intricate arrangement of keys and pulls manipulated just so, the mechanism resembled Henderson's own complex scheme to bribe and bargain his way to an empire in the West. The next morning the party headed on to Henderson's residence and finally Williamsburg, Virginia, to collect six wagonloads of goods.[11]

Attakullakulla's procession through the colony spread news of the land transaction far and wide. "The whole Province is stirred up," noted the Moravians, who watched colonists stream by on horseback and in horse-drawn carts for Kentucky. In Hillsborough, one party of emigrants marched out of town "with considerable solemnity." "Their destination seemed as remote as if it had been to the South Sea Islands!" wrote a witness. Colonists were headed for "the promised land," recalled one participant, and "every heart abounded with joy and excitement."[12]

Henderson and Attakullakulla drove their wagons laden with powder, guns, textiles, and kettles back through the Moravian towns and into eastern Tennessee to Watauga, a rude settlement situated only seventy miles from the closest Cherokee villages. Some twelve hundred Cherokees gathered there in mid-March 1775 to complete the transaction. After four days of negotiations, three Cherokee leaders—Attakullakulla, Oconostota, and the Raven—signed a deed conveying most of Kentucky and part of Tennessee to Henderson and his Transylvania Company associates.

It is worth reflecting for a moment on the dimensions of this transaction, which are so extreme that they are difficult to grasp. The Henderson purchase covered almost twenty-two million acres, making it the fifth largest colony, smaller than Virginia but slightly larger than South Carolina (excluding the colonies' fantastical claims to stretch to the shores of the Pacific). It was acquired for £2,700, a pittance then and now. Contemplating the justice of the sale, one dissatisfied onlooker said it best. After receiving a single shirt in exchange for his twenty-two-million-acre inheritance, he observed that "he could have Killed more Deer in one day upon it, then would have bought such a shirt."[13]

Henderson—judged a "man of probity and a firm friend to government" by North Carolina's Governor Tryon only a few years earlier—had brazenly defied colonial law and the king himself by purchasing a vast territory from the Cherokees. One Crown official expressed his utter astonishment: "Pray is Dick Henderson out of his head?" Cherokees may have wondered the same about Oconostota and Attakullakulla.[14]

. . .

Since the 1740s, colonists and British officers alike had been concocting ambitious and improbable schemes to carve out empires in the West, the region beyond the Appalachians known to them by rumor more than fact. The Ohio Company, the Indiana Company, the Greenbrier Company, Vandalia, the Mississippi Company, and others were all organized in the hope that the Crown would acknowledge their claims and make fortunes for their investors. The possibility of easy riches tempted the colonies' most prominent men, including Benjamin Franklin, George Washington, Patrick Henry, and the Lees of Virginia.[15]

Some of the land companies were better connected than Henderson's and therefore received less opprobrium from Crown officials. The Grand Ohio Company, soon known as Vandalia in honor of Queen Charlotte's supposed Vandal ancestors, operated under the principle that success would come if those in a position to ensure it were interested parties. Accordingly, it recruited a lengthy slate of powerful British officials. By manipulating Indian treaties and lobbying furiously in London, the company nearly succeeded in its quest, but rival land claims and the events precipitating the Revolution ultimately derailed it.[16]

On the other end of the spectrum were quixotic schemes such as Samuel Hazard's, which made Henderson's grandiose aspirations seem inconsiderable. Inspired by Benjamin Franklin's 1754 essay proposing a new settlement in the Ohio Valley, the Philadelphia businessman set out to make himself lord proprietor of an enormous new colony that would have dwarfed all others. Had it come to fruition, it would have been larger than the state of Texas. Franklin approved of the ambitious enterprise, though he deemed Hazard "not the fittest in the World to conduct such an Affair." Hazard intended to travel to London in fall 1758 to make "humble Application" to the king for a charter, but the would-be proprietor died before embarking.[17]

No matter their degree of pragmatism, all speculators were beguiled by the immense expanses of land in the West, a resource that colonists, not to mention residents of the crowded British Isles, were used to measuring by the hundreds, not millions, of acres. The colonists' sense of the region's vastness was amplified by their nebulous knowledge of its actual geography. They certainly had learned much since the previous century, when three adventurers claimed to have peered west from the crest of the Appalachians and spotted "sayles" on the South Sea. But even so, the region remained faintly exotic.[18]

Big Bone Lick, on the Ohio River just north of Henderson's purchase, encapsulated the mystery and excitement that the region generated. There, explorers found "monstrous" teeth and bones that appeared to belong to a colossal elephant or a carnivorous creature resembling a hippopotamus. How the bones had gotten there and whether such beasts still roamed the western waters puzzled experts on both sides of the Atlantic. Meeting with potential investors in London, Franklin discussed the mysterious fossils and the intoxicating possibility of establishing a colony in the area.[19]

Even armed with the best maps of the era, speculators were largely in the dark about what lay west of the Appalachians. George Washington consulted Joshua Fry's *Map of the Most Inhabited Part of Virginia*. It left the western waters uncharted but helpfully identified a "high Mountain" from which travelers could espy a gap through the Appalachians.

As late as the Revolutionary War, colonists had no better map of the Kentucky region than John Mitchell's 1755 small-scale representation of North America. What little detail it offered was highly misleading. No cartographer made more than a half-hearted attempt to publish a map of the area until 1778, long after speculators had claimed the land many times over.[20]

The combination of geographic ignorance and overweening ambition made for vague metes and bounds. Samuel Hazard had proposed a grant beginning "at the distance of one hundred miles westward of the Western Boundaries of Pennsylvania, and thence to extend one Hundred Miles to the westward of the River Mississippi, and to be divided from Virginia and Carolina by the Great Chain of Mountains that runs along the Continent from the North Eastern to the South Western Parts of America." With so much land to be had, who cared if the poorly defined line at the Appalachians was 50 miles this way or that?[21]

Official charters were more specific but still left ample room for interpretation. The southeastern boundary of North Carolina began precisely enough at a cedar stake at the mouth of the Little River but then ran northwest through "the boundary house"—which corner exactly was not specified. As the line moved west and the colonists' knowledge of the terrain faded, they abandoned landmarks for abstractions. After striking the thirty-fifth parallel, North Carolina's boundary followed the line of latitude all the way to the "south seas." The transcontinental demarcation posed two problems. First, the colony was claiming lands belonging to native peoples, not to mention to the Spanish Crown. And second, no one could locate the thirty-fifth parallel with any degree of accuracy.[22]

In his own rush to accumulate as much land as possible in an area he knew little about, Henderson seized on whatever landmark he could, with predictable results. His deed with the Cherokees referred to the intersection of mountains and rivers that do not meet and to watersheds that could be traced in theory but not practice. One boundary section took a "southeast course to the ridge of Powell's Mountain" and followed the ridge "to a point from which a northwest course will strike the headspring of the most southwardly branch of the Cumberland River," a line that even the most diligent of surveyors could not locate precisely, then or now.[23]

Such generalities were only further encouragement to make extravagant claims before the region was overrun and could be described by familiar boulders, trees, and creeks. Henderson was dismayed to find that his own purchase "abounded with land-mongers," who marked "every piece of land they thought proper." James Nourse, a woolen draper from London, was one such person. He migrated to the colonies in 1769 and six years later led a small group of neighbors to Kentucky. Not far from Boonesborough, he discovered the forests full of marked trees. His "memorandum" for locating his own claim is a monument to land fever. From Boonesborough, he reminded himself, stay on the left path past the Gists' cornfield, keep a north course "across the brows" of two or three hills, go down to a run and up the north branch "a good way." Then "keep still North," crossing "some highish" land, "trees blazed all the way." After fifteen miles, arrive at a running creek, where several trees are marked and one inscribed "surveyed 10000 acres—by order of the Council." Continue on a buffalo path. When it fails, keep going until coming to "paths that run that way." Take them to a "very plain buffalo path"; follow it to a broad run and a tree marked "J.N." Locate and take the path to the "upper corner tree." The other two corners are a "large fork elm" and a "large white oak." The tract measured thirty-seven hundred acres.[24]

At the heart of Henderson's pursuits lay what he called "the rapturous idea of property." What greater allurement could the world offer, he asked.[25]

•   •   •

No matter how audacious Henderson's western project was, it ran into the inconvenient fact that people already lived west of the Appalachians. From Boston, a skeptical John Adams called the distant colony a "Utopian" scheme. Closer to the scene, Cherokees, Shawnees, and Mingos deemed it an invasion. "Better to die like men than to diminish away by inches," a delegation of northern Indians told a receptive Cherokee audience in August 1776.[26]

When Cherokees took up arms to defend their homelands, Transylvania's colonists devised a cynical and ruthless ploy to save the speculative venture. One of them forged a letter purportedly revealing an alliance between the Cherokees and the British army. Reaction to the inflammatory though spurious document was fierce. "I hope the Cherokees will now be driven beyond the Missisipi [sic]," wrote Jefferson from the Continental Congress, where the sentiment toward the Cherokees was poisonous. North Carolina's three congressional delegates urged their home colony to "carry fire and Sword into the very bowels of their country and sink them so low that they may never be able to rise again." In fall 1776, nearly six thousand troops from South Carolina, North Carolina, and Virginia descended on the Cherokees. Leading the invasion, General Griffith Rutherford of North Carolina boasted, "I have no Doubt of a Finel Destruction of the Cherroce Nation." He intended to "crush that treacherous, barbarious Nation of Savages."[27]

Years later, one private in the Guilford County militia summarized his experience: "marched to the Cherokee Nation to suppress the Indians; burnt their town, killed and destroyed as many of the Indians as we could get hold of; remained in the nation as long as we could get provisions, and was compelled to return back." His plain description captures the event for colonists as well as any.[28]

Underlying all of the violence was the desire for western land, "the rapturous idea of property." Even before his troops withdrew, Colonel William Christian began plotting how to make Cherokee country a part of Virginia. "I like it better than the Virginia part of this side of Ohio," he wrote. Patrick Henry, whose famous call for liberty or death had resounded in the Virginia Convention the year before, reportedly wished to make a "snug little purchase" of some of the invaded land. After the Revolution, Rutherford joined a party of speculators that included two Henderson associates. He eventually claimed between twelve thousand and twenty thousand acres of former Cherokee lands and retired to Tennessee in 1792.[29]

As for Henderson, his feverish efforts ended in disappointment. Both Virginia and North Carolina nullified his deed, though not without awarding him two hundred thousand acres for his "trouble and expense." Astonishingly, the deed's illegitimacy—resolved by two state legislatures—did not prevent the United States from exploiting it to deprive Cherokees of their lands. "The parties being dead, and so much time elapsed since the date of the deed, and the country being settled, on the faith of the deed, puts it out of our power to do any thing respecting it," US commissioners instructed the Cherokees. "You must therefore be content with it, as if you had actually sold it." Ten years had passed since Henderson's illegal transaction.[30]

Eying the prospect from the crest of the Blue Ridge in spring 1775, Henderson had caught only the merest glimpse of what lay beyond. The shores of the Pacific were distant another two thousand miles, over sweeping prairies and towering mountains that dwarfed the geographic features on the Eastern Seaboard. Between the continent's far edge and the Appalachians stood thousands of towns and villages, whose millions of residents spoke diverse languages and belonged to a multitude of nations. On the eve of the War of Independence, even the most fervid of American speculators could not imagine the extraordinary events unfolding in the West.

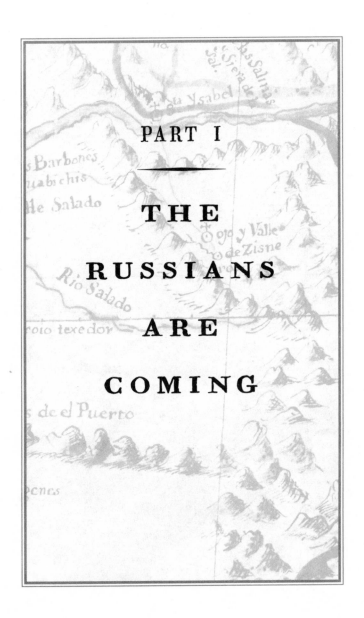

PART I

THE RUSSIANS ARE COMING

Over two thousand miles west of the Cumberland Gap, on the southeastern shore of the San Francisco Bay, an extraordinary event occurred late in the afternoon of March 31, 1776. North of what is now known as Silicon Valley, a man was carrying a bundle of edible plants called *morrén* along the tree-lined banks of San Lorenzo Creek. Suddenly he stopped short. Some forty paces away, twenty strangers were approaching. Incredibly, they were mounted on large deer—or were they elk? The man was seized with "the greatest fear describable," according to one of the strangers, and either threw himself down into the grass or collapsed in fright. He was terrorized, wrote another, "lying prone more dead than alive." The strangers suspected that up to the encounter, he had not had "even a remote notice" of any other people but his own kind—a moment of first contact that took place nearly three hundred years after Columbus had set foot in the Americas. Many of the original inhabitants along North America's East Coast had since died of disease, fled into the interior, or been killed by colonists. In the Boston area, which the British evacuated two weeks before the incident on San Lorenzo Creek, Indians had not been a significant presence for nearly a century.[1]

Observing out of the corner of one eye, the man watched one of the riders approach, lean down, and hold out some beads, strangely unlike the purple and white ones made from local sea snails. A trap? A gift? The pedestrian remained motionless. When the rider dismounted and placed the beads in the man's hand, he let them fall. He offered his *morrén*, but the strangers ignored the gesture. Then they turned and rode off. If they had not done so, wrote one of them, "I think he would have died." The strangers had come to establish a colony across the bay on the banks of the "Stream of Sorrows," the first European settlement in what would become San Francisco.[2]

Over four hundred miles down the Pacific Coast, a Kumeyaay Indian named Diego sat in a Spanish prison overlooking the San Diego River, the bay, and the ocean beyond. When Diego was a boy growing up in the 1750s, the Spanish had yet to colonize his homeland. Now, in March 1776, a few dozen Spanish soldiers commanded a small wooden and adobe brick stockade that possessed two bronze cannons. One faced the harbor to fend off European rivals. The other pointed toward Diego's native village, at least until the Indian settlement was relocated. For a time, Franciscans had also administered a mission about six miles farther upriver, but in the early-morning hours of November 5, 1775, the Kumeyaays burned it to the ground and bludgeoned one of the padres to death. It was Diego's suspected involvement in the uprising that had landed him in jail.[3]

While Diego wasted away in prison and the Spanish erected a temporary shelter in San Francisco, another remarkable story was unfolding deep in the western interior of the continent. A small party of Spanish explorers had recently set out on a fifteen-hundred-mile expedition through the Four Corners region. They became the first Europeans ever to venture into the vast area of the continent that lies between the Rockies and the Sierra Nevada. In late September 1776, shortly after the British had taken New York City from the Continental Army, the explorers reached the shores of Utah Lake, just south of the Great Salt Lake, where Ute villagers greeted them. A missionary explained the purpose of the five-month expedition: "to seek the salvation of their souls." The Utes gave the visitors a tanned deerskin painted with blood-stained men, and at the last minute, as a gesture of goodwill toward their guests, hastily added a tiny cross to each figure.[4]

Five thousand miles of open ocean separate San Francisco and San Diego from Siberia. It is another fifteen hundred miles overland from there to the dusty settlement of Kyakhta, located south of Lake Baikal, the deepest freshwater lake in the world. Kyakhta sat on a treeless, denuded plain, across from the town of Maimaicheng. (Literally "trading city," Maimaicheng is today known as the Mongolian city of Altanbulag.) Between them stood a boundary post with two inscriptions: in

Russian, "Here ends the Russian domain" and in Mongolian, "Here begins the Chinese empire."[5]

Improbably, trade between Kyakhta and Maimaicheng set off a chain reaction, which ultimately led to the incident on San Lorenzo Creek, to Diego's imprisonment, and to the arrival of missionaries on the shores of Lake Utah in 1776. To appreciate how, we must strike out for the Aleutian Islands, the Alaskan archipelago that arcs across the North Pacific. There, in early summer 1775, seven Aleuts were preparing for a hazardous five-thousand-mile journey to explore the distant country responsible for the tumultuous changes sweeping over their island homelands. They were headed toward Kyakhta.

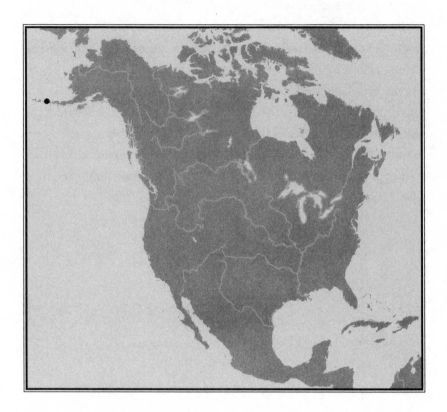

CHAPTER ONE

Soft Gold: Aleuts and Russians in Alaska

In the month of nestlings and newborn sea mammals, seven Aleuts departed their homes for lands beyond the horizon. The adventurers included a husband and wife from Samalga, a tiny sliver of an island of just 1.5 square miles, and two or three children, sent on the perilous voyage by their fathers to learn about the people who had upended their lives. On June 1, 1775, they set out westward aboard the *St. Paul*, a forty-five-foot-long Russian sloop, which was returning to Siberia with over seven thousand fox and sea otter pelts in its hold. Fifty-seven days later, Captain Ivan Solov'ev anchored his "strong & clumsy" vessel at

Okhotsk, some twenty-five hundred miles from the Aleuts' villages. This small settlement of 132 "miserable wooden houses," built on a boggy spit on the east coast of Siberia, served as the Russian port of embarkation for voyages to Kamchatka and America. The resident sailors and Cossacks drank to excess, buying liquor by "the otter," as local currency was denominated. They showed telltale signs of scurvy: pale skin, sunken eyes, and extensive bruising—the result of a diet without fresh fruits and vegetables but rich in alcohol.[1]

At the decrepit and isolated town, two of the Aleut men announced that they wished to return home as soon as possible, rather than continue on to the promised "great Russian cities." The other five, following the furs their fathers and brothers had harvested, forged ahead to Yakutsk. The 750-mile journey across rugged mountains, marshy forests, and permanent ice fields took six weeks in favorable weather; in the winter, it could drag on for two to three months. For the first time, the Aleuts saw forests—the Aleutian islands are naturally barren of trees—and dead, decaying horses by the hundreds, victims of the arduous route. The cold reached an average of forty degrees below zero every January and was unlike anything they had encountered in their homeland, where the sea moderates the climate. The frost "penetrated the body to the 'marrow of the bone,'" wrote a later newcomer, who insisted that the "phrase was no metaphor."[2]

At Yakutsk, where winter visitors found the atmosphere "constantly charged with Snow," one of the women died. The four survivors continued southwest, traveling thirteen hundred miles up the Lena River to Kachug, a tiny settlement near Lake Baikal. There they saw native Buryats, who rode and worked horned oxen, and later they passed herds of sheep and well-cultivated fields of wheat, rye, and barley. After another 150 miles, they finally arrived at Irkutsk, a huge settlement with twenty thousand residents.[3]

The city, with its hospital, theater, school, butcher shops, fish markets, and bazaar, dwarfed the Aleuts' communities; their largest village had no more than several dozen people. In fact, there were fewer Aleuts in the entire world—roughly sixteen thousand—than in eastern

Siberia's provincial capital. Each year, thousands of pelts from the Aleutian Islands and millions from Siberia funneled into Irkutsk. The scale of the vast warehousing operation was out of proportion to anything the Aleuts could have imagined. In Irkutsk, the furs were sorted by quality and the best sent on to European Russia. The others were floated across Lake Baikal to the mouth of the Selenga and then upriver to Kyakhta.[4]

By a 1727 treaty, all trade between China and Russia had to pass through Kyakhta or Tsurukhaitu, an even more remote settlement farther east that never attracted significant commerce. Kyakhta had a few fine houses belonging to wealthy merchants, a detachment of dragoons, and a rhubarb warehouse, where Chinese rhubarb (different from the common variety) was dried, grated, and sorted into different grades. The Russian state had a monopoly on the costly root, which was believed to have valuable medicinal properties, and an apothecary stood ready to approve each purchase. The rarest pieces were forwarded to St. Petersburg for use in the court pharmacy. The bulk of the imports, however, consisted of cottons, silks, and teas.[5]

In exchange, Russian merchants offered furs. Between two million and four million Siberian squirrel pelts passed through Kyakhta every year. From Siberia also came fox, sable, and domesticated cat. From the Aleutian Islands arrived fox and the most valuable of all pelts, sea otter, which trimmed the court robes of Chinese nobility. Sea otters possess the densest fur of any mammal, with an estimated million hairs per square inch, two to three times that of a fur seal and eighteen times that of a dog. Numerous eighteenth-century observers described their lustrous beauty. The "gloss of their hair excels the blackest velvet," wrote the naturalist Georg Wilhelm Steller, who accompanied Vitus Bering on his Alaskan exploration in 1741. (The meat also earned Steller's admiration: it was "rather good to eat and tasty," the females being "much tenderer and tastier.") On the Siberian coast, sea otter pelts sold for 10–15 rubles, in Irkutsk for 30–40 rubles, and in Kyakhta for 100–140 rubles—a markup of 1,000 percent. The fur trade generated almost 8 percent of Russia's customs revenues in the 1770s.[6]

Amazingly, the millions of pelts sold in Kyakhta each year did not satisfy demand, and Russian traders had to draw on another North American source. Cree trappers in central Canada, some twenty-five hundred miles east of the Aleutians, sold beaver and river otter pelts to the Hudson's Bay Company, which sent them on to London. From London, the company exported the furs to St. Petersburg, or to Arkhangelsk on the White Sea. Each year in the 1770s, some forty thousand to fifty thousand furs made their way along this circuitous route. In one of the more remarkable convergences created by long-distance trade, thousands of those pelts were carried to Tobolsk, just east of the Ural Mountains, and then sledded overland to Kyakhta, where they were warehoused with the Aleutian furs. The voyage (following the route illustrated in Figure 3) took anywhere from one to three years. Sea otter and beaver pelts, originating in North America, had traveled in opposite directions around the world—nine thousand miles east or forty-five hundred west—only to converge at a remote outpost on the Russian-Chinese border. From there, they were carted away on the backs of camels or in two-wheeled carts drawn by oxen, destined for Chinese royalty in Beijing.[7]

. . .

Only a decade earlier, Aleuts were reportedly convinced that the only Russians in the world were the few hundred exploring their islands in leaky boats. In the 1770s, sixteen Russian vessels visited the archipelago to gather furs, and each one had a calamitous impact on local residents. The *St. Paul* was not unusual in this regard. The sloop had embarked from Okhotsk on its five-year expedition in September 1770, shortly before British soldiers stood trial for the Boston Massacre on the opposite side of North America. Its captain, Ivan Solov'ev, was an illiterate but experienced navigator from Tobolsk, famed for its historic role as the base for Russia's conquest of Siberia. Solov'ev's crew of seventy-two wintered in the Kurile Islands, hunting and putting up stores for the next year, as was common practice. By the time the vessel headed for the Aleutians in July 1771, six crewmen had already died.[8]

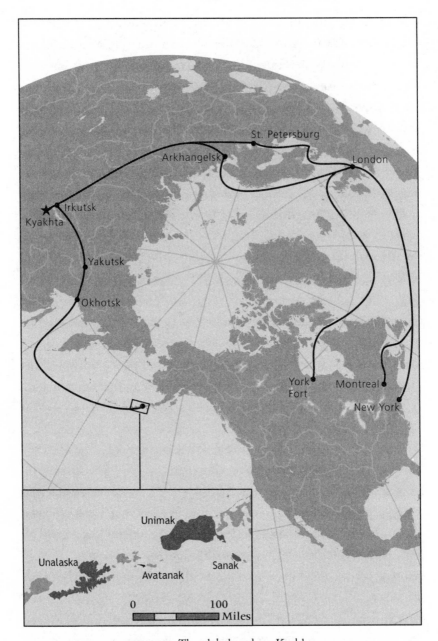

FIGURE 3 The global trade to Kyakhta.

The *St. Paul* followed a well-traveled if still hazardous route in search of furs. In the seventeenth century, trappers, known as *promyshlenniki*, had pushed across Siberia. Aided by the czar's armed forces, these newcomers pursued valuable sable furs and claimed the land for the

Russian state as they pushed eastward. Two practices lay at the heart of the expansion and were carried all the way to the Aleutians: the collection of *iasak* and the taking of *amanaty*. *Iasak* was a form of tribute to the Russian state, usually assessed in furs; to ensure payment, officials seized hostages, or *amanaty*, from local populations. The tribute was burdensome and the method of collection ruthless. Numerous peoples—the Samoyeds, Tungus, Yakuts, and Yakagirs, to name a few—suffered under the strain, and many disintegrated altogether. They were Siberia's "red men," the equivalent of North America's Indians, eighteenth-century Russians held, and Siberia was "our Peru," "our Mexico," or "our East India."[9]

By the 1670s, promyshlenniki had hunted out sable in many parts of Siberia, leaving only low-value squirrel and ermine. They pushed on, conquering the native residents, and reached Kamchatka by the end of the century. Rumors of a "Great Land" to the east and uncertainty about the geographic relationship between Asia and America led Russia's Czar Peter I and his successors to support Vitus Bering's exploration of the "Eastern Ocean" in the hopes of finding a land bridge tying North America to Siberia. Instead, the Danish-born navigator revealed the strait that is named for him, though he died near the end of his second voyage, in 1741. Surviving crew members returned with sea otter pelts from the island that now bears his name, setting off a rush for what the Russians called "soft gold." By the 1750s, promyshlenniki were trapping and trading in the Aleutian Islands, acquiring thousands of fox and seal furs and, the most valuable, otter pelts.[10]

The Aleutian archipelago arcs across the North Pacific like a giant crescent. In August 1771, the *St. Paul* approached the far eastern end of the island chain, where sea otters and foxes were still plentiful. The vessel passed by Umnak, where Mount Vsevidof rises seven thousand feet above sea level. An enormous volcanic crater that stretches seven miles across and belches dense smoke dominates the northern part of the island. Just before reaching Unimak, the easternmost and largest of the Aleutians, the vessel made landfall on Akun, a small hilly island of barely sixty square miles. Captain Solov'ev had skirted Unalaska, a much larger island to the west. Unalaska, with its deeply corrugated topography and irregular coast, had been the site of a massacre only six years earlier. Solov'ev figured prominently in the event.

In 1763, four ships, the *Zacharias and Elizabeth*, the *Holy Trinity*, the *John*, and the *Adrian and Natalie*, were visiting Umnak and Unalaska, two of the larger islands of the Aleutian chain that Russians had discovered only four years earlier. The captains collected *iasak* from local Aleuts and demanded *amanaty* to ensure prompt payment and their own safety. Then they divided their crews into hunting parties, as Aleuts from Unalaska, Umnak, and neighboring islands had expected. The Aleuts hatched a plan. As Solov'ev reported it, local residents would "live in friendship at first," but when the Russians split up to hunt and trade, they would take them by surprise. "Using this ruse," they hoped to "kill all the Russians."[11]

On Unalaska, the Aleuts ambushed the hunting parties from the *Zacharias and Elizabeth*. Four survivors, fleeing along the coast to their vessel, spotted a locker washed ashore, then bits and pieces of the ship itself, and finally the bodies of their mates, mangled and strewn about the beach. Months later, they reached the *Holy Trinity*, where they learned that, besides themselves, only three of their thirty-seven crewmates had survived.[12]

The *Holy Trinity* had also come under attack and would soon be destroyed. The skeleton crew, reduced in number and weakened by scurvy, could not control the vessel, and in heavy winds it was driven to Umnak and crushed on the rocky shore. Aleuts set upon fifty-four castaways that same night. In July 1764, the twelve survivors of that raid built a skin boat and rowed around the island, searching for the *John*, the third of the four ships that had been trading in the islands. In a steam bath constructed by the Russians, they found only a charred frame and the garroted bodies of twenty countrymen. (No one from the *John* survived to recount its story, but in 1970, archaeologists discovered the steam bath and the remains of the crew.) The refugees from the *Zacharias and Elizabeth* and the *Holy Trinity* were soon rescued by the last surviving ship, the *Adrian and Natalie*. In September 1764, relief arrived when Solov'ev anchored off Unalaska and learned of the plight of his fellow promyshlenniki.[13]

In retaliation, Solov'ev killed at least seventy Aleuts in five differ-ent engagements. "I preferred to talk them out of evil intentions so that they could live in friendship with the Russian people," he main-tained. But elderly promyshlenniki, interviewed in the early nine-teenth century, would remember differently. On one occasion, Solov'ev, after being provoked, killed one hundred Aleuts "on the spot." The bloodshed was "terrible," they recalled. On another, Solov'ev blew up a fortified structure sheltering three hundred Aleuts and cut down the survivors with guns and sabers. One trader stated that Solov'ev had killed more than three thousand in all, perhaps an exaggera-tion; another insisted that he had killed no more than two hundred. Considering that Unalaska sheltered only a few thousand inhabitants, even two hundred deaths would have represented a crushing blow to the population.[14]

Years later, Aleuts insisted that Solov'ev, above all others, was responsible for their decline. The Russian captain had killed hundreds or thousands, they said, and many others had fled at his approach. He made a practice of destroying their *baidarkas*, as kayaks are known in the Aleutians. The boats were essential for hunting, "as indispens-able as the plow and the horse for the farmer," observed one Russian. Many of the refugees died from starvation or exposure while laboring to replace the skin-covered vessels, which took over a year to build.[15]

On Unalaska and surrounding islands, Solov'ev "shot all the men," three residents recalled in 1789. He reportedly practiced a cruel experi-ment: arranging the Aleuts in a line, he fired at the first to discover how many people the bullet would pass through. On one occasion, villagers sought refuge on Egg Island, a tiny outcropping with cliffs four hundred feet high, lying in deep water just off the eastern edge of Unalaska. Its rocky shoreline hindered Solov'ev's approach, but he made landfall on the second attempt and killed the men, women, and children who had gathered there. "The slaughter was so atrocious," Aleuts said, "that the sea around the islet became bloody from those who threw themselves or were thrown into it."[16]

· · ·

Returning to the Aleutians in 1771 for the first time since the massacre, Solov'ev spent two weeks on Akun without giving details in his journal. On his departure, he "took" with him six Aleuts to serve as navigators and intermediaries, including a *toion* (village leader) named Chagusix̂, Chagusix̂'s friend Kaluu, and a translator, Vaska. Boarding the ship had both its risks and rewards, as the Aleuts would learn.[17]

Chagusix̂ and Kaluu directed the *St. Paul* through the difficult Unimak Pass to Sanak Island, known to the Russians by name only. The low-lying sea fog common on summer days, rip and flood tides, and numerous shoals made the Aleuts' local seafaring expertise indispensable. Arriving at Sanak, Solov'ev found a "low and marshy" island, with a mountain rising seventeen hundred feet on its northern point. The surrounding waters were rich with sea life. A few years later, James Cook's crew would catch close to one hundred halibut offshore in three or four hours, some of them weighing a hundred pounds. (Cook's apposite name for Sanak, "Halibut Island," did not survive.)[18]

Solov'ev explored the southern coast and found nothing but the Aleuts' empty semisubterranean earthen houses, which the Russians called *barabaras*. The residents had fled to offshore islets, high rocky outposts that offered protection from the invaders. "We moved here because we have not seen Russian people before and are afraid of them," they explained. After ascending a high bluff to speak to one encampment of some two hundred Aleuts, Solov'ev wrote that he "felt sorry for all their great troubles," though he took four hostages from the group. (They went "voluntarily," he claimed.) Sea otters were rare in the area, the Aleuts insisted. This was a thin deception, for Sanak and its surrounding islands were among the richest otter habitats in all of the Aleutians.[19]

Several weeks later, on an islet lying off Sanak's north coast, Solov'ev again found a number of Sanak residents living "as if there was some danger to them from us." They were merely gathering food, they claimed, before surrendering eleven more hostages and promising to return to Sanak. They "assured us that in no way should we be afraid of them," Solov'ev recounted, "and should travel and hunt any animal where we wish and should not fear any disturbance."[20]

It was now October, and the weather was turning. Though the Aleutian climate is moderated by the warm Japan Current and seasonal temperature swings are small, gales frequently visit the islands in the fall and winter, with winds reaching eighty miles per hour. Solov'ev's men built a yurt (really a modified version of the Aleuts' dwellings), storage shed, and forge, and then two parties set out to hunt on opposite ends of Sanak. Chagusix̂ and Kaluu returned home with gifts for their service. Around the same time, Solov'ev noticed that Aleuts were spying on his camp. Soon after, a group of Solov'ev's men went to gather driftwood and discovered a number of destroyed barabaras. Inside one of them, they found Vaska's corpse. The Aleuts had severed the translator's arm and leg tendons and stabbed him multiple times. "I killed your translator Vaska," an Aleut prisoner boasted, "because he had lived with you and he was just like you." Solov'ev directed his crew to torture the captive.[21]

Meanwhile, one of the Russian hunting parties came under attack. Aleuts shot and killed the sentry, blocked the yurt's exit, and set it afire, using dried grass and animal fat to stoke the flames. Trapped inside, the promyshlenniki somehow survived and emerged in the morning to find remnants of their furs and food stores floating in the surf. They spotted what seemed like one hundred baidarkas off the coast. "There are a lot of us now," the Aleuts shouted, "and we are going to kill all of you. Alaska is great."[22]

The attack never came, but Solov'ev's crew survived the rest of the winter in a state of siege, unable to hunt or gather food. Scurvy struck the camp, and fifteen Russians died. With little food and few healthy men, the hostages became a burden. One woman prisoner ran away with two female guards, Aleuts who were being paid for their help. After they were recaptured, they explained that many Aleuts were congregating to kill the invaders. "Why live here?" they asked. "It is better to take news about your present small numbers. For that they will reward us."[23] Solov'ev executed one of the women. The hostages, it turned out, were not the beloved children of toions but slaves to the Aleuts, captured in warfare against regional enemies. If they did not escape or pass information along to the Sanak islanders, Solov'ev later learned, they would be tortured upon their return. In the food-scarce encampment that winter, ten of them starved to death.

In July 1772, Solov'ev decided to head for friendlier islands, leaving behind a yurt, storage shed, smithy, and wooden cross planted above the dead. As the *St. Paul* sailed out of the harbor, Aleuts descended on the camp and burned down the yurt, with two of the abandoned hostages still inside.[24]

Solov'ev's skeletal account of the first Russian visit to Sanak leaves much out. Aleuts later recalled that Solov'ev had "ravaged" the island, though the details remain unknown.[25] The *St. Paul* was nearly two years into its voyage. Twenty-two of the seventy-two crew members had died (not including Vaska), and Solov'ev's promyshlenniki had killed an untold number of Aleuts. But on Sanak the ship had collected 681 foxes, 188 sea otters, and 60 otter tails. The high price of furs in distant Kyakhta made the cost of hunting on the Aleutians worth the expense—at least to the *St. Paul's* merchant owners.

. . .

The *St. Paul* headed toward Unimak, but without Chagusix̂ and Kaluu to navigate, the vessel was caught in strong winds and a flood tide. By fate, it was driven not onto the nearby shoals but onto Akun instead. From there, Solov'ev moved to Unalaska, the site of the bloodshed seven years earlier, when he had first commanded a ship to the Aleutians. A delicate relationship developed between the marauder and his victims. Solov'ev liberally distributed gifts, including a hatchet and iron knife to every man. He was even more generous with those who paid *iasak*. With the massacre still in recent memory, the toions responded in kind, at least according to Solov'ev. "No matter how many Russian people are going to be sent to our islands and settlements," the toions reportedly said, "we are going to do nothing but help and satisfy them with whatever they may need." Aware of the food shortage on Sanak, they promised to supply the Russians with fresh and dried fish. Aleuts arrived from neighboring islands, bearing discharge tickets from other

atop baidarkas "with a neatness that cannot be surpass'd," so that the equipment was "always at hand."[33]

No eighteenth-century musket matched the suitability of Aleut harpoons for hunting sea mammals. Nor did the promyshlenniki's linen, cotton, or silk shirts compare well with Aleut dress. To protect themselves against the chilling weather, Aleut hunters donned two garments—a *parka* and a *kamleika*. The parka, made of furs or puffin skins, was "indispensable," observed the missionary Ivan Veniaminov. (He is now honored by the Russian Orthodox Church as Saint Innocent.) Said to be a "manly, athletic man," Veniaminov nonetheless "suffered very much from the cold" until he began wearing one. Veniaminov admired the kamleika too, a waterproof shirt made of animal intestines and sewn with sinew. "In the worst possible weather," he declared, "nothing could be better." "Take their productions for strength and neatness," wrote one of Cook's men, "and I believe they are to be excelled by no People under the Sun."[34]

But it was perhaps the baidarka (Figure 4) that elicited the keenest

FIGURE 4 John Webber's 1778 ink-and-watercolor illustration of an Aleut and his baidarka shows the split bow that contributed to the vessel's swiftness. Webber, "Cape Newenham" (1778), UW 9193, Special Collections, University of Washington Libraries.

admiration and reflected the Aleuts' greatest adaptation to the difficult Aleutian environment. The watertight vessel was as functionally advanced as it was beautiful, and even today sailors marvel at its unequaled design. Martin Sauer, secretary to a Russian scientific expedition, first saw the boats in the late 1780s and was struck with "amazement beyond expression." "If perfect symmetry, smoothness, and proportion, constitute beauty," he exclaimed, "they are beautiful; to me they appeared so beyond any thing that I ever beheld."[35]

Constructed with "infinite toil and trouble," the fourteen-foot-long single-hatch variety was framed in cedar, joined with flexible baleen strips and bone inserts, and sheathed in translucent seal or sea lion skins. To reduce drag and improve water resistance, all but the final central seam were on the inside. A split bow (like a tuning fork) and a three-part keel made the narrow boats extraordinarily fast and flexible. Light enough to be carried by a single hunter, the thirty-pound vessels could nonetheless transport over four hundred pounds of catch through pounding waves and high surf.[36]

Aleut boys began training in baidarkas at a young age; by the time they reached adulthood, it appeared that they had been created for the vessels. Negotiating breakers that reached to their breasts, the Aleuts sported about "more like amphibious animals than human beings," said one observer. The baidarka was, many concluded, the most remarkable seacraft in the entire world, "the best means yet discovered by mankind to go from place to place."[37]

The baidarka's ingenious design and construction explains how Aleuts could navigate the treacherous Aleutian waters, chase down seabirds and otters, and travel from Sanak to Ugamak (nearly eighty miles) in twelve to eighteen hours.[38] It also explains why Solov'ev needed the assistance of Aleuts to hunt sea otters.

•   •   •

In his journal, Solov'ev remained largely silent about his thirty-five months on Unalaska and the surrounding islands, where his crew harvested the vast majority of the furs that would eventually be sent on to Kyakhta. There was "nothing worthy of notice" in the journal, declared the Russian Senate, which ordered future voyagers to keep better records. Solov'ev's reticence may have been grounded in knowledge of the fate of Ivan Bechevin, a wealthy Irkutsk merchant who was put on trial in 1764 for the actions of his company. The official investigation concluded that Bechevin's promyshlenniki—who kidnapped, raped, and murdered a number of Aleut women—committed "indescribable abuses, ruin and murder upon the natives."[39]

Nonetheless, enough details exist to reveal that relations between Solov'ev and the Aleuts rapidly deteriorated. Shortly after Solov'ev set up camp on Unalaska, he sent out two hunting parties. A detachment from the first became stranded in a cove surrounded by high cliffs. The Aleuts who discovered the vulnerable men severed their arm and leg tendons and then cut off their limbs and heads. Later, they boasted to Solov'ev, "we are going to kill all of you just like we killed Russian people before." Solov'ev ordered two Aleut captives stabbed to death.[40]

The remainder of the first party went west, to hunt on Umnak and other western islands. It met with success, according to Solov'ev. The men lived peacefully with the islanders, who "voluntarily" gave them hostages, traded with them, and paid *iasak*. "I was always happy with those foreigners and nothing bad happened while we stayed there," he stated. (*Inozemtsy*, meaning "foreigners," was the term Russians applied to the native peoples of Siberia, as well as to the Aleuts.) Their acquiescence to Solov'ev's presence may have been forged in the 1760s, when, according to one report, promyshlenniki had virtually "exterminated" the "disobedient" populations on southern Umnak and its western islets.[41]

The second party went east to Akutan, Akun, Avatanak, and Tigalda, now known as part of the Krenitzin Islands. Together not even a third the size of Unalaska, these tiny outposts with rocky coasts are rich in sea lions, seals, and otters. Until Solov'ev's crew arrived in September 1772, its local residents, unlike those to the west of Unalaska, had successfully turned back the few Russians who had tried to hunt on the islands.[42]

Among the party was Petr Natrubin, Solov'ev's "henchman," in

Veniaminov's forthright description. He was said to be both pious and "extravagantly fond" of liquor—a combination that must have fortified him against Aleut resistance. Akutan, a high, craggy island with steep shores, had much to recommend it in the spring, as Aleut place names suggest: Qawa(m)-tanangin ("sea lion rookery"), Achan-ingiiga ("salmonberry bushes below it"), and Qakiid(am)-kamga ("silver salmon's head," where coho salmon spawn)—not to mention abundant red foxes, seals, and sea lions. But in October 1772, Natrubin's party encountered heavy blizzards on the island. As Natrubin and others recounted it, by "invitation of the foreigners" they took refuge from the fierce storms in the Aleuts' barabara but were soon driven out when the residents attacked them with knives.[43]

They moved on to Avatanak, a low, narrow island eight miles to the east, with three small villages. Again, Natrubin and his partners stated they were invited into a toion's barabara. For a few weeks, the promyshlenniki and Aleuts lived uneasily at opposite ends of the house. (The largest barabaras could be over 150 feet long, cover as much as six thousand square feet, and house one hundred people, but on the sparsely populated island of Avatanak, they were probably significantly smaller, perhaps a third the size.) In early December, the Avatanak residents surreptitiously opened up several roof entrances and then, one midnight, stormed the barabara to kill the sleeping Russians. "We do not know for what offence or oppression," claimed Natrubin and his partners, who used their firearms to drive off the attackers. Several more deadly attacks followed, but Solov'ev's crew somehow persevered.[44]

Natrubin and the other promyshlenniki gave no more information about their stay on Avatanak, nor did Solov'ev recount what the hunting party did between spring 1773 and May 1775, when the *St. Paul* set sail for Okhotsk. What happened during those final two years?

In 1833, Veniaminov visited Avatanak. A skilled linguist who was fluent in the local dialect, the missionary conversed directly with elderly Aleuts about Natrubin and Solov'ev. One aged woman pointed out the remnants of the barabaras that the Russians had occupied. Others showed him a small river. "Fish came here plentifully in former times," they recalled, but after Natrubin murdered several Aleuts and cast the bodies into the stream, "not a single fish has entered it." Natrubin, Veniaminov concluded, "was destroying the Aleuts on Avatanak—unarmed and frequently perfectly innocent."[45]

Aleuts told Veniaminov one more story about Natrubin's activities in the 1770s. When Natrubin's party crossed from Avatanak to the neighboring island of Tigalda, the Aleuts took refuge on a small rock pillar that lies just off Tigalda's northwest coast. With its vertical walls and flat, grass-covered top, the rock appeared to offer protection from marauders, but the Aleuts were "ignorant of the power" of the five-foot-long rifles carried by the hunters. Trapped atop the rock, the Aleuts "became the victims of their own inexperience and were all shot down."[46]

Solov'ev was notable for his brutality but hardly unique. Some eighty ships crossed from Siberia to America in the second half of the eighteenth century, and each one of them brought disease and destruction to the Aleutians. The promyshlenniki pushed ever farther up the island chain in search of soft gold, returning to Okhotsk with hundreds of thousands of sea otter and fox pelts.[47]

The unexpected stream of wealth emanating from the "Great Land" across the Eastern Ocean excited Russian imperialists. "Russian might," speculated one enthusiastic court scientist, "will grow in Siberia and on the Northern Ocean and will reach to the main European settlements in Europe and in America." The future was bright, as long as Russia could thwart rival empires. To safeguard its hard-won geographic intelligence, akin to today's atomic secrets, Russia concealed its discoveries and released falsified maps of the Aleutian archipelago and Alaskan coast.[48] In this murky climate, Spanish, French, and British strategists struggled to gain a clear picture of the momentous events occurring in the Pacific Northwest.

So, too, did the Aleuts. In March 1776, four of the original seven who had crossed the Bering Sea with Solov'ev were awaiting a smallpox inoculation in Irkutsk before their planned departure for St. Petersburg, where they would have an audience with Catherine II. (Irkutsk improbably had one of the first centers for smallpox inoculation in the world.) A month later, Fedor Glebovich Nemtsov, governor of eastern Siberia, hosted two visitors and showed them several Irkutsk curiosities: the governor's beautiful gardens, a Kamchatka elk with exceedingly large antlers, a bird that uttered several words in Chinese and Russian, and "two savage people from America." The "dark brown savages" were lying sick with smallpox but being "treated very carefully." [49]

Nemtsov, a man who welcomed bribes and beat Irkutsk residents to extort payments, had little interest in good governance. He also had few qualms about lying to his superiors. Six months after he showed off the ailing Aleuts to his guests, he informed the distant Senate, "As for the Aleuts who had been brought here, none of them were given to me by my predecessor. And nobody told me about them." He had discovered their fate, he lied, only after investigating the matter. All of them had died. [50]

. . .

In 1759, José Torrubia was hard at work in Rome on volume ten of the official Franciscan chronicles when unexpected and exciting news arrived from Modena. The Imperial Academy in St. Petersburg had finally published a report detailing Bering's second voyage to America, nearly two decades after the event. An accompanying map showed that a narrow strait separated Asia and northwestern California. The information resonated with Torrubia, a polymath and world traveler who had recently been thinking a great deal about Pacific geography. In preparing a section of the Franciscan chronicles on the peopling of Mexico, he had gathered "authentic and remarkable" documents showing that native Mexicans had migrated from Siberia. He knew well that both Aztec traditions and Chinese and Japanese geographers suggested that the continents were only narrowly separated. And he recalled his own experience crossing the Pacific from the Philippines to Mexico in the 1730s. Three hundred miles off the California coast, he remembered, the appearance of shorebirds had indicated land to the northeast, a sign that the coastline hooked toward Asia.[51] The implication was alarming: the Russian navy could sail through the strait and descend on Spanish possessions in America.

Torrubia picked up a pen and "in a very few days" drafted an eighty-three-page tract—"small in volume," according to the papal censor, but "very large" in "erudition" and "research." Torrubia called it *I Moscoviti nella California* (*The Muscovites in California*). In breathless prose, he conveyed the urgency of the situation:

> *The Muscovites in California?* Who ever imagined? Who said so? How could it be? How are they getting there? Pray slow down, these objections are too many at once. But they don't frighten me, nor do they move me from my steadfast belief in the reality of the *crossing of the Muscovites to California*. Yes. These same *Muscovites* . . . can go above *California* with their ships; because in truth their farthest Northern Regions, which have ports on the South Sea, border our *North America*. (italics in the original)[52]

With Torrubia and others sounding alarms, Spain's ambassador in St. Petersburg was instructed to investigate, "with the greatest cunning and deceit," Russian attempts to sail to America.[53] The results would transform the California coast.

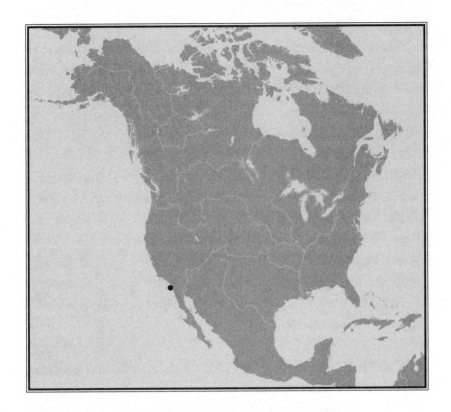

CHAPTER TWO

A War for Independence:
The San Diego Uprising

Imprisoned in a Spanish outpost at the foot of California in 1776, Diego could easily recall when the foreigners had arrived from the south by sea and by foot seven years earlier. He was probably unaware, however, that he ultimately owed his predicament to events occurring far to the north, in a region well beyond the reach of even the extensive communication channels that native peoples maintained on the West Coast. Though the Aleutian archipelago was some three thousand miles away and Kyakhta even farther, Russian activities in the North Pacific played a pivotal role in Spain's decision to establish a colony in San Diego.

As early as the 1500s, Spaniards had drafted plans to colonize California (or Alta California, as it was called to distinguish it from the Baja peninsula), but the Crown took no action until the expansion of the Russian fur trade into Alaska in the second half of the eighteenth century. At that time, a combustible mix of geographic misconceptions and imperial anxiety made colonization of the California coast appear essential to Spain's survival in the Pacific basin.[1]

Like all other Europeans at the time, Spanish officials had a murky understanding of what exactly America's North Pacific coast looked like. Perhaps it trended toward the northwest (as it, in fact, does), or perhaps the coastline ran due north. Perhaps, as some maps suggested, an enormous island the size of Great Britain sat between America and Asia. Unfortunately for Spanish officials, their anxiety was proportional to their ignorance. Even though their ambassador in St. Petersburg concluded in 1761 that Russia posed little threat to Spanish interests, it was not particularly reassuring that some Russians were already referring to the American Northwest as "New Russia." Would the colony one day rival New Spain?[2]

Whatever the precise outline of the West Coast, Spanish ministers were convinced, wrongly, that a water route of some sort connected California to the continent's interior. As one French official had pointed out years earlier, if there were no such river, it "would be contrary to all the knowledge we have of countries that are known in the world. . . . In so vast an area," he explained, "there is always some great river that traverses it."[3]

On French-influenced maps, the passage in question appeared either as a great western lake that occupied the heart of North America and emptied into the South Sea (Russia's Eastern Ocean, our Pacific) or as the fabled "River of the West" that formed just west of Lake Superior and ran straight to the Pacific. According to reports submitted by Spain's frontier officials, however, there was another possibility. Drawing on long-established geographic misconceptions, they described the existence of a navigable river that linked the Southwest or the Gulf of California to the North Pacific. How else to explain the planks that washed up on the shores of the Gulf of California, surely from a wrecked Spanish galleon whose remnants had been carried down the river into the Gulf?[4]

The precise location of this desirable river proved elusive. A 1702 attempt to find it was aborted because of a missionary's "painful flux." Another expedition in 1715 ended prematurely when a ship, outfitted to explore the Gulf of California, was nearly destroyed by a fierce storm. In 1751, one captain, who claimed to be "practically educated and particularly informed" about the geography of the Southwest, thought he had identified the river in question. As the Colorado descended to the Gulf of California, he explained, a branch forked off, trended to the northwest, coursed across the Sierras, and entered the Pacific Ocean south of Monterey, California.[5]

The rumored existence of a navigable channel connecting Spain's borderlands and the North Pacific had important strategic implications, as Andrés Marcos Burriel spelled out in an influential three-volume tome on California, published in 1757. Simply put, Spain could not control the American West without occupying the continent's Pacific Coast. There was little to fear from the "sorry canoes of the Californians," he scoffed, but if a European power made itself master of the region, Mexico itself would be at risk. Burriel advocated extending Spanish settlements into Alta California as far north as Cape Blanco, in present-day Oregon. (At the time, Spain's northernmost coastal settlement, Santa Gertrudis, was four hundred miles south of present-day San Diego.) Government censors deemed the subject sensitive enough to replace Burriel's studious map of the Pacific basin with a highly inaccurate French one. Burriel dismissed its makers, the leading French cartographers of the time, as "those Parisian boys."[6]

By the mid-1760s, Russians loomed large in the minds of apprehensive Spanish officials. One Capuchin friar in Mexico City reported on good authority that in the northernmost missions of Baja California, strangers had been spotted wearing Russian clothing and speaking what sounded like a Slavic language. A few years later, the Russian menace was illustrated on a map (Figure 5) sketched by Pedro Calderón y Henríquez, a high-ranking judge who had served for many years

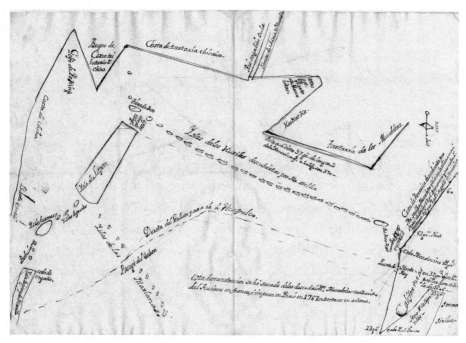

FIGURE 5 Pedro Calderón y Henríquez's map of the route from the
Philippines to northern California. From Calderón y Henríquez,
"Memorial to Don Manuel de Roda y Arrieta," 19 April 1768
(MS Vault 69), Templeton Crocker Collection. Courtesy California
Historical Society, Templeton Crocker Collection, MS Vault 69.001.

in the Philippines. Even by the standards of the day, the map, which
Calderón forwarded to one of the king's most powerful ministers, was
wildly inaccurate and uninformed. What it lacks in geographic accuracy, however, it gains as an expression of Spanish anxiety. "Tartary
of the Muscovites," or Kamchatka, hangs menacingly over the Pacific
Ocean and appears as large as the entire North American coast from
the tip of Baja California up to the Russian discoveries. The details are
even more bizarre. Calderón plotted the Aleutians in a straight line
between Kamchatka and Mendocino, California. He labeled the easternmost island Chukchi (confusing it with Siberia's Chukchi Peninsula)
and placed it a mere seventy-five miles from Cape Mendocino. As a
result, the Russians appeared to have stepping-stones leading directly
from Kamchatka to Spanish California. Arriving in the vicinity of

Mendocino, Calderón wrote, they would find a "very copious river." "By this river," he warned, "they can have access to New Mexico or the lakes along the course of the St. Lawrence River, both of which are of the greatest importance."[7]

The Spanish court needed no such notice, for it was on high alert and had already resolved to occupy Alta California. It was "of paramount importance" that no other nation establish a colony in the region, observed José de Gálvez, the talented and energetic official who oversaw Spain's expansion up the coast. After setting the project in motion, Gálvez fell ill and became delusional. According to one unsympathetic observer, the ailing Gálvez was so consumed by rumors of a Slavic presence in New Spain that he reported having personally spotted Russians in Baja California. (Gálvez in his madness, it was said, imagined himself at different times to be the emperor Montezuma, the King of Prussia, Charles XII of Sweden, Saint Joseph, and even God, in whose role he presided over Judgment Day. He eventually recovered his health and went on to become minister of the Indies and one of the most powerful and capable administrators in the Spanish Empire.)[8]

As a result of the Russian threat and Gálvez's orders, two ships dropped anchor in spring 1769 in San Diego Bay, where they awaited a pair of overland expeditions. Contagion had sickened the crew of one of the vessels, and the newcomers' first settlement was a field hospital for the indisposed. The illness soon spread to the passengers of the second vessel. Captain Vicente Vila recorded the grim results in his log: "the sick without any improvement, rather each day they find themselves worse" (May 3); "at six in the morning a sailor died" (May 6); "the sick without improvement" (May 7, 8, and 9); "at two in the afternoon a cabin boy died" (May 9); "at eight in the morning a Filipino sailor died" (May 10). A surgeon from one of the ships futilely scoured the surrounding fields for medicinal herbs, but soon two to three people were dying every day. Of more than ninety men who arrived on the vessels, only eight soldiers and a few sailors survived.[9]

Even after the arrival of the overland expeditions, the Kumeyaays observed that the Spanish were "continually burying a great number" and that many others were "prostrate in bed." In August 1769, they mounted an ineffectual attack against the weakened invaders. "I believe none of them [the Kumeyaays] were killed," wrote Junípero Serra, the Franciscan missionary; "therefore they can all yet be baptized." The struggling outpost limped on, and food supplies dwindled. In March 1770, just days from being abandoned, San Diego was saved by the timely arrival of a relief ship, whose sails appeared on the horizon during the feast of St. Joseph. Serra and others would ever after attribute their good luck to the intercession of the saint.[10]

Seven years later, Diego sat in prison. While the Continental Congress considered "certain resolutions" that its colonies were "absolved from all allegiance to the British Crown," Diego faced his seventh month of confinement. Almost five hundred miles up the coast, the Spanish were at the same time establishing their sixth mission in Alta California on the banks of the "Stream of Sorrows" in present-day San Francisco. Yet the Spanish newcomers still totaled fewer than two hundred among a native population of some sixty thousand in coastal California. In the immediate vicinity, San Diego's garrison, though recently expanded, was dwarfed by six thousand Kumeyaays. Those numbers made Diego's interrogator, Governor Fernando de Rivera y Moncada, all the more anxious to assert Spanish authority.[11]

· · ·

Diego's relations with the Spanish had taken many turns. For the first year of San Diego's existence, its two missionaries did not manage to baptize a soul. The subsequent year, they baptized sixteen young Kumeyaays, who ranged in age from three to eighteen years. The oldest of the group, Sajuil Cuylp y Meteguir, came from the neighboring *ranchería*. (The Spanish called the small native settlements they found in California rancherías, and the term is still employed today.) He was the first adult baptized in San Diego, and to mark the special occasion the missionaries asked Rivera, then second in command of the fledgling colony, to serve as the godfather. Rivera declined, but that evening, Sajuil Cuylp y Meteguir and another young boy went to Rivera's house and said, in broken Spanish, "mañana bautiza; tú, padrino." ("Tomorrow you baptize; you, godfather.") "I had no escape," Rivera recalled, and the baptism occurred the next day. Sajuil Cuylp y Meteguir was given the name Diego.[12]

Sajuil Cuylp y Meteguir's Christian name, honoring the patron saint of the Spanish outpost, reflects the high hopes that the missionaries placed in the young man and indeed in the entire colonizing enterprise. Founded amid wondrous signs in the heavens, earth, and seas, San Diego would grow and prosper, as would Diego himself—at least, so Junípero Serra imagined. Diego and his fellow convert, a thirteen-year-old boy christened Joseph María, were the first Kumeyaays to learn Spanish. "These two young Christians," wrote Serra, "serve as interpreters to the gentiles, and as teachers to the Fathers." Their progress, he noted, was exceptional.[13]

The factors that pushed and pulled Diego and other Kumeyaays to convert are obscure. The most detailed study we have of an Alta California mission—San Carlos Borromeo in Monterey—found that two forces compelled Indians to seek baptism: viruses and livestock. Old World diseases shattered families and destroyed Indian communities. At the same time, domesticated animals ruined the native subsistence base by consuming grasses, nuts, and seeds and polluting rivers. Unable to withstand the rapid collapse of both their communities and their food supply, desperate Indians sought baptism to gain access to mission crops. But the calculus must have been slightly different in San Diego for the simple reason that Spanish crops withered in the parched soil. In fact, the mission could not even produce enough food to sustain its friars and soldiers. Because of its poverty, concluded one visitor, San Diego was the worst of all the missions in Alta California.[14]

Nevertheless, by the beginning of 1775, about one hundred Kumeyaays, largely from one or two nearby rancherías, had requested baptism. Then, soon after the Spanish relocated the mission about six miles upriver, some three hundred others joined them in the span of four months. The recent neophytes, as baptized Indians were called, hailed from nine different rancherías, all within a day's walk of the mission. They came in waves. Twenty-five were baptized on a single day in July 1775, another twenty-one on a single day in September, and over eighty in the first four days of October. Francisco Palóu, a friar and chronicler of the California missions, described the "extraordinary jubilation" he felt upon baptizing a group of Kumeyaays in San Diego. When he visited their ranchería a few weeks later, the neophytes knelt before him and intoned the "Alabado," a staple of mission education: "Praise be to the Most Holy Sacrament of the Altar; and Blessed be the Immaculate Conception of the Most Beatific Virgin Mary." Palóu and his companions broke into tears of joy. Just a few days before, wrote the friar, the Indians "had been only barbarous heathen." [15]

But the rapid conversions hid a deep dissatisfaction with the Spanish presence. Around one in the morning of November 5, 1775, between six hundred and one thousand Kumeyaay Indians approached Diego's ranchería, a settlement of one hundred neophytes that sat adjacent to the mission. Vicente Fuster, one of the two friars serving in San Diego, wrote that they circled the village, but he was sound asleep at the time and had no way of knowing with certainty if the Kumeyaays surrounded the ranchería or gathered there. Soon after, the Indians descended on the mission and began looting the church. Though some of the mission structures had adobe walls, the church was built of poles and tule (a type of bulrush that once covered much of California's wetlands), and it was quickly consumed after the Kumeyaays set it on fire. [16]

Fuster awoke to the sound of gunfire and yelling, stumbled out of bed, and rushed over to the guardhouse, where he found the master carpenter and four soldiers, the mission's entire garrison. By then, only one soldier remained uninjured, and the carpenter was mortally wounded, his stomach and shoulder pierced by arrows. As the flames encroached and arrows sped by, the small party fled to another building. Fuster dashed over to Father Luis Jayme's house but found the bed empty and the burning roof near collapse.

At the mission's smithy, the two blacksmiths also awoke to find the attack under way. One emerged with a sword in hand but was promptly killed. Soldiers later found his charred remains. The second blacksmith scattered his attackers with a gunshot and escaped to join Fuster and the others. The entire group then took refuge in the only structure not yet on fire: the cookhouse, a three-sided structure made of adobe bricks and covered with a loose screen of tule. They barricaded the open side with several bundles of cloth and ropes and remained there until daybreak, dodging the rocks, firebrands, and arrows launched by the Kumeyaays.

Meanwhile, at the presidio six miles downriver (see Figure 6), another group of Kumeyaays reportedly gathered. The fort had a reduced guard and was especially vulnerable to attack. Twelve soldiers, along with a sergeant and the presidio's commander, Lieutenant José Francisco Ortega, had recently traveled some sixty miles up the coast to construct a new mission at San Juan Capistrano. Of the ten remaining at the presidio, four were lying sick and two others were in the stocks.[17]

The mission, which was visible from the presidio, was already ablaze. In calmer times, the friars regularly heard gunshots marking the changing of the presidio guard, but amazingly, that night the soldiers remained unaware of the dramatic events occurring upriver. The Kumeyaays could have taken them by complete surprise.[18] To the soldiers' great fortune, however, the locals reasoned that the garrison had already spotted the distant flames and prepared for an assault. They slipped away, without ever firing a shot.

When the sun rose over the smoldering ruins of the mission, every building lay in ashes, and the church ornaments had been burned, smashed, or carried away. Several horses, cattle, and hogs had been shot down with arrows and many others driven off. The human toll was also grim. One of the blacksmiths lay dead. Three soldiers were badly injured, as was the master carpenter, who would die of his wounds five days later. But perhaps most horrific, from the perspective of the Spanish, was Jayme's fate. The devoted friar had baptized nearly two hundred Indians over the previous four years. His body was discovered in an arroyo, a short distance from the mission. The assailants had stripped him of his frock, stabbed him multiple times, and cut out his bowels.

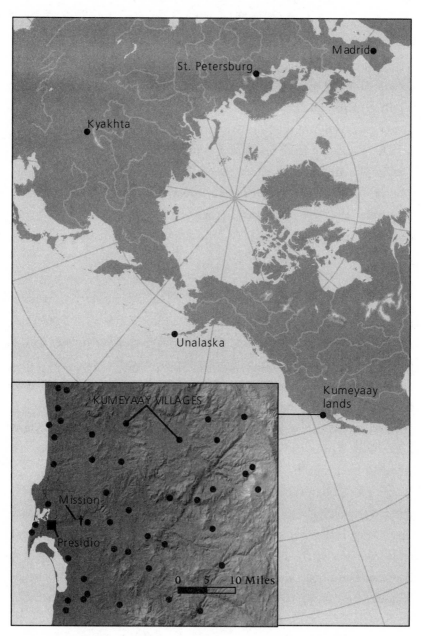

FIGURE 6 Kumeyaay land (San Diego) and the distant
locales that transformed the region in the 1770s.

They had apparently used the bloody boulder found alongside his corpse to crush his skull, and his face was bruised and swollen almost beyond recognition. Fuster succeeded in identifying his friend only by the fair complexion and tonsured pate, which remained visible. "It was indeed a stroke of fortune that they did not take his scalp off with them," Fuster observed darkly.

That same day, from his headquarters in Cambridge, Massachusetts, George Washington issued a general order against insulting the religion of Catholics. The insults were "monstrous," he wrote, given that they were "Brethren embarked in the same Cause": "The defense of the general Liberty of America."[19]

. . .

What was Diego's role in the uprising? The soldiers at the mission reported that Christian Indians participated in the attack, and one even spotted a neophyte sporting one of the missionaries' vestments. As the hostile Indians were withdrawing, three of the soldiers heard Diego yell, "adiós, Gonzalitos, guapo, ya no [h]ay azotes, ya tú y los demás *mazapá*," or "So long, little Gonzales, tough guy, there'll be no more whippings, you and the rest are as good as dead." The bilingual affront, in a combination of Kumeyaay and Spanish, targeted Alex Antonio González, who had been shot by arrows five times but would recover.[20]

On November 12, Ortega arrested four Indians, including his two interpreters, Diego and Joseph María. A day later, under interrogation, Diego insisted that he remained loyal to the Spanish. Like several others, he placed the blame for the uprising on Carlos and Francisco, two leaders among the neophytes. They had fled several weeks earlier because, it was said, they feared that the friars would punish them for stealing food from other Indians. Diego maintained that he had, in fact, told his father about the plans to attack the Spanish. But after alerting the missionaries, his father had been reprimanded and even threatened with a whipping for spreading lies—at least, so Diego claimed.[21]

The young interpreter went on to describe his devotion to the Spanish—words that must be read with some skepticism, given the

context. On the night of the attack, he became distraught upon learning of Jayme's death. "They killed my father," he exclaimed, declaring
that he would fight to the death against the Kumeyaays. His companions restrained him from acting impulsively and suicidally. As for the
insult he had reportedly hurled at González, he explained that it was a
simple misunderstanding. He had said, "Little Gonzales is brave," not
"So long, little Gonzales, tough guy." And he had observed that the
Indians, not the soldiers, were as good as dead. At daybreak, he said,
he had pursued the attackers and injured not one but two of them.[22]

Soon after Diego's interrogation, Joseph María was escorted in by
two soldiers. He, too, claimed that one of the friars had threatened to
flog him after he warned Father Jayme about the uprising. "Fear of the
heathens" had led him and others to betray the movement, he said, "and
that of the whippings to keep quiet." (Apparently, no one had informed
Fuster about the plot; as a result, no one was alive to contradict Diego
and Joseph María.) Joseph María confirmed the bulk of Diego's testimony.[23] Were Diego and Joseph María telling the truth? Or had the
two friends collaborated, concocting a story that exonerated themselves?

Ortega interrogated five other Indians and remained skeptical. "I
don't believe, nor will I believe, everything," he wrote. Yet two weeks
after the uprising, he freed Diego and Joseph María. Meanwhile, he
received reports of large clouds of smoke emerging from a valley some
seven miles from the presidio. He suspected that the Kumeyaays were
signaling another assault. Fearing an imminent attack, Ortega kept
sixteen armed and mounted soldiers and four foot soldiers on guard
every night.[24]

The extraordinary pressure led Ortega to send patrols into the surrounding mountains to capture the ringleaders and beat the prisoners.
The initial patrol returned with two women and three children. Ques-
tioned, they said that an assault on the presidio would come shortly.
Another patrol returned with Coaxín, one of the suspected ringleaders,
and he too stated that an attack was forthcoming. Ortega put him in
chains. A week later, Ortega commanded his soldiers to launch a night
raid and to fire on all attackers. Indians capable of bearing arms were to

be whipped, he ordered, so that they "feel" and "remember" the lashes. They were "accomplices," he insisted.[25]

On that last occasion, the soldiers returned with six men and seventeen women and children. Shortly after being captured, a prisoner named Culmuagua confessed that only three or four days remained until a new attack. But at the presidio, his town leader, Yguetin, contradicted him. Culmuagua is "afraid of the soldiers," Yguetin insisted, "and so he lies." Ortega issued a threat: if another attack indeed occurred, Ortega's first action would be to order Yguetin's execution.[26]

Several more patrols into the surrounding hills and valleys came back empty-handed, and on November 30, Ortega reported that he had initiated a *nobenario* of lashings to five of his prisoners—that is, twenty-five lashes on each of nine separate days. Ortega reported that the five had participated in the uprising and one had even been among the first to fire arrows—a conclusion perhaps reached because the captives were found with several church relics.[27]

The punishment was severe. The prisoners' "wounds and ulcers" had to be treated for several days before the Kumeyaays were able to return home. One prisoner never recovered. A strong stench arose from his festering ulcers, and the unfortunate victim died five days after the beating.[28]

Ortega may have adopted the same method of flogging used by his superior, Governor Rivera, in which victims were "atado a la ley de Bayona"—that is, bound in the style of the law of Bayonne.[29] Requiring no more than a single wooden pole and a whip, the punishment could be easily administered even in a remote outpost such as San Diego. Prisoners were forced to sit on the ground with their knees drawn up against their chest. A pole (or sometimes a musket) was placed in the crook of their knees, their arms pulled under the implement, and their wrists bound together around their legs. Tied in that stress position, individuals were at the mercy of the whip, as one visitor to a slave plantation in Brazil, Jean Baptiste Debret, witnessed and illustrated in the 1830s (see Figure 7).

Even a lightly administered whipping may have been especially

FIGURE 7 The law of Bayonne, as illustrated by Jean Baptiste Debret,
who witnessed the punishment while traveling through Brazil.
Debret, "Foreman Punishing Negroes," *Voyage pittoresque et historique
au Brésil* (Paris: Firmin Didot Frères, 1834–1839), vol. 2, plate 25.
Courtesy of the John Carter Brown Library at Brown University.*

humiliating for the Kumeyaays, although the Spanish were probably
unaware of the fact. According to one scholar, the native peoples of
southern California reserved flogging for individuals who murdered or
raped. The offender, after being stretched out on a rock and whipped,
became an outcast, unable to marry or participate fully in community
life. Some people reportedly committed suicide after the punishment.
What appeared to the Spanish to be a painful but not fatal flogging
could therefore seem to the Kumeyaays like a grievous and humiliating
assault on one's body and reputation.[30]

Shortly after Ortega released the five wounded prisoners, he received
troubling news: Diego was planning to flee to the rebels and was encouraging other Indians to join him. One missionary explained the cause for
alarm. Ever since Diego had convinced the Spanish of his loyalty shortly

*I wish to thank Oscar Chamosa for bringing this illustration to my attention.

after the uprising, they had placed great confidence in him. "With this neophyte united with the rebels," the missionary warned, "we should take extreme precaution."[31]

Ortega rearrested Diego and interrogated him again. "Good God! Me?" Diego exclaimed. "When did I think such things? You're being misled, Lieutenant." Ortega pushed him hard to confess, but Diego denied everything with "unthinkable deception." Ortega then placed Diego in front of several witnesses, who contradicted him. Convinced of Diego's dissimulation, Ortega extracted a confession with fifty lashes, threw him in the stocks, and placed him in solitary confinement.[32]

Even while chained hand and foot, Diego remained uncooperative. Other witnesses stated that he had visited San Luis, a neighboring Indian town, to conspire against the Spanish, but Diego insisted he had gone merely to collect acorns. Asked again why he had planned to flee the presidio, he said he had no other reason but the desire to flee. He was angry with his father-in-law for not giving him enough food, he stated, and wanted to go away to die somewhere. Diego denied all of the accusations leveled against him by the other witnesses. "The Devil tricked him," he concluded (in Ortega's paraphrase), "and he wanted to go and be killed by the heathens." Ortega added, "Such an action, even were it true, belongs to someone desperate for his life, and eager for demons to possess him."[33]

By mid-December, Kumeyaays knew that they might be beaten to death if they did not tell the Spanish what they wished to hear. In addition to the five prisoners subjected to the *nobenario*, Ortega gave all but one of the witnesses in the case against Diego thirty lashes each. In early January, two more Indians were arrested and beaten. "The whippings given were such that one of the Indians died from them and the other one was very ill," reported Pedro Font, a missionary who had recently arrived in the presidio. Font treated the survivor's wounds and was disgusted when the man soon after fled the mission, "showing little gratitude and less courtesy."[34]

.   .   .

On January 11, 1776, two days after the first copies of Thomas Paine's incendiary pamphlet *Common Sense* began circulating in the British colonies, Governor Rivera arrived from Monterey, accompanied by Juan Bautista de Anza. Anza, suspending his colonizing expedition to San Francisco, had joined Rivera in Los Angeles to help rescue the beleaguered mission farther south. They brought with them twenty-three soldiers. With rumors still flying of an impending attack, Rivera maintained Ortega's policy of sending out troops to capture Indians, often in the middle of the night. Uncowed, one town leader, perched atop some high rocks, yelled down to a party of soldiers, "I was the one who burned down the mission and killed the people, come and get me." Recounting the event, Font observed, "one could imagine the amount of trouble it would take to subdue these Indians."[35]

Rivera continued the beatings. When his sergeant returned with four prisoners on January 19, he gave each a "welcome" of fifty lashes. Rivera later released two Indians because they needed medical treatment and appeared to be innocent. A week later, the sergeant returned with nine more prisoners. On first arrival at the outpost, four of them were "handed a serving of fifty lashes" and, since the stocks were full, released. Two others were put in handcuffs and placed under guard. That same day, a party of soldiers traveled to La Soledad, an Indian settlement some ten miles up the coast, and flogged the town leader.[36]

The whippings, characterized blithely by Font as a "serving," were described with equal indifference by Rivera. The prisoners "got a good dusting," he wrote. On another occasion, one prisoner, tied in a field stock, "got a scrubbing," according to Rivera. "Although heathens," the governor protested, "they dissemble to save their skin." He told one group of prisoners that "I must know everything; that I have a medicine to make them tell the truth; that it is not nor am I like their Indian witchdoctors who peddle so many lies; that my medicine is punishment, and the great pain will force them" to confess.[37]

Rivera's were not idle threats. "I saw how poor a state an Indian, who was among the captives and had been whipped, had been left in by the lashes," wrote Font. His sores were "black and horrifying." Font concluded that it was "an extremely poor climate for the healing of sores and wounds," blaming "infected blood" and "dampness." "This poor constitution, taken together with the choler that the prisoners must have developed and their not being well adapted for whipping, perhaps led to the bad outcome of their buttocks becoming ulcerated."[38]

In mid-March, Carlos, one of the two supposed ringleaders who had eluded the Spanish for three months, appeared in the presidio church, seeking asylum. Against the warnings of the Franciscan missionaries, Rivera violated ecclesiastical sanctuary and imprisoned him. He was excommunicated for his efforts. (Rivera was later absolved, but not before suffering a nervous collapse.) At the end of April, soldiers captured the other reputed ringleader, Francisco. He was brought into the presidio with a show of force, guarded by several soldiers and tied many times over.[39] Rivera continued beating and interrogating prisoners.

Then, in early June, Rivera confronted his godson, Diego, who had been sitting in prison for over six months. Asked why he had planned to flee in December 1775, Diego responded that he had been seized with fear when he learned that Rivera was arriving. Rivera, all agreed, intended to "fight, punish, and flog everyone." As for the testimony against him, Diego claimed that the witnesses had fabricated their accusations to avoid being whipped.[40] Rivera ended the day still convinced of his godson's guilt.

From Mexico City, Antonio María de Bucareli, the viceroy of New Spain, followed and approved of the investigations: "I have had the pleasure to know that the Indians who perpetrated it are so intimidated and frightened that they now wish nothing more than peace." He announced that he would "practice mildness and gentleness rather than severity," sparing the ringleaders from execution. Rivera objected to the policy of leniency. "Being new Christians," he wrote, "they must be taught a lesson so that they know it is not the same as in their state of heathenism." Otherwise, he claimed, whenever they liked, the Indians would "eat the Padres and soldiers alive." The interrogations continued until Rivera finally left San Diego on October 14. In spring 1777, the remaining prisoners, likely including Diego, were finally released.[41]

By fall 1778, Diego was deathly ill. Serra had recently arrived at the mission, where he planned to confirm hundreds of neophytes—a sacrament performed after individuals grasp the fundamentals of Christian doctrine. Serra took "special care" that the first confirmation was Diego's. "At the beginning he had been faithful and a special favorite of mine," Serra explained. "But he turned traitor in the revolution and was one of the prisoners who they said deserved death." Too sick to walk, Diego was carried into the church, where Serra performed the ritual. Three days later, Diego received the last rites. "As he was very fluent in Castilian," wrote Serra, "it was most touching to hear how he prepared himself for death." Diego died on September 24, 1778, and was buried in the church cemetery. He was twenty-five years old.[42]

. . .

The outpost in Diego's homeland did not put to rest Spanish fears about Russian activity in the North Pacific. It was imperative to occupy and fortify the known natural harbors on the coast—that is, San Diego and, nearly four hundred miles to the north, Monterey. In early November 1769, an expedition heading to colonize Monterey had overshot the harbor and become hopelessly lost, setting up camp about one hundred miles north of their intended destination. They were just south of San Francisco but on the ocean side and entirely unaware of the great bay to their east, on the other side of the low-lying coastal mountains. A small party went out in pursuit of deer, climbing the mountains until, to their surprise, they spotted "an immense arm of the sea" that "extended inland as far as the eye could see."[43] Along the bay shore, smoke rose from countless campfires. The local residents, warming themselves on a chilly November day, were unaware that they were being watched.

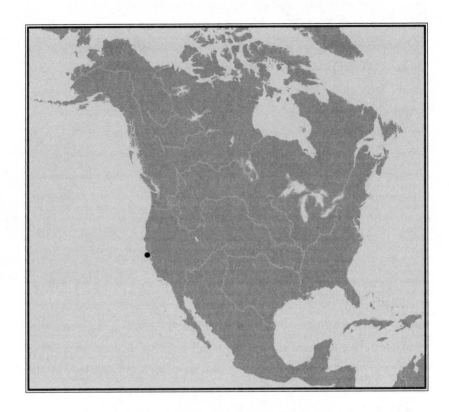

CHAPTER THREE

First Contact:
Colonizing San Francisco

After his bewildering experience with a party of mounted soldiers, the man on San Lorenzo Creek must have watched with the greatest relief as the strangers rode off, leaving him prostrate in a patch of grass. The San Francisco Bay Area native had never met Francisco Antonio de Lacy, Spain's eager ambassador to the Russian court, but in a distant way he owed his unnerving experience to the Spanish nobleman. Shortly after arriving in St. Petersburg in late 1772, the Conde de Lacy began sending alarming reports back to Madrid. Of Irish ancestry, Lacy was born in Barcelona in 1731 and had followed his father into the Spanish military, fighting in Italy and Portugal before serving as an envoy in Stockholm and then St. Petersburg. He seems to have enjoyed spycraft, and it is perhaps fitting that his only known portrait is not a likeness but a trompe l'oeil painting of manuscripts and printed papers that enigmatically capture his career and personality. Lacy possessed a fervid imagination and a writer's talent for crafting memorable details; both served him well in inflating the Russian threat.[1]

In fall 1772, Lacy reported that the Russian court had devised elaborate plans to defend the Kamchatkan port of Petropavlovsk from a foreign invasion. (Why would Spain desire a country "so harsh, so cold, and with so few resources," the Barcelona native wondered.) According to the plans—which had been stolen from the Kamchatkan archives and spirited out of the country by a duplicitous Polish exile—fifteen thousand troops were to be recruited from Irkutsk and neighboring towns and transported to Petropavlovsk on ships built especially for the purpose. A fortress was to be constructed using the peninsula's plentiful supply of timber, and local residents, including the indigenous Kamchadals, were to prepare dogsleds to haul supplies and munitions. Lacy concluded his report with a "singular" fact. Catherine the Great, standing with a high-ranking admiral before a map of her dominions, had told the officer that if Asia and America were joined by land, she would extend her territorial conquests into that part of the globe; if separated by a strait, she would expand by sea.[2] (None of these ambitious plans to defend Petropavlovsk were ever enacted.)

Other disquieting revelations followed. A Russian officer had recently completed an expedition to America, Lacy ascertained. His papers were triple sealed, and he and his secretary were sworn to "keep the deepest silence" about the discoveries. Despite the Russian court's secrecy, Lacy learned that the officer had acquired European coins in America. The unstated conclusion: the Russians were within striking distance of Spanish colonies. A few months later, Lacy warned of a Russian plan to send a fleet around the Cape of Good Hope and across the Indian Ocean to capture Spanish possessions in the Pacific. Russia had a greater right to America than any other power, said one adviser to Catherine II, "because that country was once peopled by Siberians." "The projects of this court are so vast," Lacy marveled, "that it has formed a plan to invade China with twenty-five thousand men" and launch a simultaneous maritime invasion of Japan.[3]

According to Lacy's sources, Russia was also considering the possibility of forming an alliance with Britain against Spain in the North Pacific. Britain's interest reportedly lay in defending the possessions of the Hudson's Bay Company, the London-based outfit that held a monopoly on the fur trade in western and upper Canada. The HBC controlled Indians from Baffin Island to the Bering Sea, Lacy exaggerated, and "kept a profound silence about its trade." (In fact, some twenty-five hundred miles of the most inhospitable terrain in North America separated the HBC's westernmost outpost from the Bering Sea.) If Lacy's geography seems hazy and the prospect of a grand Russian-British alliance in the Pacific far-fetched, the rumors were nonetheless startling.[4]

While Lacy relentlessly built up the Russian threat, a Spanish reconnaissance of San Francisco Bay returned with pivotal news in spring 1772. The explorers had stumbled upon a great river that probably originated in the vicinity of New Mexico. (They were badly mistaken, for the river's source was close by, in California's Central Valley.) "We cannot but fear the gravest harm to the Spanish Crown should any foreign nation establish itself at that harbor," a high-level Franciscan warned New Spain's viceroy. By following the course of the river, interloping nations could obstruct the Spanish and, even worse, "possess themselves of what is already subject to our Catholic Monarch." With alarms sounding in St. Petersburg as well as in northern California, the viceroy set in motion plans to occupy the bay, selecting Juan Bautista de Anza, a "prudent and zealous conquistador," for the job.[5]

Born in Sonora in 1736, Anza had long dreamed of establishing a direct overland link between his homeland in the Southwest and the Pacific Coast. In 1774, the career military officer accomplished the feat with a small party, crossing the Colorado Desert at the foot of California to Mission San Gabriel (the future site of Los Angeles) and then turning north to Monterey. (Native peoples in southern California perhaps

FIGURE 8 This rock art in the Anza-Borrego Desert in southern California may show Anza on horseback during one of his two expeditions through the region. Courtesy of the Agua Caliente Cultural Museum.

memorialized the event, as suggested in Figure 8.) A year later, he set out with a much larger group, three hundred colonists, on the same route. This time, he carried instructions to continue to San Francisco Bay to establish the first colony in the area.

On January 2, just before the colonists reached the Pacific Coast, the missionary Pedro Font paused at a large sycamore tree near present-day Ontario, California, and carved, "YEAR 1776. The San Francisco expedition came here." (On the opposite coast, the siege of Boston was then in its ninth month, and Washington was welcoming his newly reorganized forces. With fresh recruits arriving from around the thirteen colonies, he observed, the army "in every point of View is entirely Continental.")[6] At San Gabriel, the party was delayed by news of the Kumeyaay uprising in San Diego. Anza and his soldiers rushed down the coast to reinforce the outpost, and the colonists did not resume their journey northward for eight weeks. In early March, they reached Monterey, Spain's northernmost mission and presidio.

Though Monterey was then entering its seventh year, it did not give the impression of permanency. The Royal Presidio consisted of a stockade and a few buildings constructed of wood and mud. "The whole thing amounts to very little," scoffed Font, who found himself lodged in a "very dirty little room full of lime." A few miles away, near the mouth of the Carmel River, stood Mission San Carlos. In Font's assessment, its church, though made largely of tule grass, was "somewhat roomy and well built"—a grudging compliment from the judgmental and disagreeable missionary. The surrounding stockade was closed each night by lock and key, but as Junípero Serra dryly observed, "an entrance can easily be effected by knocking down or pushing aside some of the poles." Somewhere between three hundred and four hundred Christian Indians resided there. Anza suspected that most of them had accepted baptism because "they like our grains and gifts."[7]

After pausing briefly in Monterey, Anza set out to scout the San Francisco Bay to identify sites for a presidio and two missions. (He would select the location for the presidio but only one of the missions.) Accompanied by Font, twelve soldiers, and six muleteers, he headed north-northeast, skirted the Santa Cruz Mountains, and entered the heart of what is now Silicon Valley. The San Francisco Bay Area is defined by a break in the coastal mountain range, a narrow strait of only a mile across called the Golden Gate. The ocean washes through the strait and fills what was once a vast river plain, stretching north–south. Anza would venture up the southern peninsula to the Golden Gate and then head back down and around the bay. In the course of his travels he would pass through the homelands of some sixty autonomous tribelets, as anthropologists call the indigenous communities in the region, each composed of a few hundred individuals occupying an area about ten miles in diameter. Most of the people he would encounter spoke one of the seven Costanoan languages, as different from one another as are French, Spanish, and Italian. In the greater Bay Area, Costanoan existed alongside seven other language families, which were mutually unintelligible. After a day's travel from Monterey, the Spanish were already stymied by the linguistic diversity. "They had a great deal to say," Font wrote of a group of hunters, "but we could not understand any of it."[8]

The Spanish camped about twenty miles southeast of present-day San Jose. They were mystified by what they found at the site. Six months earlier, a small Spanish exploratory expedition had pitched tents on the same ground, and the missionary Francisco Palóu had said mass beneath a makeshift arbor. What remained of the arbor was now encircled with stakes and poles adorned with feathers, arrows, and balls of seeds and acorns. Costanoans had made similar offerings to a cross in Monterey. The reason, one local resident explained, was that it "might not be angry with them."[9]

Anza and his party headed northwest the next day, passing numerous wary residents, who made sounds and gestures that seemed intended to discourage the Spanish from proceeding, but as they moved up the San Francisco peninsula, the residents became more welcoming. One "long-bearded chief" cheerfully recognized one of the officers from an earlier expedition. Others, deemed "quite ugly" by Font, nevertheless were docile enough to earn his patronizing approval: "A good, developed mission could be formed with them," he wrote.[10]

As they approached the end of the peninsula, the tree cover thinned out, exposing green rolling hills and, farther on, the enormous sand dunes, some rising over one hundred feet, that once covered much of present-day San Francisco. Blanketed with low, thick vegetation with only the occasional stunted coast live oak, the inhospitable dunes supported a population of under two people per square mile, a third of the density found farther south. Only two "useful and serviceable" Indians came to visit the strangers at their Mountain Lake camp, a mile and a half from the southern footing of today's Golden Gate Bridge.[11]

After overlooking the Golden Gate—"a wonder of nature," according to Font—the party circled the peninsula. Toward the sheltered and sunnier bay side, where Anza decided to establish a mission, the captain found "numerous and docile heathen," who accompanied him "with great pleasure." The Spaniards' warm reception continued as they returned south along the bay shore. At present-day San Mateo, the Indians were "quite attentive and courteous and even bothersome," wrote Font. "They would be easy to convert," he predicted. Farther on, Costanoans were "saddened" when the Spanish did not accept their enthusiastic invitation to visit their village. Curious residents watched Font use a graphometer (a semicircle inscribed with angles) to calculate the height of a towering redwood, the famous *"palo alto"* that gave the present town its name. The "quiet and attentive" Indians were "struck with wonder at seeing what I was doing," wrote the missionary. Anza concluded that all of the people north of the Palo Alto region were indeed "very friendly, content, and joyful" and anxious to assist the Spanish in every way.[12]

But as the party skirted the bottom of the south bay, local residents became less welcoming. One group exhibited a "great deal of fear," and the women stayed hidden in their huts. They and another village warmed up after Anza presented them with glass beads, but other Costanoans remained antagonistic. One elderly woman stood at her doorway until the Spanish departed, reciting what appeared to Font to be incantations. She ignored the beads that Anza offered. Other Indians "fled like wild beasts." Soon after, the man on San Lorenzo Creek spotted Anza and his party. He threw himself down into the grass, hoping to remain undetected.[13]

Heading up the east side of the enormous bay, the expedition reached the Carquinez Strait, where the San Joaquin and Sacramento Rivers enter the ocean waters. (Once again, the Spanish were fooled by the region's geography. After careful observation, Anza and Font determined that the two great rivers did not exist and that the strait was instead an inlet.) Unlike the Costanoans farther south, the Huchiuns greeted the travelers with "indescribable jubilation," bringing firewood in the evening and food, song, and dance the next morning. They were neither wonder-struck nor intimidated. When the Spanish approached the banks of the strait, fishermen ignored them and their insistent requests to trade, at least until Anza held a colored handkerchief aloft. The discriminating Indians had no interest in beads and fishhooks but greatly desired cloth.[14]

Following the strait east toward the distant snowcapped Sierras, Anza's party encountered fishermen laden with salmon. Farther on, they met a group of hunters carrying an elk head; one of the men, painted fawn color, intended to place it over his head to help him sneak up on and kill tule elk. At one village near present-day Antioch, the women and children took to the water in their reed boats as soon as the strangers approached, while the wary men stayed behind to treat with the visitors.[15]

The Spanish did not progress far into the interior, despite Anza's intention to reach the Sierras. On the western edge of the "boundless" San Joaquin Valley, the vast tule marshes proved impenetrable. Mules sank deep into the muck, and men, it was said, could drown and disappear forever beneath the mud. Anza and his party turned back, cut through Livermore Valley, and headed south to re-join their outgoing route below present-day San Jose. The dry, hilly interior was less populated. They passed some abandoned "wretched little huts" and spotted a single person in the distance, who, said Font with his usual disdain, fled "like a deer." Reentering the populous Silicon Valley, the travelers were greeted once again by local residents, who brought them food. On April 8, they arrived back in Monterey.[16]

The colonizing enterprise was now turned over to José Joaquín Moraga. In late June 1776, the officer led a party of soldiers and colonists back up the peninsula to the banks of the Arroyo de los Dolores, the homeland of the Yelamu people, where Anza had decided to establish a mission. Not far from the geographic center of modern San Francisco, they erected fifteen bell-shaped tents, and the next day they built a shelter of branches and set up a portable altar. Nearly three hundred cattle grazed along the lagoon; curious residents did not yet perceive the deadly impact of the exotic animals.[17]

.   .   .

The newcomers arrived with a panoply of strange but fascinating things: horses, cows, pigs, firearms, iron, sailing ships, woolen textiles, corn, wheat, liquor, dyes, chocolate, and a host of other goods. Equally intriguing to local residents, Spanish missionaries practiced unfamiliar and perhaps powerful rituals. Native inhabitants saw opportunity in their arrival, the possibility of appropriating and harnessing new ways of controlling and shaping the world. That promise explains why they so often welcomed the strangers—at least at first.

During the initial overland expedition to northern California in 1769, locals were "very friendly and cheerful." It was as if "they had always dealt with us," wrote one of the Spaniards. Near present-day Santa Cruz, they welcomed the strangers "with great affability and kindness." The Spanish repeated the same refrains: the Indians were of the "best disposition and temper," received them with "a great deal of hospitality and pleasure," were "anxious for them to come," and brought them "a great many large black very rich pies," which, the hungry soldiers reported, would have gone well with a spicy pipián sauce.[18]

When the *San Carlos* became the first European vessel on record to sail through the Golden Gate in July 1775, residents stood at the water's edge to assuage Spanish fears and encourage the crew to come ashore. Watching from shipboard, the missionary Vicente de Santa María confessed, "We summoned our courage because we had to, lest fear make cowards of us." Native peoples revealed no such misgivings. Visiting the sixty-foot ship, they were "in great delight," "marvelling" at its structure and wondering at the pens of lambs, hens, and pigeons. One of the Costanoan phrases recorded by Santa María sums up the pleasure that local residents took in the encounter: on being given a cigar, an individual aboard the Spanish vessel demanded, "Give me a light to start it with."[19]

To be sure, not everyone was unperturbed by the arrival of the foreigners. In 1769, the Spanish deemed one party of unwelcoming hunters to be "not in the mood." Another group of "amazed and confused" villagers north of Monterey "had no notice of our coming," though after some negotiation, the women set to work making food for the visitors, who gave them beads in return. On the shores of the East Bay, there was no such rapprochement. There, people of "evil disposition" reportedly received the Spanish "very badly."[20]

The reasons for such variations in behavior are surely complex. In 1769, local residents may have been horrified by the enormous purple bruises covering the soldiers' skin, their bloody mouths (a result of bleeding gums), and grotesquely swollen limbs. Scurvy had set in just as the Spanish were approaching the Monterey area, and soon eight soldiers were incapable of walking. Two received their last rites, but the fresh food gifted by locals relieved the worst of the symptoms. The emaciated soldiers survived, only to come down with fevers and severe diarrhea, caused by eating raw acorns.[21]

Moraga's founding expedition in 1776 suffered no such misfortune, and the Yelamus initially went frequently to trade with the newcomers, exchanging mussels and grass seeds for glass beads and Spanish food (excepting milk, which they refused to taste). In late August, a ship arrived with supplies for the new presidio and mission, and the Spanish began constructing a chapel and the living quarters for the Franciscan fathers. Three miles to the northwest, just inside the Golden Gate, they laid out the presidio, nearly 250 feet long on each side. Impressive in its size and uniformity, it was nonetheless made almost entirely of palisades and mud, and in 1779 heavy rains would wash away most of the structure.[22]

On September 17, the day after Washington's troops held their position on Harlem Heights in Manhattan, the Spanish took formal possession of San Francisco Bay. Two missionaries performed a solemn mass, church bells were sounded, and cannons and muskets fired. The *San Carlos*, anchored offshore, responded in kind with its swivel guns. All felt "joy and happiness," wrote the missionary Francisco Palóu, though local residents vanished during the festivities and did not appear again for several days. In early October, another ceremony marked the official founding of the mission. "The only ones who did not enjoy this happy day," Palóu noted, "were the heathens."[23]

Though language barriers made communication nearly impossible between natives and newcomers, the Yelamus soon realized that the Spanish intended to remain in their homelands. Ninety miles down the coast, Monterey served as an unnerving illustration of what might befall them. At Mission San Carlos, the Spanish took disciplinary actions against baptized natives that were disconcerting and even terrifying. In early 1775, for example, the Spanish spotted a convert "in actual fornication" with a colonist along the Carmel River. Both were locked up and interrogated, and the colonist was whipped. A month later,

Spanish soldiers hunted down a neophyte who had fled the mission. In December 1775, soldiers once again pursued an Indian fugitive, but he shot one of them with an arrow and escaped. Just as alarming was the fact that even the Spanish found cause to flee from the colonial outpost. When Anza reached the marshes on the outer edge of the San Joaquin Valley, his men recognized the area from earlier sorties in search of fugitive soldiers.[24]

News of this astonishing behavior—which perhaps seemed far more incredible than Spanish technologies—traveled far and wide and certainly reached people living on the San Francisco peninsula. In May 1776, the missionary and explorer Francisco Garcés met an Indian who asked him in Spanish for paper to roll a cigar. "I had a suspicion that he might be some Christian who had just fled from the missions of Monterey," wrote Garcés, "since he made signs of shooting and of flogging"—actions that the Indian must have described in detail to his hosts. (Garcés later confirmed his supposition that the cigar smoker was indeed a fugitive.) The encounter occurred in the foothills of the Sierras, well over one hundred miles from the closest mission.[25]

Alongside those individual accounts of flight and captivity, Bay Area residents may have pieced together a general picture of the terrifying mortality rates in the missions. Except for 1774, demographic statistics are lacking for the early years of Mission San Carlos. In that year, twenty mission Indians died—a death rate of eighty-five per one thousand, which was extraordinarily high even for the eighteenth century. In later years, for which statistics are more complete, the annual death rate averaged seventy-nine for every thousand mission Indians, enough to prevent the population from reproducing itself. By comparison, in revolutionary-era Philadelphia, thirty-five of every thousand white residents died each year; for black residents, including the four out of five who were enslaved, the death rate was twice that. A grim list of often fatal diseases permeated mission life: dysentery, whooping cough, diphtheria, pneumonia, measles, influenza, tuberculosis, syphilis, gonorrhea, and the occasional devastating outbreak of smallpox.[26]

At Mission San Antonio de Padua, about 175 miles south of San

Francisco, the year 1775 was especially deadly. The resident missionaries later compiled a grammar of the local Salinan language, and included practical sentences such as "o missina?" (Do you feel sick?) and "que°onióu̯cᶜ zo peᵃ Padre peᵃ quissíną" (The sick man was given medicine by the Padre). Some Indians at San Antonio de Padua blamed the Franciscans for the widespread illnesses that year. The "insolent" Salinans enticed Christian converts from the mission and sheltered them in the mountains, complained the Franciscans, where word of the frequent deaths and the suspected malevolent sorcery of the missionaries must have spread from village to village. The situation became so tense that the missionaries were unable to travel safely to native villages to proselytize.[27]

By the time the Spanish ceremoniously took possession of San Francisco, many Yelamus had already fled across the bay or taken refuge on its uninhabited islands. Their visits to the mission became infrequent, occurring only when individuals passed by while hunting ducks on the lagoon. In December, relations turned hostile. One Yelamu man tried to kiss the wife of a soldier. Another threatened to shoot the missionaries' cook, a native convert from Monterey. A third killed a pig that had been foraging on Yelamu land, eating the roots and seeds that local women harvested. The commanding sergeant bound and flogged the man and pursued two others who had tried to rescue their companion. The situation escalated the next day, when the Spanish shot dead one individual on the bay shore and captured and whipped two more. The Yelamus disappeared for three months. Then, in late June 1777, a full year after the Spanish had erected their tents on the Arroyo de los Dolores, a twenty-year-old named Chamís became the first local resident baptized at the mission. He was renamed Francisco.[28]

Indians were usually "caught by the mouth," observed the missionary Pedro Font—a statement that must be understood in the broader context of the region's stingy environment. Scarce resources had led to a long-term trend of resource intensification in the four millennia before contact. That is, to support a growing population, native peoples increasingly extracted more calories per square mile and exerted more energy in doing so—to the point that they had destroyed local breeding grounds for certain birds, overhunted large game, and reduced the population of sea mammals. One ingeniously designed study of a midden in present-day Emeryville, next to the San Francisco–Oakland Bay Bridge, found that native peoples overexploited the sturgeon population, forcing residents to turn to less productive species, such as mollusks.[29]

Perhaps the surest sign of resource intensification was the dependency on the acorn, as important to Californians as corn was to natives of the Southeast and Southwest. Though acorns are high in fat, oak tree production is sporadic, and toxic tannic acid must be leached out before the nuts are edible, as Spanish soldiers learned from hard-won experience. Given the labor investment necessary to process acorns, they were not a preferred food but a fallback exploited only after population size and density outgrew other resources. The trend in acorn consumption, and thus in resource intensification, is reflected by the increasing frequency of mortars and pestles in archaeological sites over the four millennia preceding contact. By the time the Spanish laid claim to San Francisco, inhabitants were concentrated in locations where oak trees thrived.[30]

As a result of the scarcity of food sources, Bay Area residents suffered from dental decay, arthritis, nutritional deficiencies, and a host of infectious and deadly diseases. One study of precontact Costanoan burials in the East Bay measured bone and tooth deformations and found that 30 percent of the population suffered from nutritional stress during childhood; 25 percent were afflicted by staph infections, yaws, or nonvenereal syphilis; and over 50 percent had either anemia or vitamin B_{12} deficiency, brought on by poor diet, unsanitary living conditions, disease, or intestinal parasites.[31]

To survive in such an environment, local residents developed a number of effective measures to extract food from the land. Though they were not farmers, they burned, coppiced, pruned, sowed, tilled, transplanted, and weeded wild plants. California, observes one scholar, was not a wilderness but a garden. On the San Francisco peninsula, inhabitants hunted and fished, harvested shellfish, and gathered wild grass seeds, acorns, berries, and onions. Yet they had little surplus and were especially vulnerable to the environmental damage inflicted by Spanish cattle and hogs. Outside of the view of Spanish missionaries, they began to starve.[32]

They had nowhere to go. They would not take "a step outside of their respective territories," according to Anza, "because of the enmity which is common among them." Font observed that villages often fought each other for access to mussel beds, and one Costanoan proved the point by showing off a fresh arrow wound in his leg. The neighboring tribelet, Font deduced, was "very fierce." When one Indian arrived at Anza's encampment near the Carquinez Strait with a scalp dangling from the end of a pole, Font stated the obvious: it "smelled like warfare."[33]

Since then, archaeologists have confirmed that violence was widespread in the Bay Area. At one burial site in central Silicon Valley, fully 17 percent of the skeletons bear signs of healed fractures and penetration wounds—a rate higher than that found anywhere else on the continent. At another site on the southeastern side of the bay, skeletons reveal that facial and skull wounds were common and that injury by projectiles was unusually high compared to other precontact North American populations. Though the Yelamus drew on their alliances as best they could, their flight across the bay was a desperate response to a dire situation.[34]

Chamís's baptism was "to the greater honor and glory of God," wrote San Francisco's missionaries, the culmination of their yearlong labors among the heathens.[35] For local residents, by contrast, the ceremony was one defeat in a debilitating struggle that had begun when the Spanish arrived with their portable altar in June 1776.

• • •

The Spanish represented both an opportunity and a threat. They possessed unfamiliar and appealing new technologies and seemed, by dint of their immune systems as well as their weapons, unusually powerful. Yet they appropriated valuable land, created permanent outposts, and refused to permit residents to leave; they hunted down and beat fugitives; they punished women and men who had sexual relations outside of marriages presided over by missionaries; and they enforced a regimented labor system and compelled people to attend church. The missions were disease ridden. When locals were starving, they went there to die.

With the establishment of Mission Dolores and the Presidio of San Francisco (Figure 9), exotic European goods and technologies became ordinary. California Indians integrated both of them into their lives and languages. They adopted Spanish terms for *beeswax*, *dog*, *iron*, *ax*, *orange*, *mule*, *chicken*, and a host of other things once unknown to them. Along with Spanish goods and technologies, Spanish authority and endemic disease became ordinary too. To describe their new world, Bay Area natives needed new words that the colonists' language conveniently supplied: Spanish equivalents of *drunkard*, *devil*, *fever*, *work*, *rifle*, and *soldiers*.[36]

The demographic collapse that followed was swift and terrible. In 1807, twelve Aleut baidarkas slipped into the San Francisco Bay. Carried south by Russian-employed traders to scour the harbor for its numerous sea otters, the Aleuts hugged the northern shoreline to avoid the

FIGURE 9 A new world of foreign goods and technologies. A view of the Presidio of San Francisco in 1816 by Victor Adam, after Louis Choris. Beinecke Rare Book and Manuscript Library, Yale University.

Spanish presidio's looming canons.[37] The coast was nearly deserted. On the northern peninsula, the Huimens, who had greeted the first Spanish ship to enter the Golden Gate in 1775, were no longer. The tribelet had sought refuge in Mission Dolores in the 1780s. Across the water on the San Francisco peninsula, the Yelamus had long since joined the mission as well. South to the end of the bay, the Urebures, Ssalsons, Lamchins, and Puichons had also been subsumed into the mission population. A long list of other peoples had also entered the missions or simply disappeared: the Alsons, Tuibuns, Yrgins, Jalquins, Huchiuns, Pruristacs, Chiguans, Cotegens, Olpens, Oljons, Partacsis, Quirostes, Achistacas, Cotonis, Uypis, Sayantas, Somontacs, Tamiens, and Ritocsis.

Missions created cataclysms that radiated across the land, wiping out the closest villages first and then, in order of distance, destroying those situated farther away, as Figure 10 illustrates. By the time the Aleut hunters entered the bay in 1807, the outer boundary of the devastation extended to the western slope of the San Joaquin Valley, some fifty miles east of the Golden Gate. The boundary ran northwest along the valley's edge, skirted the Sacramento–San Joaquin River Delta, and circled the north bay. The epicenter was Mission Dolores. In the thirty years after Moraga founded the colony in 1776, a total of six hundred individuals were born and baptized at the mission; during the same period, more than four times that many died there.[38] Perhaps the man from San Lorenzo Creek was among the dead.

· · ·

In early 1773, Junípero Serra weaved through the market stalls, garbage heaps, and gallows in Mexico City's central square and entered the massive viceregal palace, where the public had established a saloon, gaming tables, and a sex market, whose patrons marked the walls with nicknames and lewd illustrations.[39] Serra had come to see Antonio María Bucareli, the viceroy of New Spain, who governed dozens of colonies from Guatemala north to California and Louisiana, and east to Cuba. The Franciscan father brought with him a long list of "suggestions" for how the viceroy might strengthen the fragile missions on the Pacific

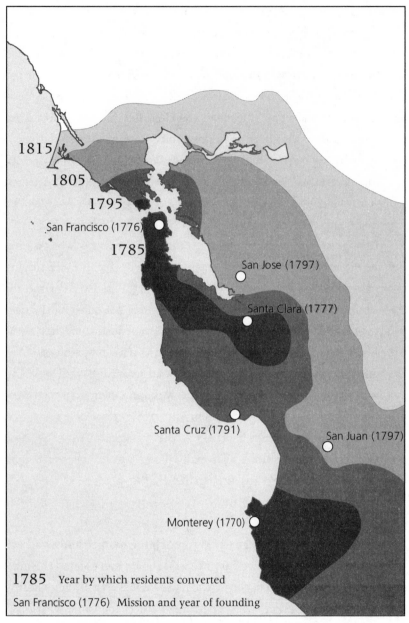

1815

1805

1795

San Francisco (1776)

1785

San Jose (1797)

Santa Clara (1777)

Santa Cruz (1791)

San Juan (1797)

Monterey (1770)

1785   Year by which residents converted

San Francisco (1776)   Mission and year of founding

FIGURE 10 The San Francisco Bay Area, with Spanish
missions founded before 1815 marked by circles. The shaded
areas show the progression of Indian conversions.

Coast. But first and foremost, he explained, there was an immediate and pressing crisis: food was running desperately low in the missions, and supplies needed to be rushed to California from San Blas.[40]

Plagued with torrential rains and a sickly environment, San Blas could not have been more poorly situated to support the missions, though the port had been established precisely for that purpose in 1768. Ocean voyages from the Pacific outpost to Alta California regularly took from fifty to over a hundred days, and contrary winds and countercurrents sometimes carried vessels far off course and into the ocean. Fighting strong headwinds, one ship took seven months to travel half the distance between San Blas and San Diego.[41]

The journeys were often exercises in futility, as illustrated by the *San Carlos*. In late 1768, after crossing the Gulf of California and making port in La Paz in Baja California, the newly constructed vessel was already in a sorry state. Short of crew and taking on a half foot of water per hour, it arrived with its tackle and rigging in shreds and anchors broken. Its cargo was damaged too. Despite undergoing repairs and taking on fresh supplies at La Paz, two of the crew died on the voyage to San Diego and were thrown overboard; another seven were buried on arrival. In 1771, the vessel set out again from San Blas, heading for California with a group of missionaries. Shortly after embarking, it was blown hundreds of miles south and beached on the Mexican coast, its rudder broken into pieces and planks opening at the seams. The following year, the *San Carlos* sailed as far as Monterey but, fighting fierce headwinds, could not make landfall and had to slip back to San Diego. In 1773, the vessel did not make it even that far and was forced to land in Baja California with a damaged rudder. No wonder Indians at the Monterey mission called it the "sad ship." Nonetheless, it was more fortunate than the *San José*, a "new and beautiful packet boat" that disappeared on a voyage to Monterey and was never heard from again.[42]

Despite the insecurity of yearly shipments, Spanish California depended on San Blas for just about everything. Serra ran down a list of groceries that were imported: chocolate, beans, lentils, peas, rice, meat, butter, biscuits, sugar, greens, vinegar, soap, tobacco, and so on.

Elsewhere, he described the hardware that colonists needed to survive, including saddles, iron, gunpowder, muskets, plows, axes, saws, kettles, and cauldrons. (One secular official observed that there was a shortage of families in Spanish California too; colonists in Monterey were "condemned to a perpetual and involuntary celibacy.") Even when shipments did arrive on schedule, Serra complained, they often did so in short measure. Perhaps just as well, since the corn often was full of grubs and maggots, and the meat "maggoty and putrid." Flour, "the most basic for the sustenance of life," was packed in burlap sacks of such poor quality that much of it was lost in the shipping.[43]

Though each mission had its own fields, the crops often failed. Shortly after Anza arrived in Monterey in spring 1776, the missionaries began holding public prayers for rain; "we are," they said, "in a terrible plight." California was unlike either Spain or New Spain, observed the colony's governor. Along the entire five-hundred-mile coastline from San Diego to San Francisco, rains were irregular and rivers, water holes, and springs few and far between. The Spanish outposts had little useful water nearby, making cultivation difficult, and fields only a short distance away demanded an armed escort to protect the laborers. Serra added that the missions could not even come to each other's aid, since pack animals were in short supply. The soldiers had deserted with some, and Indians had eaten others.[44]

Serra suggested two alternatives to the erratic San Blas supply line. One was to establish an overland route from Sonora, as Anza would do the following year. The second and preferable option was to open direct communication with Santa Fe, far to the east on the Rio Grande. "According to the best of my information," wrote Serra, "if they start straight west from Santa Fe, with a slight deviation to the south, they will strike Monterey."[45] Yet no Spaniard knew what lay between the two settlements. Deserts, mountains, great lakes, and hostile Indian nations all posed potential barriers. Since measuring longitude was still exceptionally challenging, no Spaniard even knew exactly how far apart the two colonies lay. Seeking to answer these questions, in July 1776 an expedition would strike out from Santa Fe into lands unknown.

CHAPTER FOUR

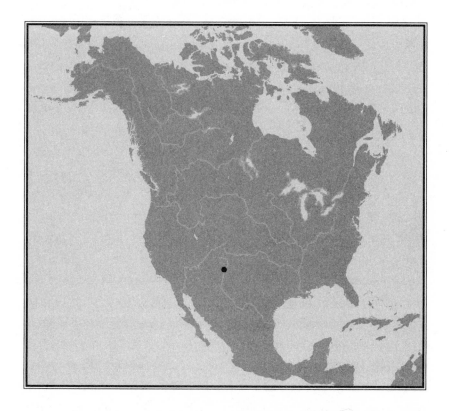

Across the Colorado Plateau

Viceroy Antonio María Bucareli found nothing but frustration in New Spain's northernmost territories. "Ask God to grant me strength to disentangle myself from the chaos of difficulties which enclose me in the confused management of these vast provinces," he wrote to a friend. "I walk in shadows." Assiduous and devoted to his work, Bucareli claimed that checking Russian aggression on the northern frontier occupied most of his attention, yet the faraway region, a thousand miles from his office, remained in disarray and vulnerable to attack. Fewer than two thousand soldiers defended a line nearly eighteen hundred miles long, presidios were collapsing, and corruption was rampant. Apaches and Comanches dominated the lands and treated the Spanish like dependents.[1]

The Spanish Crown, eager to strengthen its defenses against foreign invasion, approved a systematic but unworkable plan to space presidios at hundred-mile intervals from "sea to sea," from the Gulf of Mexico to the Gulf of California. The well-ordered cordon appealed to the mind but had little practicality. As Bucareli smartly observed, "Not everything believed possible on paper is possible in execution, especially in so vast an area." Moreover, New Mexico and Alta California stood well above the line of forts. The two colonies were exposed like fingers on a hand, and there was no way for Spaniards to move between them without traveling down and around, hundreds of miles out of the way.[2]

A short walk from the viceregal palace, two other influential administrators—Rafael Verger and Isidro Murillo—shared Bucareli's preoccupation with New Spain's northern provinces. Verger was the head of the College of San Fernando, a Franciscan institution dedicated to training missionaries for the field, and he supervised the missions in Alta California from his office on the outskirts of Mexico City. He had not always looked kindly on the California enterprise. The entire undertaking was unsound, he had complained, and would cost lives, ships, and money. Barring a miracle (not to be ruled out, of course), nothing good could come of it. By 1773, however, Verger was more hopeful. Conversions were numerous and crops healthy, he claimed, perhaps too optimistically, but supplying the missions remained expensive and difficult. The matter needed to be addressed with urgency.[3]

Not far from the College of San Fernando stood the Church of San Francisco, from where Isidro Murillo, minister of the Province of the Holy Gospel, supervised the New Mexico missions. In the sixteenth and seventeenth centuries, the province had earned martyrdom and fame by evangelizing the Aztecs and carrying the gospel north into New Mexico, but the missions in the distant Pueblo lands had since become a source of embarrassment. Comanches and Apaches regularly raided the impoverished Spanish outposts, and the demoralized missionaries rarely bothered to learn Pueblo languages. Some of them were dedicated more to embezzling funds than to spreading the gospel. Even worse, in 1772 a friar based in El Paso was found to be soliciting sex in the confessional from both women and men. After he was spirited out of the colony, his replacement initiated an affair with a married woman. The New Mexico missions were in desperate need of revitalization.[4]

Bucareli, Verger, and Murillo all reached the same conclusion: a connection must be established between Monterey and Santa Fe. The road would serve "both Majesties," God and Charles III, by solidifying Spain's hold on the region, strengthening the California missions, and revitalizing those in New Mexico. Junípero Serra observed that the conquest of the lands in between would be hastened as well, "assuring a harvest of many souls for heaven."[5]

The convergence of interests in Mexico City had profound and long-lasting consequences in lands fifteen hundred miles to the north. Beyond the mining operations in Zacatecas and Durango and north into the Chihuahuan desert, the colonial population began to thin out, disappearing altogether in some areas. Approaching the Rio Grande (the present-day border between Mexico and the United States), Spanish authority receded almost entirely in the face of Apache supremacy. At El Paso, the last Spanish colony for two hundred miles, besieged residents were subject to the dominion of the region's native peoples and lived in a state of "miserable panic."[6] After a long and dangerous trek up the Rio Grande, travelers reached the outer edge of the Spanish empire, the impoverished and isolated colony of New Mexico.

New Mexico was then a thin and weak settlement, clinging to the Rio Grande. The capital of Santa Fe possessed about two thousand residents and, with its adobe houses and one "quasi-street," was "mournful" in every respect, according to one disdainful visitor from Mexico City. New Mexico as a whole was an assemblage of modest farms and huts and had ten thousand individuals of Spanish ancestry and nine thousand native residents. To the east and north, the colony was hemmed in by the Comanches. Though new arrivals to the region, they had expanded rapidly and "destroyed many Nations" in the process, in large part because they surpassed all others in their dexterity on horseback.

To the west, the colony bordered the numerous Navajos. Like Comanche horsemen, Navajo shepherds had integrated Old World animals into their economy, and they were already renowned for weaving wool blankets. Below the Navajos, New Mexico adjoined Moqui, the land of the Hopis, who had expelled the Spanish in the great Pueblo Revolt of 1680. A century later, the Hopis still maintained their autonomy.[7]

The deliberations of Franciscan and Crown officials in distant Mexico City echoed hundreds of miles beyond New Mexico, in lands entirely unknown to Europeans. Encouraged by their superiors, two Franciscans met in Santa Fe in June 1776 and discussed opening a road from the New Mexican capital to the Pacific port of Monterey. "It was so necessary and proper," wrote one of them, "that from that very night we made a pact for the two of us to undertake the journey." The five-month expedition would take the two missionaries on a trek of seventeen hundred miles through one of the continent's most distinctive landscapes. Crossing the high deserts, striated escarpments, and deep canyons of the American Southwest, they would explore a region equal in size to all of the colonies then in rebellion along the Eastern Seaboard. The departure was set for the fourth of July.[8]

· · ·

Francisco Atanasio Domínguez, the elder of the two leaders, was a thirty-six-year-old Mexico City native who had been appointed by the Province of the Holy Gospel to inspect the crumbling missions of New Mexico. Before his arrival in spring 1776, there is no record that he had ever spent time in New Spain's destitute outer reaches; it does not appear that he enjoyed the experience. His companion, Francisco Silvestre Vélez de Escalante, was a decade or so younger and, since the beginning of 1775, had been serving in Zuni Pueblo, an Indian settlement of under two thousand people situated on the New Mexico frontier. The energetic missionary had taken a particular interest in the people and lands to the west and had made several inquiries into the subject.[9]

If all went as planned, they would set out from Santa Fe bearing northwest and cross out of New Mexico into unfamiliar lands two days later. After traversing the rugged highlands of the Colorado Plateau, they would turn west and enter the vast barrens of the Great Basin, which extends from western Utah across Nevada. At the end of a four-hundred-mile-long trek through the desert, they would reach the imposing Sierras. They would climb and descend the mile-high peaks, venture through California's fertile San Joaquin Valley, and finally reach their destination on the Pacific Coast.

Yet not a single one of those geographic features appeared on their maps, fantastical creations made by individuals who had never set foot in the area. Where ignorance reigned, they let their imaginations run wild. The Southwest was fancied to be the location of Teguayo, the mythical homeland of the Aztecs; the Sierra Azul, a mountain rich in minerals such as quicksilver; and Quivira, a fabulously wealthy city. One 1760 map of New Mexico located all three sites but acknowledged that that part of North America "is incognita to the Spanish." [10]

Domínguez and Escalante enlisted eight New Mexico residents for the adventure, including Bernardo Miera y Pacheco, on Escalante's recommendation. Miera, sixty-three years old, was an artist and cartographer who had recently completed an altar screen and two sculptures for Escalante's Zuni church. Remarkably, the two men had grown up some twenty-five miles apart in the province of Cantabria, on Spain's northern coast. Following two very different paths, both ended up in New Mexico, five thousand miles from their homeland. Escalante, much the younger of the two, called Miera his "paisano" and deemed him "clever enough" to be in charge of mapping the unfamiliar lands. [11]

Domínguez was less enamored of the man, associating him with the "gossipy vulgar herd." Miera's statue of St. Philip in the church of San Felipe was "not at all prepossessing," he gibed, and the sculpture was further tarnished in his eyes by the exceedingly high price demanded by the artist. Domínguez also damned Miera's Zuni altar screen with faint praise. It was "as seemly as this poor land has to offer," wrote the Mexico City native. [12]

Despite Domínguez's doubts, Miera would make an outstanding contribution to the expedition, producing a magnificent "Geographic

Map of the Newly Discovered Land to the North, Northwest, and West of New Mexico" (Figure 11). Nearly three feet wide and more than two feet high, it charts over 175,000 square miles in the Four Corners region of the American Southwest. Like other cartographers of the time, Miera inherited the medieval tradition of creating "visual encyclopaedias of the world," and his map is bursting with illustrations, symbols, and narrative legends. It remains one of the key sources of information about the expedition and one of the most influential maps in American history.[13]

The expedition of ten men set out from Santa Fe for their far-off destination not on July 4, as originally planned, but on July 29. After two days of traveling northwest over rough road, the group arrived at Abiquiu, situated on a hill overlooking the Rio Chama. Only a few hundred people lived at this northernmost Spanish settlement, most of them detribalized Indians known as *genízaros*. In the fall months, the settlement hosted numerous Ute traders, who journeyed across the Colorado Plateau to exchange deerskins and sometimes captives for horses. Domínguez was scornful as usual. The residents were "weak, gamblers, liars, cheats, and petty thieves," he wrote, examples of what happens when "idleness becomes the den of evils."[14]

From Abiquiu, the party continued northwest toward the Colorado Plateau, following a trail known to Spanish and Ute traders. The Colorado Plateau is a high desert, ranging from five thousand to eleven thousand feet in elevation, and is cut through with steep canyons and layered with precipitous escarpments. The explorers would follow its outer edge for the next two and a half months, hemmed in first by the towering Rocky Mountains along the eastern and northern limits of the plateau and then, as they circled around, by the Great Basin on the plateau's western edge.

After several days' journey, they spotted the snowcapped San Juan Mountains in the distance on their right. Part of the Rockies, the 175-mile-long mountain chain begins in Colorado's southwestern corner and, like a comma, curls down into New Mexico, where it rises almost eight thousand feet above the surrounding plateau. On his map, Miera

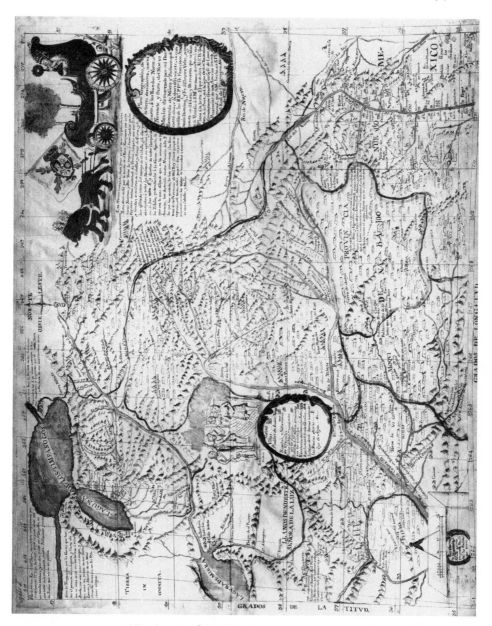

FIGURE 11 Miera's map of the Four Corners region, completed in 1778.
© The British Library Board, Additional Manuscripts 17661-D.

represented the mountains with steep, hachured cones and saw-toothed lines and the plateau tablelands with short trapezoids. His three decades in the Southwest made him a keen observer of the landscape, and he was perhaps the first European to distinguish flat-topped mesas from peaked mountains on a map.[15]

A week into the journey, the travelers were 150 miles northwest of Santa Fe and moving deeper into Ute lands. In early August, they camped about twelve miles from the thirteenth-century cliff dwellings at Mesa Verde but were apparently unaware of the spectacular ruins. Soon after, they were overtaken by two genízaros, Felipe and Juan Domingo, who had fled their masters in Abiquiu to join the expedition. They would come to play an important role in its survival.

For the first three weeks of the trek, Domínguez and Escalante relied on Andrés and Lucrecio Muñiz to guide them. The two brothers had traveled this part of the route before, and Escalante referred to them with sarcasm as "the experts." Only six days into the journey, they "lost the trail—and even the slight acquaintance they showed to have had with this terrain," Escalante sniped. The explorers' unfamiliarity with the land led to a series of setbacks. On the scorched canyon lands of the Colorado Plateau, the friars sent out a reconnaissance team to locate water, but it was unsuccessful. That night, the horses became so thirsty that they wandered off in search of a pond or stream. The next day, by a stroke of luck, the expedition found and followed a "well-used" trail that led them to an abundant water source. Meanwhile, Miera became temporarily lost, forcing his companions to wait for him until midnight. Then, on August 19, trapped in the steep channel formed by the Dolores River in southwestern Colorado, the travelers "put [their] trust in God" and chose a direction by casting lots.[16]

The game of chance led them to retrace their steps to the channel's exit, but more trouble ensued the next day. Entering a large ravine, they followed a footpath carved into the sediment but then foolishly abandoned it to ascend a nearly impassable rocky incline that drew blood from the horses' feet. Reaching the top, they stumbled upon a water hole amid the sagebrush. A path led directly to it—the same one they had turned off of to climb the escarpment. Local residents took the easier route to the water source.[17]

The string of misadventures came to an end in the open woodlands of the Rocky Mountain foothills, east of present-day Uravan, Colorado.[18] Since leaving Santa Fe three weeks earlier, they had traveled about 250 miles to the northwest, skirting the San Juan Mountains, and then turned to the northeast and trekked another fifty miles across the Uncompahgre Plateau, a distinctive section of the larger Colorado Plateau. As the party struggled up a steep ascent, a Ute man caught up with them. Anxious to trade but suspicious of the outsiders, he at first refused to divulge anything about the country, but after some negotiation, he agreed to guide them to the Gunnison River area, thirty miles to the north, where there was a Ute encampment.[19]

Atanasio, as the Franciscans imperiously called the Ute, was the first of several guides who ensured the survival of the expedition. With a local resident leading the party, the journey became easier. Atanasio, whose real name was not recorded, escorted the Spanish down steep but "not difficult" trails and over "good terrain . . . without any laborious slope" until they reached the Uncompahgre River, which flows northwest down the San Juan Mountains.[20] They followed it down to the steep-walled Black Canyon of the Gunnison and then pushed up to the top of Grand Mesa, some eighty-five hundred feet above sea level and thirty-five hundred feet above the riverbed. There, on September 1, they were greeted by eighty mounted Utes. The explorers stood about 140 miles due west of the future location of Colorado Springs.

Visiting the Indians' nearby encampment, Domínguez took the opportunity to proselytize, without success. The friars' more important accomplishment was to recruit another guide, whom they had met two days earlier. Known as both Panchucunquibiran (meaning "Great Talker") and Red Bear to the Utes, the friars called him Silvestre.[21] He was from the area around Utah Lake, situated some thirty miles south of the Great Salt Lake, and would guide them the more than 350 miles to that location.

With evident irony, the Utes mocked the Franciscans. "The padres could not get lost," they said, "because they carried drawn on paper all the lands and routes of travel." In fact, when the Utes pulled up camp the next day, the expedition's reliance on its native guides became embarrassingly clear. Panchucunquibiran had second thoughts about escorting the party and remained behind. The Spanish were at a loss and helplessly trailed after the Utes—heading in the wrong direction, as it turned out—until Panchucunquibiran called them back and led them to the correct route.[22]

.   .   .

Bearing northwest once again (Figure 12), the travelers soon came to the upper reaches of the Colorado River, which the Spanish called the Río de San Rafael. Across the river, they saw the layered sandstone and shale walls of the Tavaputs Plateau. The chain of high cliffs, wrote Escalante, "are of white earth from the top down to the middle and from the middle down evenly striated with yellow, white, and not too deeply tinged red ochre."[23] The explorers climbed to the top of the arid plateau on its rugged south side, which is cut through with ravines and escarpments, thousands of feet high.

On the plateau, Miera noted the presence of "Yutas Zaguaganas ultimos y fronterizos a los Cumanchis" (last Sabuagari Utes bordering the Comanches). The Comanche threat introduced some dissension into the small group, and several men, including Miera, began looking for excuses to reverse course. For decades, the Comanches had stolen livestock and abducted or killed colonists and Catholic Indians in New Mexico, and by 1776 they had nearly drained the colony of horses and mules. On his map, a series of decayed settlements "ruined by the enemies" appear along the colony's southeastern and northern borders. Reassurance came when the travelers met a party of Utes, recently returned from rustling Comanche horses. The Utes reported finding tracks indicating that the much-feared raiders were headed east, toward the Arkansas River.[24]

Traveling through canyons and over ridges, the explorers moved north across the Tavaputs Plateau and down into the desiccated

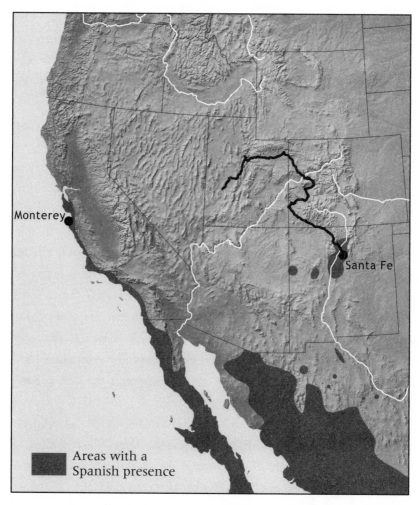

FIGURE 12 Progress of the expedition between July 29 and
October 7, 1776, with state boundaries superimposed.

scrublands of the gentler Uinta Basin. They were fortunate to find
running water at the bottom of one arroyo. Now over forty days into
their trek, they were running short of provisions. When they found
the tracks of a lone bison, they pursued the animal and killed it. They
paused for a day to jerk the "grand supply" of meat.[25]

On September 13, six weeks into their journey, the Spanish arrived
at the Green River, which they called the San Buenaventura. The water-
course flows from its origins in western Wyoming almost due south

before joining the Colorado in southeastern Utah. This was as far north as they would venture. They stood some 380 miles northwest of Santa Fe and at this point turned west toward Monterey, their destination on the Pacific Coast. (They were just north of present-day Jensen, Utah, in the far northeastern corner of the state.)

The mapping of the Green River would lead Miera to make an enormous geographic blunder. Since leaving Abiquiu, the expedition had crossed eighteen rivers and several smaller streams. In most instances, the travelers forded each one only once and therefore could not determine the location of either its headwaters or its mouth. As a result, Miera relied on local residents to describe the topography.

The expedition's first guide, Atanasio, had patiently explained that the lower rivers flowed into the Colorado, but the Spanish had crossed the Colorado a week earlier.[26] Where, then, did the sizable Green River discharge its waters? The Spanish followed it some thirteen miles downriver and then spotted its junction with the White River. Miera made note of its southwestern bearing and the large volume of water moving through the channel. Later, he would encounter the Green River again—or so he would believe.

The party turned west and soon crossed the divide between the Colorado River and Great Basin watersheds. The Colorado Plateau, despite its awesome spire-like mesas and deeply etched canyons, made some sense to the travelers. Its rainfall drains into the Colorado, which carries the water to the Gulf of California. The Great Basin is altogether different, and its hydrography was entirely incomprehensible to Europeans. Rivers that enter the Great Basin do not escape; they seep into the sands and vanish. Even a century after the expedition's arrival on the rim of the Great Basin, the fate of the region's water remained a puzzle to non-native peoples. Mark Twain marveled at how the Carson River, from its lofty origins in the high Sierras, expired in a Nevada desert in "a shallow melancholy sheet of water some eighty or a hundred miles in circumference." The river, he wrote, "is lost—sinks mysteriously into the earth and never appears in the light of the sun again—for the lake has no outlet whatsoever."[27]

The travelers encountered one of the Great Basin's mystifying land-locked bodies of water on September 23, when they passed through Spanish Fork Canyon and entered the expansive valley formed by Utah Lake, where Provo, Utah, is now situated. Utah Lake was the largest body of water they would encounter, measuring some twenty miles long and eleven miles across at its widest point. The Spanish were impressed with its potential for colonial settlement. The area boasted ample freshwater, abundant pasturage, fertile soils, and plentiful fish and waterfowl.[28]

This was Panchucunquibiran's homeland, and Utes had been send-ing up smoke signals for at least a day to announce the arrival of visitors. After several different camps gathered to greet the party, Domínguez proselytized and then asked for another guide to lead them to the next nation. The friar appeared to be successful on both counts. The Utes said (as it was translated) that the Spanish should return and "build their homes wherever they pleased."[29] They also promised to designate one of their own to guide the expedition.

Given the cultural distance and the language barrier, the Utes could not have made much of the abstractions of Catholic theology: the "salva-tion of souls," the belief in a "single true God," the necessity of baptism, and so forth. Their enthusiasm for Christianity more likely resulted from an interest both in Spanish trade goods and in availing themselves of the powers that the Spanish seemed to possess through their foreign technologies and exotic religion. Even Domínguez and Escalante, despite their "unutterable joy" at seeing such "wonderful docility," betrayed some doubts about Ute motives. In fact, European and Indian promises and professions of friendship, made through imprecise translators, could van-ish in an instant when reality intruded. Ten days after departing Lake Utah, their Ute guide would abandon them without a word.[30]

Miera learned from local residents that Lake Utah was connected to a much larger body of water (the Great Salt Lake) by a "narrow pas-sage," later named the Jordan River by Mormons. As a result of poor translation or wishful thinking, Miera also understood from his hosts that a "very large and navigable" river flowed *from* the Great Salt Lake,

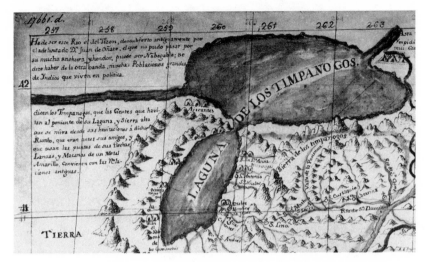

FIGURE 13 Utah Lake, the Great Salt Lake, and the mythical Río del Tizón. © The British Library Board, Additional Manuscripts 17661-D.

or the Laguna de los Timpanogos, as he called it. On his map, Miera depicted the river as wide as the Colorado and conveyed its depth with a dark green hue that appears nowhere else on the map (Figure 13). "If it is as they say," he noted, it must be the Río del Tizón, discovered by New Mexico's founder Juan de Oñate and therefore, by Oñate's own description, capable of carrying boats. Where did this river, of "great width and depth," lead? Conveniently, Miera did not have to say. He sketched the river running due west, alongside the forty-second parallel, and let the map's frame hide the answer.[31]

Yet the implication was clear. As all Europeans understood, every sizable lake drained into an ocean, and what was true in Europe must also apply to the Great Basin. For rivers west of the Continental Divide, there were only two possibilities: they emptied either into the "South Sea" or through the Gulf of Mexico into the Atlantic. As for which of those oceans received the Río del Tizón, Miera tipped his hand in a letter to the king in which he recommended the establishment of a colony at Lake Utah. "In a short time," he supposed, "a very beautiful province would be formed, and it would serve to promote and supply the nearest ports of the coast of California."[32]

· · ·

It was now late September. Far away on the East Coast, Washington's troops were slowly losing their grip on New York and would soon abandon the city altogether. Back in Ute lands, meanwhile, the expedition had reached the fortieth parallel and planned to descend two hundred miles to the thirty-seventh and then turn west again toward Monterey. In the "great heat," they marched south over salt flats and arid hills, through the bed of ancient Lake Bonneville, which had once covered twenty thousand square miles in western Utah. On September 29, they came to the Sevier River. The river, shaped like a shepherd's crook, originated 130 miles due south of them and hooked to the southwest just past their crossing point. Then it meandered ninety miles through salt plains before terminating in Sevier Lake in western Utah. Miera, perhaps with conscious irony, named the brackish pool the "Miera Lagoon."[33]

It was near this point that Miera made a major error. When a group of Utes visited the Spanish encampment, the explorers recognized the local name for the Sevier River; they had heard it two weeks earlier on the banks of the Green River. Though the Sevier and Green never meet, running parallel to each other some hundred miles apart, Miera took his Ute informants at their word—or so he thought—and merged the two rivers, calling his apocryphal creation the Río de San Buenaventura. On his map, the San Buenaventura begins in the Rocky Mountains, bears southwest, and discharges into the Miera Lagoon (Laguna de Miera), whose western shore is cut off by the map frame (Figure 14). The implications were extraordinary. After pooling at the lagoon, the river must continue west. (Indeed, local residents said so.) For two centuries, Europeans had searched fruitlessly for the elusive and long-sought passage from the continent's interior to the Pacific Ocean.[34] Now they had finally found it.

Miera's willingness to accept local descriptions of the topography—even though seemingly garbled in translation, as in the case of the San Buenaventura and the Río del Tizón—reflects his long

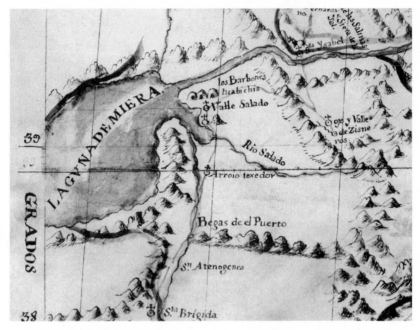

FIGURE 14 The Río de San Buenaventura, or Green River, emptying into the Laguna de Miera. © The British Library Board, Additional Manuscripts 17661-D.

history of working with the region's indigenous people. He borrowed artistic techniques from them (how to make a "perfect" azure paint), and perhaps employed them in his studio and sold them paintings of the saints.[35]

An event that occurred later in the trek reflects Miera's broad-minded attitude. One evening after the missionaries went to sleep, Miera and his companions visited a nearby camp of Southern Paiute Indians "to chat." (Southern Paiutes and Utes were politically distinct but spoke related languages.) Miera was suffering from a stomach illness, and "one old Indian" offered or agreed to help him with "chants and ceremonials." Escalante was scandalized by the "wholly superstitious" medical interventions and aggrieved when Miera and his companions "hailed them as indifferent kindly gestures."[36]

The event led Escalante to pen a long diatribe against the moral turpitude of his traveling companions. Some of them, he charged, traded illegally with the Utes. Others "go after the flesh which they find here for their bestial satisfaction." One wonders if he was equally scandalized by the two bare-breasted Southern Paiute women who appear on Miera's map (see Figure 15). They, at least, wore skirts that fully covered "what one cannot gaze upon without peril," unlike the women Escalante would meet on the trail. To the Franciscan missionary, those cross-cultural encounters corrupted native people and explained why it was so difficult to spread the gospel. But the encounters also suggest that newcomers and natives exchanged geographic information, along with goods and sex.[37]

Continuing south through Lake Bonneville's bed, the party skirted salt marshes, pausing to explain "God's oneness" to a group of friendly Southern Paiutes. On the morning of October 5, their guide, who

FIGURE 15 Southern Paiutes. © The British Library Board,
Additional Manuscripts 17661-D.

had been with them since Lake Utah, ran off after witnessing a fight between one of the Spaniards and his servant. For the remainder of the journey, they would be without a native escort and would suffer terribly for it. Near starvation and without water, they would enter impassable canyons and backtrack, cross desiccated plains, and spend days in search of a ford across the Colorado River.[38]

In the evening a heavy snow covered the plains of western Utah, forcing the expedition to halt for two full days. Their camp was on the edge of the Great Basin in what is today western Utah, fifty miles from the Nevada border. The desolate region is startlingly flat and supports desert shrubs and grasses and little else. Scrub-covered mountains rise on either side. Blanketed in snow, the area was especially bleak to the weary travelers, who were short of supplies, without a guide, and in "great distress" from the extreme cold and want of firewood.[39]

In these trying circumstances, the simmering tension between the missionaries and their companions erupted. They had been on the road for over two months and had traversed a thousand miles of rugged terrain on foot and horseback, yet by Escalante's reckoning, they were only about a third of the way to Monterey and a mere 360 miles west of Santa Fe.[40] (They were in fact about halfway.) The success, if not survival, of the expedition seemed in doubt. Domínguez and Escalante reached a decision: they ought to abandon their journey to the Pacific Coast.

Before departing Santa Fe, the two Franciscans had considered the possibility of failure and concluded that, at worst, they would return through the Grand Canyon region, using the opportunity to proselytize the Havasupai people who lived there. In fact, Escalante had confessed that Monterey "never seemed attainable to me with so few men." But from the frozen camp in western Utah, their traveling companions suspected that the Franciscans were placing God before mammon. Miera had conceived of "grandiose dreams of honors and profit from solely reaching Monterey," vented Escalante, "and had imparted them to the rest by building castles in the air of the loftiest." Their companions—even the servants, groused Escalante—began acting

"very peevishly." Miera reportedly promised that if the expedition persevered, it would arrive in Monterey within a week.[41]

The discord led Escalante and Domínguez to suggest they draw lots.
One result would point ahead to Monterey, the other to the Havasupais
and Santa Fe. The contest would reveal God's will, according to the friars. Nevertheless, Domínguez petulantly declared that should Monterey
be selected, Miera, and only Miera, would have to lead them. They began
praying and then cast lots. The return route prevailed (see Figure 16).[42]

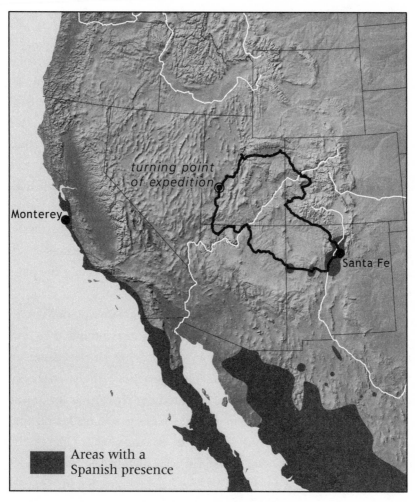

FIGURE 16　Route of the expedition, showing the turning
point, with state boundaries superimposed.

· · ·

Although the explorers had abandoned their destination on the Pacific Coast, their journey was far from over. Its most difficult challenge and one of its greatest achievements still lay ahead. The expedition moved south, out of the salt and mud flats, over high plateaus, and into the land of the Southern Paiutes, whose contact with the Spanish was still indirect. Unlike the Utes, they had not adopted the horse and were terrified to see the arrival of equestrian strangers. One group fled in panic. A Paiute man, chased down and thrown upon a horse, was forced to lead the expedition. He was joined by an "ancient individual" who also agreed to guide the strangers. But after allowing time for their families to flee into the mountains, the two Paiutes vanished around a corner while the encumbered Spanish labored through a narrow fault in the volcanic rock.[43]

Since leaving Lake Utah, the expedition had traveled over lands between forty-five hundred and fifty-five hundred feet high. Just before crossing the present-day Utah-Arizona border (near Cedar City, Utah), the travelers dropped down to follow the Hurricane Fault, which marks the edge of the Colorado Plateau. The region, with its towering mesas, incised ravines, and steep cliffs, is among the most breathtaking in North America. For premodern travelers, it was also among the most challenging.

They were now completely bereft of supplies and unacquainted with the rare water holes in the area. A group of Paiutes promised to lead them toward a crossing at the Colorado River, but the locals ran off when the Spanish mounts were unable to negotiate the steep, rocky paths. In desperation, the explorers scoured the scrublands for greens to staunch their hunger but found only enough to sustain Miera, who was almost too weak to speak. That night, the missionaries named the camp "San Ángel"; the ailing Miera simply called it "On the Mesa."[44]

The lost travelers were spared a worse fate when five Paiutes spotted them from atop a mesa. After Escalante and Domínguez approached and "begged" the Paiutes to guide them to water, the residents took them to an arroyo with two water holes deep within its recesses. The next day, more locals arrived at the camp to sell cactus pear and seeds and furnish them "vague directions" to a ford on the Colorado. Despite the circumstances of his own party, Escalante was struck by the Paiutes' poverty; they were not horticulturalists and depended on seeds, wild plants, and small game for sustenance.[45]

As the Spanish traveled east toward Santa Fe, they met other Paiutes, but no one would guide them to the crossing of the Colorado. On October 26, about twelve miles below the present-day Utah-Arizona border, they arrived at the immense river and its gaping canyon. There began twelve days of fruitless attempts to cross, first by swimming, then by fashioning a raft, then by probing higher up the canyon. They slaughtered and ate a horse while waiting for various reconnaissance missions to return. The weather turned to snow and hail.

Just north of the present-day Utah-Arizona border, in an area now covered by Lake Powell, they finally found a section of the river that was relatively accessible and both broad and shallow enough for the horses to walk across. They cut steps into the stone cliff to descend to the riverbank with their mounts and lowered their equipment down with lassos and ropes. The two genízaros, Felipe and Juan Domingo, who had joined them uninvited after the expedition's brief sojourn in Abiquiu, were the best swimmers in the party and the first to venture across the mile-wide channel. One of them (Escalante does not specify who) then returned to lead the Franciscans, who remained mounted on horses. Laboring all day, the entire expedition crossed the great river on November 7. They were about 250 miles downstream from where they had forded the San Juan River three months earlier. Miera wrote simply, "This river is deeply encased in very steep, rocky red escarpments." The terrain was so challenging and confusing that he did not attempt to trace their exact route.[46]

Within a few days of the crossing, the expedition encountered signs of cattle and horse herds and soon spotted the animals themselves, which belonged to the Hopis. The exhausted travelers were now heading southeast across the rocky canyon lands of northeastern Arizona. They were thirsty and cold. Miera was "ready to freeze on us," wrote Escalante. After making a dinner of toasted horsehide one evening, the explorers shared a single porcupine the next day. A central goal of the Franciscans was to proselytize the Havasupais of the Grand Canyon region. But over one hundred days and some fifteen hundred miles after their departure, they could no longer bear the frigid temperatures and deep hunger and thirst. They hurried toward home.[47]

At the Hopi pueblos, they purchased provisions and were given lodging, awaking to baskets of flour, beef tallow, and maize paper bread. They paused three days at Oraibi, Shongopavi, and Walpi in a fruitless attempt to lure the Hopis to the Catholic Church. Alternately confessing their love for the Hopis and expounding the "gravity of eternal punishments," they made no headway among people who had generations of experience with Spanish conversion efforts. If the Hopis failed to submit, the Franciscans threatened, "they would have to suffer without letup in hell." The Hopis calmly responded that they desired friendship but not Christianity. The "ancient ones had told them and counseled them never to subject themselves to the Spaniards."[48]

Racing through blizzards and freezing weather, Domínguez and Escalante crossed into New Mexico ahead of their companions and arrived on November 25 at the pueblo and mission of Zuni, where they recuperated for several weeks. Since the Spaniards' departure from Santa Fe four months earlier, the British had driven the Continental Army out of New York and were now pursuing Washington's troops through New Jersey. "These are the times that try men's souls," wrote pamphleteer Thomas Paine; the time for the mere "summer soldier and the sunshine patriot" was gone.[49] Washington counterattacked, crossing the Delaware on Christmas night and surprising the Hessians in Trenton on December 26. On January 2, 1777, he withdrew from the site of his stunning victory. That same day, the Domínguez-Escalante expedition arrived in Santa Fe, completing the circle.

• • •

Miera's map of the 1776 journey through the Southwest helped shape the geographic imagination of the nation born that same year in Philadelphia. Though the chart was never published, it influenced cartographers and beguiled white Americans for the next six decades. Alexander von Humboldt, working in the archives of Mexico City, produced a map of New Spain that contained Miera's two westward-coursing rivers: the Río del Tizón and the San Buenaventura. Humboldt shared a copy with Thomas Jefferson; Zebulon Pike saw Jefferson's copy and incorporated it into his own *Map of the Internal Provinces of New Spain*. The Laguna de los Timpanogos (the Great Salt Lake) "opens wider to the West," Pike wrote. He pictured the San Buenaventura entering the Laguna de Miera and, like Miera and Humboldt, left the shape of the western side of the lake a mystery.[50]

Other cartographers reduced the uncertainty. Cartographer John Melish, for example, offered solutions to the drainage of both the Miera Lagoon and the Great Salt Lake in his 1816 *Map of the United States with the Contiguous British and Spanish Possessions*. Along a river that ran from the Miera Lagoon, Melish wrote, "Supposed Course of a River between the Buenaventura and the Bay of San Francisco which will probably be the communication from the Arkansas to the Pacific Ocean." It emptied into today's Carquinez Strait, the passage that connects the San Francisco Bay to the San Joaquin and Sacramento Rivers. A second waterway, the Multnomah (Miera's Río del Tizón), ran all the way from the Great Salt Lake to Puget Sound via the Columbia River. A later edition of Melish's map, "improved to 1823," introduced more errors in a futile effort to correct the earlier version. Now the San Buenaventura coursed across "Unexplored Country" (the Great Basin) and entered the Pacific Ocean north of San Luis Obispo. And not one but two rivers drained the Great Salt Lake—one going to the San Francisco Bay, the other to a point north of Cape Mendocino.[51]

When the first wagon train set out for California in 1841, the emigrants carried maps that showed two rivers, both larger than the Mississippi, running from the Great Salt Lake to the Pacific Ocean. The rivers were the direct descendants of Miera's Río del Tizón. One westerner advised the emigrants to carry tools to construct canoes. If the country became too rough for the wagons, he explained, the migrants could descend one of the rivers to the Pacific.[52]

Miera's errors were finally extinguished when the explorer John C. Frémont struck out from California across the Great Basin in 1843. Among other goals, he wished to locate the San Buenaventura, which, he wrote, formed "agreeably to the best maps in my possession, a connected water line from the Rocky mountains to the Pacific ocean." Instead, he found only a vast desert, stretching across Nevada and western Utah. It was, he said, a "Great Basin" from which no waters escape. Nearly seventy years after Miera had heard the Utes call the Green and Sevier Rivers by the same word, Frémont put to rest the mythical Río de San Buenaventura.[53] Subsequent maps corrected Miera's errors.

Miera's westward-coursing San Buenaventura seemed to confirm Americans' Manifest Destiny to expand to the shores of the Pacific, which explains why it persisted on maps for so long. A different attribute of Miera's map proved inconvenient to the young nation, and it had a much shorter life. The map is divided into nations, much like the familiar multicolored National Geographic world maps. Broad, yellow-hued borders separate New Mexico, the Navajo Province, Moqui, Southern Paiute lands, and Ute lands. Referring to the Utes, Escalante put into words the meaning inherent in Miera's map: they "compose a single nation, or let us call it kingdom."[54]

The same prominent borders exist on Spanish maps of the region from the late 1770s and 1780s, but by the nineteenth century they had vanished. In Humboldt's hand-drawn chart of 1804, red lines define the provinces of New Spain, but beyond those distinct borders, Indian ethnonyms and geographic labels are jumbled together, as if mountains, rivers, and Native Americans were equally part of the landscape. American cartographers embraced Humboldt's design, and the sovereign

Indian nations delineated by Miera disappeared from the land. Some mapmakers did not bother to record the existence of Utes and Paiutes in any form, erasing even their names.[55]

Those events lay in the future. In 1776, Miera looked forward to the extension of Spain's dominion in the Southwest; the Utes anticipated deepening their commercial ties with New Mexico; and the Hopis strategized how to retain their independence. Back east, George Washington rallied his diminished army. Few could have foreseen how Miera's map would soon be edited, copied, and reinterpreted, reflecting the appearance of a new nation on the continent, intent on extending its sovereignty to the shores of the Pacific.

. . .

In 1823, Russian carpenters at Fort Ross laid the keel of a new two-hundred-ton brig. Obtaining lumber for the project was an arduous task. Laborers often had to haul massive timbers more than a thousand feet to the shore, and then Aleuts in baidarkas floated the logs along the coast to the shipyard. The brig boasted four cannons, sent down from Sitka, but the weapons could not hide the fact that, like other ships built at Fort Ross, it was already rotting before it was launched in late summer 1824. In the damp climate, its soft wood would not last for more than six years.[56]

On its maiden voyage, the vessel entered Monterey Bay to take on flour at the Mexican settlement. (Mexico had won its independence from Spain only a few years earlier.) During the ship's short life, it traveled up and down the California coast, making stops at Monterey, Santa Cruz, and San Francisco, and also sailed north to Sitka, Kodiak Island, and the Aleutian archipelago.[57] Spanning the distance between Russian Alaska and Mexican California, the brig was a conspicuous reminder of the imperial rivalries and international trade networks that had spurred colonization of the Pacific Coast and prompted exploration of the Colorado Plateau a half century earlier. It was named the *Kyakhta*.

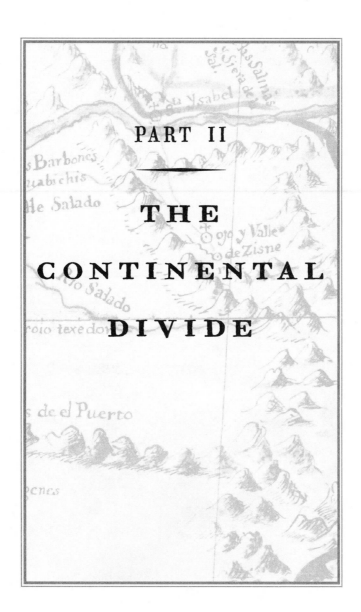

PART II

THE
CONTINENTAL
DIVIDE

W hile visiting Paris in 1763, a British traveler noted that the
city contained two kinds of men. The men of letters passed
evenings at home in "agreeable and rational conversation" with a few
friends, before retiring early. By contrast, the "most fashionable," who
were privileged by birth and fortune, dined "in numerous parties" and
whiled away their time "both before and after supper" playing games
of chance.[1] The aristocrats who gathered in Paris in February 1763 to
divide up North America belonged to the gambling sort.

Nine years earlier, a skirmish between France and Britain in the
Ohio River Valley, famously involving a young and inexperienced officer named George Washington, had exploded into a worldwide conflict, retrospectively named the Seven Years' War or French and Indian
War. The imperial powers attacked each other's colonies across the
globe—in the Americas, Africa, India, and, after Spain foolishly and
belatedly joined as France's ally, the Philippines. By 1763, Britain had
emerged victorious, if nearly bankrupt, and all that remained was to
finalize a peace.[2]

Representing France was the Duc de Choiseul, whose magnificent
residence on rue de Richelieu was barely a half mile from Louis XV's
palace. Among his diversions: his "delicious" mistresses and drinking
with the Duc de Richelieu into the early hours of the morning. ("I like
my pleasure like a twenty-year-old," the middle-aged minister declared
in 1760.) His residence was furnished with gaming tables, and during
the last three months of 1762—as he was finalizing the treaty with
Britain and Spain—he lost over 8,000 livres at cards, more than one
hundred times what he paid some of his servants over the same period.[3]

The Spanish ambassador, Jerónimo Grimaldi, may have rivaled his
friend Choiseul in opulence. Because of the "elegance of his person,"
the former cleric from an illustrious Genoese family had earned the

nickname "the handsome abbot" in the court of Philip V, but he had long since abandoned the ecclesiastical habit and gone on to become one of the most powerful men in Spain. He kept an open house, wrote one visitor to Grimaldi's residence in Aranjuez, south of Madrid, and guests could always depend on "meeting with numerous company, cards, and conversation." In Paris, the "magnificence" of his weekly parties was said to be exceeded only by their "politeness & elegance."[4]

By contrast, the Duke of Bedford was at a disadvantage, and not just because the fifty-five-year-old British emissary, sent across the English Channel in September 1762, had to rent and furnish a house in haste. The gout-ridden duke was said by one embarrassed Englishman to possess an unfortunate combination of stateliness and avarice. Though his residence included several gaming tables, he almost never kept a "publick table" and was reportedly "the joke of Paris."[5]

In the course of the lengthy negotiations, the adversaries traded islands and continents like poker chips. Minorca for Guadaloupe and Gorée; Louisiana for Martinique; Florida for Havana and the Philippines; St. Lucia ("indispensable," declared Choiseul) for Grenada, Tobago, and St. Vincent ("worth absolutely nothing," groused Britain's secretary of state). Demands flew back and forth: evacuate Bunghun on Sumatra and Ostend and Nieuport in the Austrian Netherlands; dismantle the logwood settlements on Central America's Gulf Coast; cede rights to Canada's cod fisheries. The emissaries bargained and plotted, deceiving their enemies as well as their allies.[6]

From the perspective of North Americans, the most important provision of the treaty was the one that divided their continent between rival empires. Choiseul proposed "an imaginary line" lying somewhere between the Mississippi and the Appalachians and "capable of easy and clear execution." The French minister pointed out that there were numerous precedents for a border defined by geometry rather than geography, including the meridian that had apportioned newly discovered lands between Spain and Portugal in 1494. (He chose a poor example. The meridian dividing Spanish and Portuguese possessions could not be precisely located, leading to lengthy disputes.) Unlike the

Appalachians, which extended "in a very irregular manner" and "are ill represented on ordinary maps," he said, an artificial line would "leave no subjects for controversy."[7]

Britain pushed instead to divide the continent along the Mississippi River for the same reason: with each nation "keeping to its side," the line would "forestall all disputes." The logic seemed faulty even to those who espoused it, for the river had multiple channels and its eastern bank was "mix'd and complicated with certain Spanish settlements." Britain won the day, however, and the Mississippi became the border (see Figure 17), with the occupants of both sides having the right to navigate its waters. To obtain Spain's acquiescence, France's Louis XV gifted his portion of the continent to Charles III. "I say, no, no, my cousin is losing altogether too much," Charles is reputed to have said; "I do not want him to lose anything in addition for my sake." Despite his protestations, Charles accepted the present, some 820,000 square miles of prairies and forests that were the homelands of numerous Indian nations.[8]

In the evening of February 9, 1763, the ambassadors attended a ball at Grimaldi's palace that carried on through the night until ten o'clock the next morning. After recovering from the revelry, they reassembled in the evening at the Hôtel de Grinbergen, the Duke of Bedford's residence, and, under crimson draperies and a portrait of Britain's King George III, signed the "definitive" treaty that shaped the fate of North America.[9] Before the war, France had claimed an immense domain stretching from the St. Lawrence to the mouth of the Mississippi; Spain had possessed the Southwest and greater Florida, which included present-day Alabama and Mississippi; and Britain had presided over its Atlantic colonies. In the treaty's aftermath, the political geography was vastly simplified. Everything west of the Mississippi River belonged to Spain and everything east of it to Britain, with the important exception of New Orleans.

Though the line splitting the continent down the Mississippi was easy to describe and simple to delineate, its impact on North Americans remained obscure to the European aristocrats who conceived of it. George III, who became sovereign of a vast new swath of the continent,

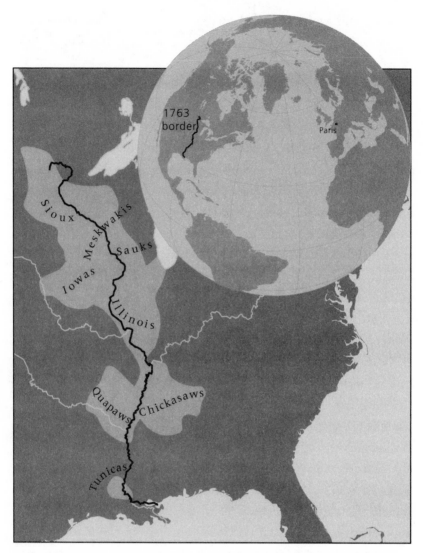

FIGURE 17 Paris and the 1763 border down the Mississippi, with a close-up
identifying some of the people whose homelands spanned the river.

reportedly confused the Mississippi with the Ganges.[10] (He was right
about one thing: Indians lived along the banks of both rivers.) His ministers may have been better informed, but even in the densely populated
colonial centers that they knew well, the treaty's consequences were

too numerous and too complex to predict. As for the millions of acres beyond, imperial officials were in the dark.

Ignorance did not breed caution. Instead, the enormous North American land transaction galvanized British subjects of all sorts. Merchants and traders schemed and plotted how to wring profits out of the tens of thousands of Indian consumers now under British dominion. Crown officials drew up ambitious plans to administer the vast territory that a day earlier had belonged to Louis XV. And from Fort Pitt to Fort Detroit, smug garrison commanders began to command native peoples like subordinates. British troops had "carried victory wherever they advanced their Standards," wrote one flag-waver, "and drove the armies of both *French* and Natives before them." Every imperialist was convinced that Britain ought to have its way with the Indians who remained.[11]

On the face of it, the claims of European monarchs to vast North American domains were absurd, as even some colonists recognized. Britain, said one, had no more right or title to the continent "than she had to the Empire of China."[12] Yet for local residents, the massive land transaction had very real consequences with complex and varying ramifications that took decades to unfold. Across the Atlantic and deep in the heart of North America, the fortunes of native peoples rose and fell as a result of the land transfers negotiated by indifferent aristocrats in faraway Paris.

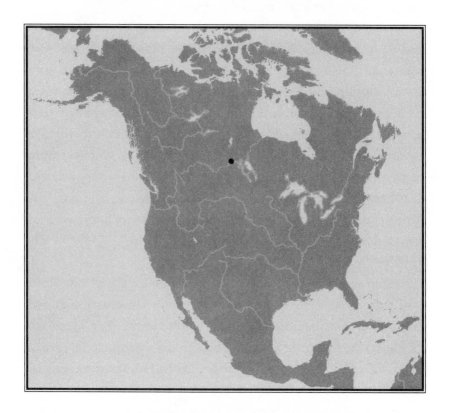

CHAPTER FIVE

A Forest Transformed:
The Hudson's Bay Company
and Cumberland House

E ighteenth-century London seemingly had a coffeehouse for every
mercantile interest. The Jamaica Coffeehouse was frequented by
West India traders, the East India Coffeehouse by East India traders,
and the Virginia Coffeehouse by Chesapeake traders. London contained
an African Coffeehouse, a Hamburgh Coffeehouse, and a Carolina
Coffeehouse, each visited by region-specific merchants. There was even

an Antigallican Coffeehouse, patronized by "foreign merchants" including, oddly, French ones.[1]

There was no Canada Coffeehouse, however. The land acquired from France north of the St. Lawrence did not yet have an established network of London-based merchants to serve it. To rectify the situation, a group of enterprising traders formed the Canada Committee, which met regularly at the New York Coffeehouse, just around the corner from the Bank of England in the heart of commercial London. There, the committee strategized how best to take advantage of the tremendous commercial opportunities created by Britain's newest colony.[2]

Among the committee's members was Brook Watson, the "wooden-legged commissary" who had supplied British troops in New France during the Seven Years' War. (The wood replaced a leg that had been severed by a shark in Havana Bay—an event famously captured by the American artist John Singleton Copley.) Perhaps Watson's wartime experience had opened his eyes to the profits to be had trading in that part of North America.[3]

Their order of business was twofold. Over the course of the recent war, New France had printed paper bills by the millions, and the currency was now nearly worthless. Members of the Canada Committee and other speculators bought large quantities from French colonists at 15 percent of face value. Then they relentlessly lobbied the secretary of state to pressure Louis XV of France to redeem the paper. Their second scheme was to deregulate the Canadian fur trade and open it up to all British newcomers, but most especially to themselves. They were successful on both counts.[4]

Employing their profits from currency speculation, they invested in an expansive market situated thousands of miles away in central and northern Canada, a land of few residents but exceptionally valuable resources. The Hudson's Bay Company had long enjoyed a trade monopoly on the region of nearly 1.5 million square miles.[5] Chartered by the Crown, the staid, hundred-year-old corporation shipped cheap manufactures and consumables to a series of posts along the shores of Hudson Bay, the huge inland sea stretching from the Arctic down into Ontario and Quebec. There, its employees took shelter from the frigid winters and stoically awaited the arrival of Assiniboine and Cree Indians bearing furs. The furs, packed in bales, shipped across the Atlantic, and auctioned off in London, returned a substantial profit to the venerable company.

Backed by members of the Canada Committee and other merchants, independent traders began infiltrating this entrenched commercial operation in the late 1760s. Making a mockery of the HBC monopoly, they traveled deep into native territory in Manitoba and Saskatchewan, set up temporary winter camps to trade with the residents, and sent their furs down to Montreal the following spring. HBC officials could not fathom why Indians preferred to do business close to home rather than undertake a month-long journey through barren forests, risking both their merchandise and even starvation, to reach the company's forts on the shores of Hudson Bay. Indians "Manifest an Uncommon Indifference about coming down," one employee protested.[6]

Nor did it help that the "pedlers," the derisive name that the HBC attached to independent traders, were often British-financed Frenchmen. The French, wrote one HBC employee, "are masters of all the Indian languages & have greatly the advantage of us." They had "adopted the very Principles and Ideas of Indians, and Differ from them only a Little in Colour." Unconstrained by corporate directives, they intimidated and undersold the HBC's rule-bound "servants," as the company called its low-level employees.[7]

The expanding competition had a measurable impact on the HBC. At York Fort, the collection point for pelts from most of Manitoba and Saskatchewan, the number of furs traded annually dropped precipitously from thirty thousand before the Seven Years' War to half that in the 1770s. HBC officials, asleep "by the Frozen Sea," as one hostile former servant had charged, responded to this alarming decline by establishing the company's first-ever inland post.[8]

Cumberland Lake, on the border of Saskatchewan and Manitoba, was four hundred miles southwest of York Fort, the closest permanent

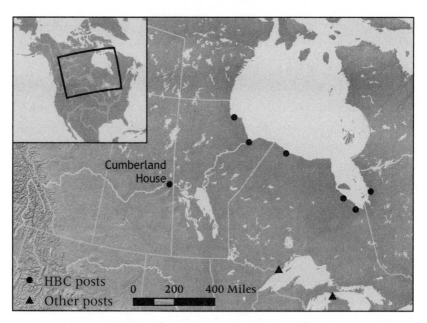

Cumberland House

• HBC posts
▲ Other posts

0   200   400 Miles

FIGURE 18 Cumberland House and other trading posts,
with state and provincial boundaries superimposed.

colonial settlement, and four thousand miles west of London. After an arduous, month-long journey up numerous rivers and around dozens of falls and rapids, three HBC employees pulled their canoes up to its grass-lined shore in September 1774 and began constructing a small log fort that they called Cumberland House (Figure 18). They had selected the site after "a long Consultation with Indian Chiefs," who insisted that it was "more commodious" for them than one farther east proposed by the HBC. Surrounded by "fine Strait Pine," poplars, and birch, the fort had a commanding view of the lake.[9] From this advantageous location, the HBC hoped to retake control of the beaver trade in the Canadian prairies.

• • •

The great naturalist Georges-Louis LeClerc, Comte de Buffon, famously argued that all creatures in the New World were weaker and smaller than their Old World counterparts—with the exception of the beaver. New World animals "shrink and diminish under a niggardly sky and an unprolific land," he asserted. America's native people were no better off, for they were "timid and cowardly," with "no vivacity, no activity of mind." In America, even men's "organs of generation" were "small and feeble," he surmised. But beaver were different. They had been hunted out of most areas of Europe, and the few survivors in the Old World were "dispersed, forlorn and timid creatures." Not so *Castor canadensis*. Granted, in a "state of nature"—that is, in the "prison" in which Buffon kept a lone specimen sent over from Canada in 1758—the creatures were "gloomy and melancholy" and generally unimpressive. But in America, Buffon owned, they were marvelous and astonishing, "superior to all other animals."[10]

He was not the only European to admire the rodent. The beaver's industriousness tended to appeal to the entrepreneurial spirit of New World colonizers, giving rise to a number of encomiums. Andrew Graham, a longtime servant of the HBC, lauded the animals' vigilance, strength, prudence, and industry. Beaver feats of engineering earned constant admiration. Their dams were nearly impregnable. Their lodges, spacious and sturdy, "woud puzle a good workman to do the Like." A 1750 publication, *The Wonders of Nature and Art*, commented on the "Sagacity and Beauty" of the "little Cities" of beaver spread across North America.[11]

The seemingly hierarchical and well-ordered world of the beaver, depicted in Figure 19, particularly resonated with diverse leaders and investors who lamented the freedom and individualism so evident among generations of colonists. The honeybee, a traditional emblem of industry and orderly cooperation for European moralists since ancient times, now shared the stage with a larger member of the animal kingdom. Graham observed that the industrious beavers were "constantly employed . . . laying up stores of provisions for the winter." (He ordered HBC servants to do the same.) Even workplace safety earned a compliment from Graham, who reported that a designated beaver kept watch and warned the others before each tree crashed to the ground. He wrote approvingly that in large communities, enslaved beaver were made to do the hard labor. For Robert Beverley, a Virginia gentleman, beavers'

FIGURE 19 "View of ye industry of ye beavers in making dams to stop
ye course of a rivulet," inset in *A New and Exact Map of the Dominions
of the King of Great Britain*, by Herman Moll (1731). Variations of
this unintentionally comical image appeared in texts throughout
the eighteenth century. Library of Congress, gm 71005441.

"regular Form of Government" had special appeal, for it was "something
like Monarchy." In the fanciful projections of this slave master, a "Superintendent" oversaw daily labor among the beaver, and on their toilsome
march bearing timber to the dam or lodge, a "Governor" walked "in
State" beside them, beating those who failed to bear the burden.[12]

Among naturalists who authored accounts of the beaver, there
seemed to be a contest "who shall most exceed in fiction," wrote one
jaded HBC employee at the end of the 1700s.[13] He singled out *The
Wonders of Nature and Art* for its fervid exaggerations, but unbeknownst
to him, the genre was still in its infancy, not reaching its zenith until

the end of the nineteenth century. Among the tomes then published was Horace T. Martin's *Castorologia, or the History and Traditions of the Canadian Beaver,* "an exhaustive monograph, popularly written." (Beaver in the United States already had their own extensive volume, Martin explained, by way of justifying his northerly focus.) *Castorologia* opened with a "Salutation from the King of Beavers," by Canadian poet George Martin:

> This great Dominion raised our name,
> Emblazoned on the scroll of fame;
> A choice that to the world attests
> The base on which its greatness rests,
> Our one transcendent, special gift:—
> Persistency of honest thrift.[14]

The subject demanded a broader perspective, for in 1914 there appeared *The Romance of the Beaver: Being the History of the Beaver in the Western Hemisphere,* authored by A. Radclyffe Dugmore. Objective: "to provide a book on the subject free from exaggeration." Dugmore, a naturalist and adventurer, wrote from the point of view of a beaver family, headed by a watchful "father" who was concerned for the safety of his "wife" ("Mrs. Beaver") and their three children. When not working, the family sat for "afternoon tea" and held "animated" discussions. Beaver skills surpass that of any other animal but man, wrote Dugmore—and even then, it was doubtful to Dugmore that man "in his lowest form" was as accomplished.[15]

Martin and Dugmore composed their tributes at the nadir of the beaver population in North America. Much like white Americans lamenting the disappearance of Indians, they used the occasion of the beavers' demise to praise the animals they had done so much to destroy. With "a pathetic appeal in their mild eyes," wrote Dugmore, the creatures "simply put up their little hands above their heads as though to ward off the fatal blow of the axe or club."[16]

No matter how much they admired the beaver's achievements,

however, Europeans esteemed their fur even more. Before the arrival of Europeans, it is estimated that there were between sixty million and four hundred million beaver industriously damming rivers and constructing lodges in North America. By 1900, the animals were nearly extinct.[17] The Canada Committee belonged to part of a much larger, centuries-long undertaking to turn the semiaquatic rodents into hats.

If Washington wore a hat when he crossed the Delaware on Christmas night to rout the Hessians at Trenton, it was made of beaver. ("Mans best Beaver Hatt for a pretty large head" was how he described a 1773 purchase.) In the eighteenth century, every self-respecting Englishman had to have one. The British were not alone in their desire for the headwear. Men also sported the hats in Spain, Portugal, the West Indies, East India, and Africa. England exported over 100,000 beaver felt hats in 1775 (down from half a million in 1760), along with 80,000 beaver pelts and 1,322 pounds of beaver wool. Trapped, skinned, shaved, pressed, rolled, blocked, singed, steamed, and polished, *Castor canadensis* in hat form traveled the world over.[18]

Beaver felt hats had become increasingly popular over the course of the seventeenth century. In the early 1600s, they were still a luxury item, worn by courtiers who aspired to be "beaver gallant."[19] The rodent became synonymous with the hat itself and took on connotations of nobility:

> I saw young Harry with his beaver on,
> His cushes on his thighs, gallantly armed.
> (*Henry IV*, Part 1, 4:1:104–5)[20]

Shakespeare's hat would have been high-crowned and broad-brimmed, but after Charles I was beheaded, such ostentatious headwear was replaced by the sober, conical-shaped hat made famous by the Puritans. With the Restoration of Charles II, a broad-brimmed, flattish, and feathered slouch hat, borrowed from the French court, became fashionable in decadent cavalier London. In 1663, the great diarist Samuel Pepys recorded purchasing a "new Beaver, which altogether is very noble." He wore it to church, with his "best black clothsuit, trimmed with Scarlett ribbon, very neat," a "cloak lined with Velvett," and black silk knit leggings.[21] Women, too, occasionally wore beaver felt hats, but more often they chose head coverings made from straw, silk, linen, or sheep's wool.

By the eighteenth century, the flamboyant slouch hat had become democratized as the cocked hat, inspired by military headwear. At the time of the Revolutionary War, the three-cornered, cocked hat predominated, though some American radicals preferred a round hat, associated with simple country living. Image-conscious Benjamin Franklin wore one. For his first portrait after arriving in France in 1777, however, this master of public relations donned an even more rustic fur cap (beaver again)—just right for causing a sensation in Paris.[22]

·   ·   ·

From its establishment in 1774 (the same year that the Quebec Act and other intolerable acts of Parliament pushed British colonies south of the St. Lawrence Valley closer to rebellion), Cumberland House encountered severe difficulties. To the frustration of HBC servants, the region's native peoples were not at all dependent on them. "I must needs say," wrote Samuel Hearne, who was sent inland in the summer of 1774 to establish the post, "that it gave me no little uneasiness to see so many fine fellows of Indians and their Families not only Cloath'd with the Canadians goods finely orniminted, but ware also furnish'd with every other Necessary artical, and seem'd not to be in want of any thing."[23] Hearne attributed their disregard for the HBC to the presence of merchants working out of Montreal. But the truth was that Saskatchewan natives were not dependent on any European traders, whether Canadians, HBC employees, or others.

In the mid-1700s, in the vast area west of the Ontario border, only five hundred to eight hundred Indians traded annually with the HBC. Though some of those men acted as brokers, transporting European merchandise farther inland to trade with the Blackfeet and others, the total volume of goods was relatively small. Each Cree trader, for example, purchased on average only six pounds of gunpowder and twenty pounds of shot per year—not enough to get through a winter, let alone to supply others in any quantity. York Fort, which serviced the enormous expanse between Hudson Bay and the Rockies, traded on average only 165 guns each year to a population numbering in the tens of thousands. Since gun locks frequently broke and gun barrels often failed in the subzero Canadian winters, only a fraction of those weapons reached first-time buyers. Even if Indians were "mad for guns, Knives, Hatchets &c," as one HBC servant insisted, they evidently could survive just fine without them.[24]

Europeans who assumed that local residents depended on them found themselves in an awkward position. A week after the thirteen colonies declared independence from Britain, the head trader at York Fort grudgingly half acknowledged his own dependence on native peoples. Indians "Know, nay, they say, We cannot do without them; and having neither Honor or Generosity, imposition is all they aim at."[25]

Several factors combined to make HBC "chiefs"—so the principal officers commanding each fort called themselves—dependent on the native chiefs who traded with them. Foremost among those factors was the winter weather. The extreme cold astounded the British sojourners when it did not kill them. In the comfort of the meeting room of the Royal Society of London, the Canadian winter was a recurring subject of scientific curiosity and wonder. In 1742, for example, gentlemen had attended a learned presentation titled "The Effects of Cold." "The Air is filled with innumerable Particles of Ice, very sharp and angular, and plainly perceptible to the naked Eye," reported Christopher Middleton, a ship captain with the HBC and Royal Navy, recently returned from a brutal winter in Hudson Bay that had killed several of his crew. "Bottles of *strong Beer, Brandy, strong Brine, Spirits of Wine,* set out in the open Air for Three or Four Hours freeze to solid Ice." In the mornings, a layer of frost coated servants' bedrooms, to be removed with a hatchet.[26]

York Fort was indeed "shockingly cold," said its chief. Farther north, at Churchill, the "pureness of the Air," along with the wholesome diet, led a few to think that they were living in the healthiest place on

Earth. "Some of us think that *we never grow any older*," wrote the chief at Churchill in winter 1777, though he admitted that "we may be greatly mistaken." Indeed, he was. Seven months later, he was suffering from "a foul ulcer" at the back of his nostrils and was "spitting out" his lungs. The symptoms, he confessed, were "very alarming."[27]

More commonly, the bitter cold simply froze people, sometimes to death. Despite wearing three pairs of socks, a pair of moccasins, three pairs of stockings, three jackets, a fur gown, a double-layered large beaver cap, gloves, and elbow-length mittens, laborers frequently returned to their HBC fort with frostbite. "We think nothing to have our face, point of our nose, under the chin, points of our fingers, and the laps of our ears froze a little," wrote Andrew Graham, who worked for the HBC for over twenty-five years and almost lost his own feet to frostbite. A common treatment was to "lay open," or slice through, toes that were "froze to the Bone." That remedy disabled Robert Longmoor at Cumberland House for a month and a half. There was no treatment for snow blindness, which also incapacitated HBC servants.[28]

One trader, on crossing a river in eastern Saskatchewan, fell through the ice, losing his guns, blankets, shoes, and provisions. He wrapped his feet with pieces of his coat and found sustenance by eating three pairs of old horsehide shoes. Four days later, he arrived at Cumberland House, spared death by the unusually mild weather. Another, leaving Cumberland House for the prairies, was overtaken by the intensity of the cold. One morning, he and his two companions, sleeping together under the same skin, found themselves beneath a foot of snow. Their fire had gone out, and they managed to gather wood and light another only with great difficulty. Continuing their journey, they subsisted on boiled water, tinctured with a bit of chocolate. They were spared starvation when they stumbled upon the remains of an elk carcass, abandoned by wolves.[29]

In the winter of 1775–1776, the coldest temperature at York Fort reached forty-nine degrees below zero. The following May, when spring was turning to summer in revolutionary Boston, seven Indian women froze to death as they approached Fort Prince of Wales at Churchill, and twenty more arrived with their extremities almost frozen solid. That June, the snow was still two feet deep at Albany Fort, on James Bay. It is "a most Shocking thing and a Dismal object," confessed one chief, "to see a man when first found froze, as hard as a Rock."[30]

The long and difficult winters meant that HBC servants could not feed themselves, and they were, to their dismay, literally dependent on Indians for their sustenance. Forts on Hudson Bay were less vulnerable than their inland counterparts, since there were more workers stationed along the shore and the posts could seek assistance from each other. Even then, without Indians to hunt geese and ducks, factory chiefs were at a loss. "I know not *which way to turn for next Winters stocks*," admitted the chief at Albany Fort, after Indians abandoned the area for the summer and fall.[31]

Inland, the situation could become dire without Indian assistance. Cumberland House was on reduced allowances shortly after its establishment, and although the master, Samuel Hearne, was little alarmed, his men were certain that "entire famine must Ensew." That same winter one hundred miles to the north, one independent trader took to eating moose skins to survive. One or two of his companions starved to death, and a third ate one of the corpses and as a result was shot to death by native residents. That calamity may have convinced Hearne that his men unavoidably had to be separated and put out to live with Indians each winter to provision themselves—a practice that became customary. Even then, they complained of "having been almost Starved at times."[32]

Famished traders stocked with valuable but inedible merchandise presented Cree and Assiniboine people with a golden opportunity. At Cumberland House, Indians sent spies to assess the stock of provisions. "If they find you in want their demands are extravagant," one master reported, advising his successor to always appear well supplied, even if not the case. Cumberland House also had to deal with competing traders, who concocted a strategy in fall 1776 to destroy the post by paying exorbitant prices to corner the provisions market. HBC servants were forced to survive on fish that winter. Several years later, Crees and Assiniboines devised another way to exploit the situation at inland posts. They reportedly set fire to surrounding prairies to profit from the ensuing scarcity of game.[33]

Equally vexing to HBC employees was their "very great dependance" on Indians for transportation inland. If Indians did not wish to accompany them, the servants could not proceed. If they wanted to pause and hunt, the servants had no choice but to dawdle too. If they resolved to head for a different destination, the servants reluctantly went to that destination as well. When Crees transported furs from Cumberland House to York Fort, they sometimes divided the bundles, thereby increasing their pay, since they were remunerated by the bundle. When they returned to Cumberland House bearing trade goods, they embezzled along the way. They demanded compensation on departure and again on arrival, denying that they had been paid the first time. On top of that, they insisted on large numbers of presents. "This I think is too much," protested the chief at York Fort, "yet [I] am obliged to comply, or all would be in a *Flame*." He suggested that "a Manly firmness mixed with a little condescension" could alleviate the worst of the abuse, but that dubious advice did not address the root of the problem: the HBC recruited from the Orkney Islands, and no Orkneyman could manage a canoe. Nor, according to Samuel Hearne, Cumberland House's first master, did any of them endeavor to learn how to do so.[34]

No journey captures the futility of HBC ambitions in Indian country better than Matthew Cocking's. Cocking departed York Fort in July 1774 with two other HBC servants and five canoes manned by Crees and laden with goods for the establishment of Cumberland House. The Crees began complaining immediately about the weight of the cargo and the helplessness of the three HBC employees. After two days of "incessant requests," they persuaded Cocking to leave one of the employees behind. Over the next few weeks, they continued to grouse about the burden, but Cocking, who expected to carry nothing, was "obliged to dissemble" and refrain from telling them that they were merely indolent. ("It was their own choice to carry the Goods," he protested to himself.) A month into the voyage he seemed dispirited: "It gives me much uneasiness to think that our Lives are so much in the power of Villains and our Situation such that we have it not in our power to resent any Injuries we may receive." His impotence continued to weigh on him, along with his own goods, which the Crees made him carry at the portages. Even worse, they forced him to shoulder some of their own. "We have indeed been miserable Slaves to these People," he wrote in dismay.[35]

Then, in early August, the Crees refused to proceed any farther. "I am obliged to comply," Cocking wrote, lest he and his companion be left behind, "where we may very probably be starved for want of natives to provide for us particularly in the Winter." "If the Natives would not carry Us, what could I do?" he asked in a letter to Hearne, which the Indians then failed to deliver. By mid-October, some two months after he was to have met Hearne to establish Cumberland House, Cocking and his guides had entered the parkland west of Lake Winnipegosis and were several hundred miles away from his intended destination. He wintered with the Crees along the upper Assiniboine River. Finally, in late June 1775, almost a full year after departing York Fort, he returned to his point of origin, never having reached Cumberland House. "There will be as I have found no End to the Natives Demands in general when they know the Company's Servants cannot do without their assistance," he concluded. Until then, he wrote, "a Trader will be a continual Slave to all their Humours."[36]

Cocking's misadventure was protracted but hardly unique. Indians escorting HBC servants to and from Cumberland House almost always exploited the situation. Hearne complained that the Crees, to support their "private drinking bouts," methodically siphoned one hundred gallons of brandy out of his kegs and replaced the missing alcohol with water. In a second, more successful trip to Cumberland House, Cocking was obliged to tap the kegs and to give away his gun when his escort refused to proceed. (He later recovered the firearm.) Joseph Hansom was abandoned "privately" at night by his guides. He fared better than

Robert Flatt, who was robbed by his, beaten by two Cree women, and left to "starve by himself."[37]

Humphrey Marten, chief at York Fort, used Flatt's ordeal to argue that HBC servants ought to travel in larger numbers. "We, for want of strength are obliged to suffer Insults tamely, and suffer Villains to go unchastized," he wrote. But when the Indian who had robbed Flatt arrived at York Fort to trade, Marten's resolve flagged. Marten decided to drop the affair "and use him kindly," since "he hath much sway in his Country." After that humiliating encounter, Marten salvaged his pride by remembering his obsequious behavior as a stern rebuke. When Flatt's tormenter returned again the following year with "a fine parcel of Furs," a delighted Marten crafted a fictitious lesson: "This plainly shews, that a little roughing now and then is absolutely necessary to make the Native humble and servicable."[38]

•   •   •

Viewed from its substantial headquarters near the Thames ("a very fine brick building, adorned with pilasters, architraves, &c."), the HBC looked like a formidable English enterprise. Capitalized by British investors and staffed by British citizens, it was one of a handful of corporations with a royal charter. But viewed from Saskatchewan, the HBC seemed more like a local endeavor. Crees, Assiniboines, and others hunted rodents—which at least for a time seemed to multiply endlessly—and sold the skins to much-abused HBC servants, who had abandoned their homes and families in Britain to come supply the needs of America's native peoples. Ironically, because supple pelts were easier to process into felt, Europeans often preferred well-worn furs that had been softened by months of sweat. In exchange for the greasy and unremarkable pelts, native peoples received luxury goods and state-of-the-art implements, manufactured at great expense in Europe and shipped a thousand miles across the Atlantic. "The English have no sense," delighted one Indian in the seventeenth century; "they give us twenty knives like this for one Beaver skin." It was clear who was getting the better end of the deal. From a British perspective, the four beavers on the HBC crest advertised the company's purpose; from an Indian's, the crest might have just as accurately displayed a keg of brandy and a roll of Brazil tobacco.[39]

The Canadian side of the enterprise began in winter, deep in the Saskatchewan and Alberta grassland, or farther north, at the edge of the boreal forests. There, indigenous traders—often Cree and Assiniboine families—purchased moose, wolf, marten, and beaver pelts from Blackfoot, Athapaskan, and Inuit peoples. Like commercial exchanges in London at the opposite end of the fur trade, the purchases were sometimes made on credit. In early spring, when flocks of geese and swans appeared overhead migrating to their northern breeding grounds, the indigenous traders began gathering on the banks of particular rivers. "Every Evening," wrote one witness, "Feasting &c, smoking, dancing and singing." While young men hunted and women butchered and dried the game, elderly men set to work building canoes. After the frames were completed, men began collecting the birch bark sheathing. Toward the end of April when the river ice broke up, the native families packed the furs into bundles and set off on the long journey to Hudson Bay.[40]

Traveling in groups of as many as seventy canoes, they fought off mosquitoes and hunger. The mosquitoes could be swept away by the bushel, and if not careful, a traveler might end up with a head swollen as large as a "tilterkin," or kilderkin, an eighteen-gallon cask. One HBC employee who accompanied the traders judged the mosquitoes "worse than cold weather"—an assessment perhaps shared by Indians. A Cree legend told of a man who mistreated mosquitoes and as a result was devoured entirely by the insects. Hunger was also a regular part of the trip, since hunting was difficult in the boreal plains. Along the way, Indians ate their dogs when fish and game were scarce.[41]

After the ice melted, the rivers were full of travelers. Indians stopped to trade with those who did not wish to make the trip downriver, purchasing some furs outright and taking others on consignment, with instructions to purchase specific trade items. The profits could be enormous. On the return trip, these indigenous traders would sell a gun for fifty beaver, a hatchet for six to nine, and a kettle for twenty—markups of between 150 and 800 percent over what they paid for the goods at York Fort.[42]

After traveling for several weeks, they made contact with Europeans for the first time, the peddlers who established camps along the major trade routes. There, native peoples obtained alcohol, kettles, blankets, and other goods, acquired in kind, on credit, or as fulfillment of a debt obligation that the peddlers had incurred to them the year before. In many ways the peddlers served native peoples. Chiefs "obliged" them to gift liquor and other goods, and some apparently took by force what the peddlers were unwilling to give. Even the most experienced peddlers had to furnish valuable presents, including furs, to "troublesome" Indians. In spring 1773, Matthew Cocking's guides boasted that Indians took several items in broad daylight from a peddler named Bruce. The theft, "through fear, was connived at." Bruce admitted that "as they had got the Goods in possession he was obliged to content with his loss." The most successful traders inevitably "curbed their indignation" on numerous occasions.[43]

After selling their prime furs to the peddlers, the Indian traders continued on, perhaps stopping at Cumberland House, where they were encouraged to go to York Fort. Near the bay, the land transitions from bedrock to swampy lowlands, and the rapids and falls forced travelers to carry their canoes, or chance their way through dangerous currents. When Anthony Henday accompanied dozens of traders in 1755, they "padled thro' falls & betwixt Rocks" but lost several canoes in the process. The next day, they hauled the remaining canoes and cargo around six falls.[44]

Finally, two months after setting off, the traders arrived at York Fort, where they were saluted with a cannonade and greeted by the governor. Courtesy of the HBC, the most important Indians were dressed in a blue or red suit trimmed with lace, a shirt, and a pair of stockings and shoes. The outfit was crowned with a hat (ironically made from beaver) ornamented with multicolored feathers and a silk handkerchief. The captains—as these leading Indians were called—dined on bread and prunes, drank brandy, and smoked tobacco on the governor's account. Halberd and ensign bearers, marching to the beat of a drummer, then escorted the captains to their tents. After further ceremony and inspection of the weights and measures, the trading room was formally opened.[45]

The native traders picked over the goods carefully, purchasing what was unavailable from the peddlers. They especially desired Brazil tobacco, the HBC's single greatest attraction. James Isham, a governor at York and Churchill in the mid-eighteenth century, recorded a hypothetical discussion between an Indian and an HBC factor: "This tobacco has a bad taste, I will not trade itt," states the Indian, to which the factor replies, "I will ope'n another." Later an Indian observes, "Your tobacco is bad itt's very dry." Indian traders were "so Nice and Difficul in the way of Trade that I admire to see it," wrote one HBC servant.[46]

In this extensive and far-reaching indigenous enterprise, Cumberland House could offer Indian traders the convenience of proximity, but that advantage disappeared when self-employed European peddlers rowed by the post and headed upriver with several barrels of alcohol. Hearne wrote that his own escort, who had accompanied him from York Fort to Cumberland Lake to establish the new trading post, was so enticed by the smell of rum that he followed after the peddlers even before they were out of sight. Despite the inflated prices of peddlers' goods, Hearne learned, brandy and rum induced the Indians to trade with them.[47]

With such large profits to be had, native traders must have seen little reason to be frugal and abstemious, especially since more furs seemingly could always be gotten. So while HBC servants implied that peddlers were taking advantage of intemperate Indians, Indians were merely purchasing what they wanted, and doing so, as Hearne observed, "at their own Doors." (It should be noted that HBC servants also drank to excess.)[48]

In the currency devised by the HBC, Cumberland House purchased a total of about forty-five hundred "Made Beaver" in its first two years of operation.[49] At the beginning of its third year, in fall 1776, the outpost received word that the colonies were "in a state of open Hostility with Great Britain." Its master was instructed to keep a "strict watch" and to put the post "on the most respectable Footing possible." But the real threat to Cumberland House—which lay fifteen hundred miles northwest of the territory seized by the "Conqueror of the Northwest," George Rogers Clark—came from the peddlers, who were intercepting trade along the Saskatchewan River. (In 1779, Clark famously led a group of American militiamen against the British in the trans-Appalachian West.) The "Pedlers are all got up so soon," complained the master, "which has induced me to send my Men away by themselves."[50]

The servants ventured inland to various locations that winter. In all, they brought in almost a thousand beaver, raising Cumberland House's total trade in its third year to over six thousand Made Beaver. That was a small fraction of HBC exports and an even smaller fraction of all beaver exports from North America, which amounted to around a hundred thousand. But Cumberland House was the HBC's first step in a cross-continental race for *Castor canadensis*. Peddlers continued to push up the Saskatchewan, and within a few years, Cumberland House would establish an outpost of its own, 450 miles farther inland.[51]

. . .

The trade in beaver changed the continent in surprising and far-reaching ways. Beaver are what ecologists call ecosystem engineers or geomorphic agents because the rodents create, destroy, and modify habitat. One ecologist has observed that until relatively recently (about ten thousand years ago), the "surficial changes" wrought by beaver surpassed those produced by humans. Indeed, entire valley floors have been raised by beaver activity.[52]

Beavers build dams to flood their surroundings. The dams, made of alder, aspen, thicket, leaves, mud, stones, and other debris, can be enormous, regularly stretching 225 feet across with a thickness of 6 feet. One dam in Montana measured an astounding 2,300 feet. Another rose 16 feet high. In favorable environments, there may be as many as thirty dams per mile of stream, and up to 40 percent of all streams may be modified by the obstructions.[53]

Depending on the geography, the immediate effect of damming is to give fast-running streams a stair-step profile, marked by periodic ponds. In flatter areas, the dams create floodplain wetlands or multithread channels. When dams collapse decades after the demise or migration of beaver colonies, the sediment-rich ponds drain and become fertile meadows. Single dams can flood up to 250 acres and retain as much as 1.7 million gallons of sediment (the volume of about two and a half Olympic-size swimming pools). On an entire watershed, they can retain five hundred times that amount.[54]

The natural history of the Kabetogama Peninsula, in northern Minnesota, has given ecologists the opportunity to observe how the animals transformed the land. Beaver began recolonizing the peninsula in the 1920s, and six decades later they had converted fully 13 percent of its 116 square miles into ponds and meadows and increased the area of aquatic habitat by over 400 percent—an astonishing feat of geoengineering. In maintaining wetlands, their presence is more important than variations in temperature and precipitation, even when severe droughts strike.[55]

Though dams may take centuries to collapse, by hunting out beaver, indigenous peoples and their colonial trading partners transformed North American forests and streams in ways that we still do not fully understand. One study of the impact of beaver in the Adirondacks found that the animals increased the number of species of herbaceous plants by over a third. Their effect on trees is equally as great. A single beaver will eat through almost 220 trees per year, and within a hundred yards of its pond, a colony will annually cut over a ton of wood. By eliminating deciduous trees and leaving behind shrubs, the rodents change the amount of light reaching the stream channel, the quality of litter returned to the soil, and the composition and quality of nutrients in groundwater draining to the stream. Indirectly, they eliminate spruce and fir trees, since those conifers depend on a particular fungus that cannot survive in waterlogged soils. Even after the ponds drain and dry up, spruce and fir will not return. That is because the red-backed vole, which disperses the fungus, does not favor beaver meadows.[56]

Nor do blackflies, which prefer fast-moving, well-aerated water. In North America, blackflies can transmit pathogens to birds and mammals and are a scourge to ungulates. In Saskatchewan and Alberta, blackflies exist in such large numbers that they torment cattle, reducing weight gain and milk production. The most severely afflicted animals will die from fluid loss. Humans who come under attack may get blackfly fever, an assemblage of symptoms that include headache, fever, nausea, and painfully swollen lymph glands. Flies were reportedly so thick around Hudson Bay in the 1740s—perhaps because of the success of Indian trappers in eliminating beaver—that "a man Can not see his way for them" and was "Lyable to be Joack't [choked]." Travelers could find relief from their vexations only by standing in the smoke of a campfire.[57]

Beaver alter the landscape so profoundly, affecting so many species, that it is impossible to unravel the consequences of their near extermination. A healthy beaver population will create a landscape of intact, abandoned, and collapsed dams, a pond-filled environment that fosters both an abundance and a diversity of fish. Beaver activity leaves behind fresh speckled alder leaves in streams, an important food source for aquatic invertebrates. The loss of aspens, felled for dams, makes neighboring white pines susceptible to attacks from white-pine weevils. Certain bark beetles thrive in the dead wood surrounding beaver dams. Frogs and toads, unlike salamanders, multiply rapidly in beaver ponds. Numerous birds depend on the decaying trees in beaver ponds for nesting sites. River otter benefit from beaver dams and lodges in several ways, and the recent increase in the otter population of the United States may be a consequence of the reemergence of beavers. Deer, elk, and moose all prefer aspen and birch shoots, which are common in active beaver areas. The effects, great and small, of the near elimination of beavers cascaded through Canada's boreal forests in the eighteenth century.[58]

The cascade was set in motion by the Indian yen for alcohol, tobacco, textiles, and guns, and the globe-spanning desire for beaver felt hats.

Between 1765 and 1800, about six million beaver pelts were exported from North America. Soon after, native hunters began using steel traps baited with castoreum, a pungent, oily substance obtained from the beaver's sexual glands. With this "infallible" method, native and white trappers pushed farther north and west, denuding the continent of *Castor canadensis*. Beaver "were the gold coin of the country," reminisced one HBC employee in the mid-nineteenth century, when the population was at a historic low. Only the growing preference for silk hats in the 1840s saved the animal from ultimate extinction.[59]

. . .

Soon after the Canada Committee took up residence at the New York Coffeehouse, the Bank of England began a major new expansion of its headquarters around the corner on Threadneedle Street, adding two new wings that were designed according to exacting Palladian standards. The original building, erected in the early 1730s, was simply too small to accommodate all of the business engendered by funding England's frequent wars. The Seven Years' War had kept the bankers especially busy. The government financed the enormous cost by borrowing thirty-seven of every hundred dollars it spent on the conflict, taking out massive loans that towered over all others in the country's history. Almost daily at the Bank of England, a vast crowd of jobbers and brokers pressed into the transfer room to buy and sell government certificates. Every transaction was processed by the bank—for a fee, of course.[60]

Interest rates stayed low throughout the war, indicating that investors remained confident in England's ability to honor its obligations, but the mounting public debt weighed on the Treasury. Emergency loans needed to be secured annually, and disaster always seemed to loom ahead, at least in the mind of the Duke of Newcastle, whose job it was as First Lord of the Treasury to secure the funding. "The real cause of the misfortune," he fretted (a few months before England's great victory in Quebec in 1759), "is that we are engaged in expences infinitely above our strength; and the people do not see any end of it." The Treasury delayed payment on less critical obligations, threatened to issue unbacked bills, and considered rigging the market—all with an eye to securing commitments from the "mony'd men" who ruled the City.[61]

Newcastle's fear of default meant that in the early 1760s, the commander in chief of British forces in North America, Jeffrey Amherst, labored under two disadvantages. One was the pressure to reduce expenses, even while securing the immense new territory now under his command. The other was his own pride and vanity, "of which," said one critic, "he had a tolerable share."[62] He loathed Americans, whether native or not.

Where his concern for cost savings and his contempt for Indians overlapped, Amherst seized the opportunity. "To save unnecessary expenses to the Government & our provisions I got rid of the Indians," he wrote on one occasion in 1759. His native allies were "as idle good for nothing a crew as ever was." More generally, he economized by cutting gifts to Indians; there would otherwise be "no end to it." The money-saving initiative violated centuries of diplomatic protocol in North America. He also seized on a clever but flawed plan to trim the cost of supplying frontier garrisons by encouraging colonists to establish farms on the lands surrounding western forts. "This fell Severely upon those Nations who had been in our Alliance," wrote one longtime observer of Indian affairs, "and from who we had conquered nothing."[63]

Amherst's subordinates shared his sentiments about the local population. Indians, they agreed, were "fickle and Wavering," "dogs" and "bastards"—in short, a race of "Inhuman Villains." After the French evacuated in 1759, Hugh Mercer, the commander at Fort Pitt, relished the opportunity to put native peoples in their place. "We can now talk to our new Allies in a proper Stile," he delighted, "as their services are not Necessary."[64]

Mercer was no longer in command in May 1763, when Delawares and Mingos killed and scalped two soldiers at Fort Pitt's sawmill, leaving behind a tomahawk. It "means I think, a declaration of war," wrote his successor. Three British forts south of the Great Lakes had already fallen to the region's native residents, and six more would do so in the coming weeks. Amherst recorded the events in his journal—first dismissively, then with increasing disgust at the Indians' perfidy and his own officers' "ill-judged confidence" in them.[65]

From his headquarters at the southern tip of Manhattan, Amherst, who had never been west of Oswego, New York (on the eastern end of Lake Ontario), struggled to understand the events unfolding in Ohio country. Native peoples, rather than expressing gratitude for the privilege of becoming George III's subjects, appeared to be deeply angry about the arrival of the imperious British. Finding common cause, Ottawas, Senecas, Delawares, Miamis, Ojibwas, Shawnees, and Mississaugas had joined together to evict the newcomers from their homelands. The English "regard us as dogs," protested the Shawnees, expressing a feeling shared widely by native peoples. They seek "to become Masters of all," the Delawares declared, "and would put us to Death." Amherst wanted to blame the French for the Indians' disaffection, but as British forts between Pittsburgh and Green Bay came under attack, he recognized that the affair was "more General" than he had thought.[66]

With the conflict in full swing, Amherst's loathing of native peoples got the better of his war strategy. His opponents were "more nearly allied to the Brute than to the Human Creation," he wrote. There should be "no Prisoners," he underscored. When one officer suggested using dogs to hunt down "the Vermin," Amherst instead advised that blankets infested with smallpox might be more effective. "Try Every other Method, that can Serve to Extirpate this Execrable Race," he urged.[67]

But the commander in chief of the British armed forces had lost the confidence of his superiors and would not have the opportunity to see the end of the conflict. Invited to return to England, he boarded the *Weasel* for London in November 1763 and never again returned to America. The war, subsequently named for the eloquent Ottawa leader Pontiac, dragged on through fall 1765 before it drew to a quiet close that left both sides in an uneasy truce.[68] The consequences of Pontiac's War would extend into the 1770s and resound as far west as the Black Hills.

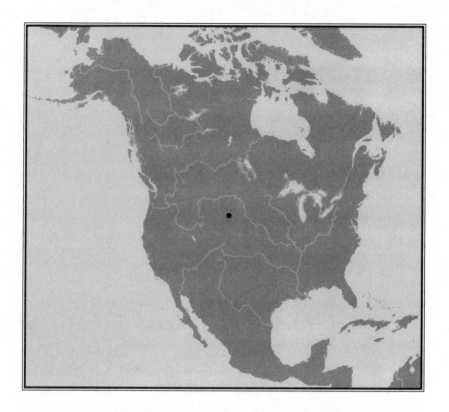

CHAPTER SIX

The Discovery: The Black Hills and the Lakota Nation

I n the 1700s, the Lakota people, the westernmost of the three Sioux political divisions, set out westward from their homelands in what is now Minnesota. Traversing gently rolling grasslands, they reached the steep gullies, high bluffs, and knife-edged ridges that descend to the Missouri River. They crossed the river and moved onto the semi-arid Missouri Plateau. Toward the south, sand, clay, and volcanic ash have washed onto the plains from the Black Hills and Rocky Mountains. Where eroded, the desiccated escarpments and buttes create an inhospitable environment, the Badlands of South Dakota. Continuing still farther west, the Lakotas arrived at the Black Hills.

Standing prominently above the surrounding plains, the Black Hills are composed of four distinct geological zones that form concentric rings around an inner core. The outermost ring rises gradually out of the grasslands until it reaches four thousand feet above sea level. Numerous streams cut through the formation, creating gaps or long valleys that provide access to the interior. Aptly named Hogback Ridge, it terminates in a steep escarpment, which drops down to a grassy depression several miles wide. The depression, or trough, circles the Black Hills and is called the Red Valley or, more evocatively, the Racetrack. Within its bounds sits the Limestone Plateau. Most of the plateau rises higher than six thousand feet above sea level and is well watered by numerous permanent springs. Its cliffs tower some eight hundred feet over the innermost formation of the Black Hills, the deeply eroded Central Basin, which consists of rugged granite mountains, a congeries of spires, knobs, and outcrops. One mountain, Harney Peak, has resisted the elements and remains the single tallest in the Black Hills. It commands boundless views of the surrounding lands.[1]

The Black Hills became sacred to the Lakotas. The mountains were the first place created on the world's surface, they say, and the point from which the Lakota people emerged. In 1876 the United States seized control of the Black Hills, less than a decade after setting them apart in the Treaty of Fort Laramie "for the absolute and undisturbed use and occupation of the Indians." As a young warrior, the Lakota leader American Horse signed the treaty that formalized the land transfer. The cession was costly, both spiritually and, after the discovery of gold, economically. "The only place we had to run our hands in the ground and pick up money, your people have filled it up full," American Horse chastised Congress.[2]

A year after that distressing event, American Horse was present when a soldier fatally stabbed Crazy Horse through the back. Crazy Horse had famously led his people against Custer in 1876 but was living under the watch of the US Army at the time of his death. His parents wrapped their son's body in a red blanket, carried it to Camp Sheridan in northwestern Nebraska, and placed it in the branches of a small tree atop a bluff. Perhaps the plank fence surrounding the tree was still standing in 1879 when American Horse sat down with William Corbusier in the bluff's shadow to share a Lakota winter count.[3]

Painted on animal hides and later on sheets of paper, winter counts mark the passage of time by memorializing each year with an unusual or memorable event. The term derives from the Lakota phrase *waniyetu wówapi*, referring to the span of a year from first snow to first snow and to "something that is marked." Lakotas also call winter counts *hekta yawapi*, or "counts back," because by counting backward, it is possible to calculate the number of years before the present that a particular event occurred.[4]

American Horse marked 1879 with a sketch of a wagon, explaining through a translator that the federal government had given them wagons that winter. He represented the previous year with a picture of Crazy Horse, pierced by a bayonet and bleeding profusely. And so on back in time, the Lakota leader recorded the passage of the years, memorializing periods of starvation, episodes of warfare, the arrival of deadly epidemics, periods of unusual weather, and other such events, some trivial, some momentous.

After he finished copying the calendar, Corbusier or someone else numbered the images from 1 to 104 and, starting with the last and most recent picture, added calendar years, counting backward until reaching the initial entry. As Figure 20 shows, it marks the beginning of history, as remembered by American Horse, and spans the first snows of 1775 and 1776, when Washington captured Boston, Thomas Paine wrote *Common Sense*, and Congress declared independence. In that same period, explained the Lakota leader, Standing Bull discovered the Black Hills.[5] Two nations were born that year.

· · ·

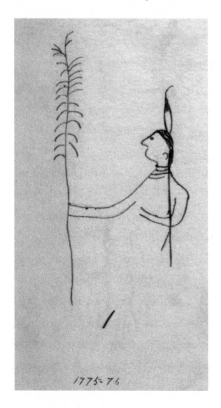

FIGURE 20 According to American Horse's winter count, Standing Bull discovered the Black Hills in 1775–1776. This image is a powerful mnemonic device if Standing Bull is holding part of a Ponderosa pine, which reaches its easternmost extent in the Black Hills and in nearby Pine Ridge. The tree's needles are much longer than the white, jack, and red pines that the Lakotas were accustomed to, its bark has a distinctive yellow hue, and from a distance its needles look almost black—hence "Black Hills," the English translation of the Lakota name *Paha Sapa*. American Horse Winter Count (1879). National Anthropological Archives, Smithsonian Institution, inv. 08746923.

Looking east from the Minnesota River, Pontiac's War appeared a lot different than it did looking west from Manhattan Island. Where Amherst saw an unjustifiable challenge to British power launched by treacherous savages, Standing Bull's people identified a grave threat to their access to Atlantic trade. Every spring the Sioux held a great commercial fair on the banks of the Minnesota. (After the Lakotas' westward migration, the gathering moved to South Dakota's James River.) "Hear [sic] was Sport of All Sorts," a British trader wrote after visiting a similar fair on the Mississippi. The Sioux rendezvous, as it was called, attracted over a thousand lodges and more than ten thousand individuals. "Each man brings different articles, according to the places over which he has wandered," explained one observer. Indigenous products—bison hides, tipi covers, and leather shirts and leggings from the prairies; catlinite pipes from southwestern Minnesota; bows made

of Osage orange from the south—were plentiful. But British manufactures such as guns, powder, and kettles were not. The Indians were
"destitute of Goods," recalled one British trader.[6]

In part, the scarcity was simply a product of distance. Before reaching Sioux country, British goods had to pass from the Hudson's Bay
Company into the hands of Assiniboine Indians to the Great Lakes or
upper Missouri River. Alternatively, the goods could be ported up the
St. Lawrence through the Great Lakes to the British trading post at
Michilimackinac, at the junction of Lakes Huron and Michigan, and
then on to Green Bay; or they could be carted overland to Pittsburgh,
ferried down the Ohio to the Mississippi, and then rowed upriver to
Fort Chartres, near the junction of the Illinois River. "The Enormous
Expences attending it, at Times makes us almost Sick," wrote a group of
traders. Even after those circuitous thousand-mile journeys, it was up to
the Sioux to travel the final three hundred miles from their homelands
to obtain the goods. "The Traders go no farther then these falls," one
map indicated in a location well to the east of the Sioux homelands.
Another route, ascending the Mississippi, was made impractical by
Spanish control of New Orleans, on the river's east bank. "I fancy this
was not well understood by the Peace Makers" at the Treaty of Paris,
wrote one snide British officer, who concluded that the "free Navigation
of the Mississippi is a Joke."[7]

More immediately, the scarcity was caused by Pontiac's War, which
cut off Sioux access to Atlantic trade networks and was the latest in
a series of obstructive conflicts that included the Seven Years' War.
Fort Michilimackinac, Britain's gateway to the West, fell in early June
1763, when Ojibwa lacrosse players hooked a ball over the pickets and
stormed in after it. "Nothing could be less fitted to excite premature
alarm," wrote one witness, who had become accustomed to the sport's
intensity. Once inside, the Ojibwas took the garrison by surprise. A
few weeks later, the British abandoned their westernmost outpost, Fort
Edward Augustus on Green Bay, without a fight. Even after peace formally returned in 1765, commerce resumed slowly, and native peoples

continued to plunder British traders. Local residents were "ungovernable and rapacious," imperial merchants complained.[8]

Far from Amherst's New York headquarters, Standing Bull's people grappled with the consequences. The Dakota leader Wabasha spoke energetically and repeatedly about "the necessity . . . of maintaining and opening a corispondence with the English." (The Dakotas were the easternmost of the three Sioux divisions.) Said by one acquaintance to be "a lively aspiring genius," the sixty-something headman reached out to the British in 1767 and again in 1775. A Dakota embassy also descended the Mississippi to Spanish St. Louis, an initiative that ended poorly when five of the delegates succumbed to disease on the return trip.[9]

A year later, in 1776, with commerce disrupted yet again by imperial warfare, Wabasha and some five hundred other natives traveled to Montreal to help the British retake the fur-trading center from Continental troops. They arrived after the American retreat, but the resolute Dakota leader continued down the St. Lawrence to Quebec with the goal of securing a military and commercial alliance. There, he smoked tobacco with the governor, enjoyed a state dinner, and received an eight-gun salute from the H.M.S. *Isis*.[10]

While the Dakotas sought a solution to the erratic trade by looking east to the British Atlantic, the Lakotas turned west. By the sixteenth century, indigenous trade west of the Mississippi had coalesced around three major centers. They defined the points of a triangle covering half of North America. Several smaller trade fairs stood within and beyond its bounds, tying together the continent in a hub-and-spoke system, formed not by airlines but by footpaths, horse trails, and river routes.[11]

The bottom point of the triangle stood on the Pueblo and Spanish villages of the Southwest. Shortly before setting out across the Colorado Plateau, Francisco Atanasio Domínguez visited Taos, a small colonial and native village of barely four hundred people that became a bustling market when Comanches arrived. Firearms, tobacco, hatchets, slaves, bison hides, horses and mules, corn, and a host of other items exchanged hands, sometimes multiple times in a single day.[12] Taos was one of several markets in the region that drew people from hundreds of miles away.

A second point was situated a thousand miles to the northwest at The Dalles, where the Columbia River cuts through the Cascade Mountains on its way to the Pacific Ocean. Salmon were easily speared in the miles of rough rapids, and perhaps as much as five hundred tons of dried fish was prepared there every year. In a visit to one of the shoals during the off-season, Lewis and Clark saw five tons of dried fish, "tied up very Securely in large bundles" and resting on scaffolds by the river. The bounty drew people from both sides of the mountains. Congregating at The Dalles, they exchanged fish, skins, furs, feathers, shells, roots, and other goods from up and down the Pacific Coast and throughout the Great Plains.[13]

It was the third point, a thousand miles due east of The Dalles, that interested the Sioux. Centered on the Missouri River, it encompassed the Arikara villages in present-day South Dakota and the Mandan and Hidatsa villages 150 miles upstream. The trade that passed through the region was continental in scope, with goods arriving from both coasts and from many places in between. The cultivation of corn by the Missouri River villagers ensured their commercial importance in a region of nomadic peoples who did not farm. They received an unexpected boost in the eighteenth century, when they found themselves situated at both the eastern edge of the Plains Indian horse market and the western edge of the European gun trade. From this advantageous location, Arikaras, Mandans, and Hidatsas controlled the east–west flow of two of the most coveted commodities in the midcontinent.[14]

Drawn to the concentration of wealth, the Lakotas became a common presence along the Missouri River. By 1804, one area in the midst of the Arikara homeland would be known as the Sioux Pass. That year, William Clark disembarked "to See this great Pass of the Sioux and Calumet ground," located just south of the Big Bend, the great horseshoe on the Missouri River located due east of the Black Hills. Walking along the Missouri's precipitous east bank, he came to a small creek, where he saw signs of Sioux camps "for many years passed." At that place, "all nations who meet are at peace with each other," he wrote.[15]

Yet the Lakotas' intentions were not always peaceful. According to traders who visited the Missouri River at the end of the eighteenth century, the Arikaras "feared and dreaded" the Sioux. "Their very name causes terror," observed Jean Baptiste Truteau, "they having so often ravaged and carried off the wives and children of the Ricaras." Truteau himself was certainly terrified. To avoid the "ferocious" Lakotas, he hid in a hole by day and traveled across the prairie by night, skirting the river altogether. He did not breathe easier until he was well outside of the places most frequented by the Sioux.[16]

A second trader, Pierre Antoine Tabeau, noted that the Lakotas saw the Arikaras as "a certain kind of serf, who cultivates for them and who, as they say, takes, for them, the place of women." Mutual interest kept hostilities brief, he stated. Though he was contemptuous of the "weakness and stupidity" of the Arikaras, who, he believed, were abused constantly, there was some irony to his observation, for he tolerated similar ill treatment for the privilege of trading. The Arikaras threatened his life, plotted his assassination, stole his goods, and demanded gifts. "However tenacious a trader may be," Tabeau conceded, "it is impossible for him to escape having to give, sometimes, a knife, a mirror, an ounce of vermilion, some charges of powder and balls, and gradually these gifts have an effect upon a store so moderate." To avoid the annoyance and expense of feeding his Arikara hosts, he finally walled himself off in their earth lodge and ate alone behind a locked door. His actions, he wrote, "at first caused murmuring."[17]

To counter the frequent raids by Lakotas and others, the Missouri River villagers began constructing defensive fortifications in the middle half of the eighteenth century. (The fortifications were associated with the rise in the gun and horse trade, though the degree of correlation is a matter of debate.) Consisting of palisades, deep and wide trenches, and "well flanked" bastions, they impressed one European, who remarked that there was "nothing savage" about them.[18]

Nonetheless, the defenses were not up to the task, as excavations at the Larson site suggest. The remains of the fortified Arikara village sit on the east bank of the Missouri River, on a high terrace overlooking the floodplain, about five miles south of the present-day border between North and South Dakota. Archaeologists have recovered the bones of seventy-one individuals and estimate that several hundred more corpses may rest in unexcavated lodges. The bodies were not formally interred, but trapped when burning roofs collapsed on top of them.[19]

Removing a scalp with a sharp knife often leaves no skeletal evidence, but done with a blunt-edged weapon, it produces a telltale line across the cranium, still visible two centuries after the event. Because the tissue is cut rather than torn over the top of the head, dull blades also leave nicks on protruding bone irregularities. Of the forty-one skulls recovered at Larson, seventeen show signs of scalping, and thirteen more were too badly damaged to make a determination. At least eight of the victims were women, seven were between the ages of ten and nineteen, and one was about five years old.[20]

A number of the skeletons were decapitated, and some facial bones contain only the roots of the incisors, suggesting that the attackers knocked out teeth with a club. One young woman, between sixteen and twenty years old, was brutalized. Assailants scalped her, severed one of her hands, smashed her right arm in two, and slashed her torso and legs multiple times. The cuts were so deep that they reached the bone.[21] Other individuals, still buried under the fallen lodges, may have suffered a similar fate.

According to some winter counts, the Lakotas burned down and destroyed a Missouri River village, perhaps Larson, sometime between 1771 and 1773, just after Pontiac's War had shut down Sioux access to Atlantic trade networks.[22] If the accounts are accurate, then the Lakotas were establishing their supremacy on the Great Plains around the time British colonists disguised themselves as Indians and dumped tea into the Boston Harbor. For both peoples, the next few years would be pivotal.

• • •

Pontiac's War was by no means the only reason for the Lakotas' westward advance. Like all great migrations, this one had multiple causes, though reconstructing the story poses special challenges. Unlike the British colonists who crossed the Atlantic, the Lakotas did not keep journals. The first person to describe the Black Hills in writing, the trapper Jedediah Smith, arrived in 1823, a half century after the Lakotas' momentous entrance into the region. (The visit was a painful one for Smith. A grizzly bear tore off his scalp and broke his ribs.) In the absence of contemporary accounts, the story of the migration must be pieced together from contextual evidence.

The Missouri River was but one stop on a longer journey. West of the river, the Lakotas encountered enormous herds of bison, a resource that, unlike British manufactures, appeared to be limitless. One herd, drawn to the high-protein short grasses in the region, reportedly stretched the entire 150 miles separating the Mandan and Arikara villages. Between the Missouri River and the Black Hills, bison were said to be "countless."[23]

The awe-inspiring bounty persuaded Lakotas to reorient their economy. Rather than hunting game for the eastern trade, they would pursue western bison, a roving market on hooves whose various parts provided sustenance, clothing, and shelter, as well as an array of tools and implements. By most measures, the decision made perfect sense. Bison were plentiful; horses, by extending a hunter's range, made them even more so; and equestrian Plains Indians were flourishing.

In fact, by the mid-nineteenth century, Plains Indian men were taller than any documented population in the entire world, standing about a half inch above European Americans and towering a full two to five inches over their sickly European counterparts. The Cheyennes, who were the tallest of all, were the same height as well-nourished American men in the late twentieth century. Their impressive stature is attributable to the profits of the bison economy. By comparison, Missouri

River farmers fared poorly. In the second half of the eighteenth century, the Arikaras suffered from increasing malnutrition and disease, with predictable consequences: low birth weights, fragile bones, and overall higher morbidity. Before the 1730s, about 43 percent of the population survived to the age of twenty; after 1760, only 32 percent did.[24] For the Lakotas, the choice of sedentary farming, toiling for the Atlantic market, or nomadic hunting was an easy one.

Pulled by the enormous bison herds, the Lakotas spent more and more time west of the Missouri. On the undulating and relatively tree-less plains, the Black Hills stood out, an oasis in a sea of grass. Genera-tions of humans have been struck by the natural beauty of the ancient uplift, as thousand-year-old rock art on its sandstone cliffs attests. But to the bison-hunting, equestrian Lakotas, the Hills also had a very practical appeal. Rainfall is the key to the bison population. More rain produces more grass, and well-watered grass has higher levels of protein and phosphorus and is more nutritious than its parched equivalent. (The eastern Great Plains are wet, but the climate produces tall grasses, which bison do not favor.) Wet years generate healthy cows and calves and larger herds. In the wettest years, the short-grass plains produce twenty times more forage than in the driest years and can support herds twenty times as large. Conversely, droughts strike the ungulate population hard; a single dry season can ravage the bison population, which will not recover for years.[25]

Precipitation decreases steadily from east to west across the Plains, with one exception, as illustrated in Figure 21. The Black Hills, where annual rainfall is significantly higher than in the surrounding area, receive as much precipitation as areas lying more than three hundred miles to the east. The Black Hills are the most fertile area in the mixed and short-grass prairie that stretches from southern Saskatchewan to Texas. They have cooler summer temperatures, which improve grass production, and milder winters than other parts of the Dakotas. More-over, compared with the drought-prone prairies, the Black Hills also have lower year-to-year variability in rainfall.[26]

Consequently, the mountain uplift offers thousands of acres of lush

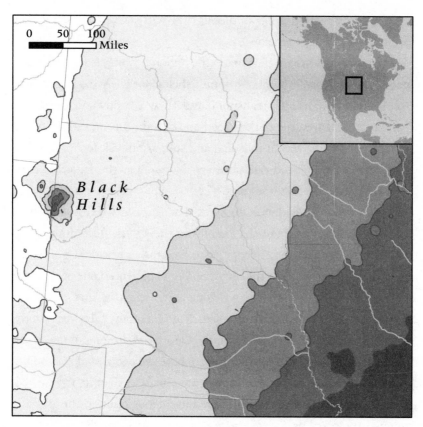

FIGURE 21   Moving east to west, average annual precipitation decreases
in the northern Great Plains, shown here with darker shading
representing wetter areas. The Black Hills stand out as an oasis.

pasture, as white ranchers discovered in the late nineteenth century.
Valuing the forage over the region's lucrative mines, ranchers boasted
that there was "more gold from the grass roots up." Along the Belle
Fourche River, hugging the northern Black Hills, the grass was said
to be three feet high even in November. The valleys were "an ocean of
surging grass."[27] When droughts struck, the hills produced the best
pasture within hundreds of miles and offered relief to emaciated bison.
In severe winters, the river valleys sheltered the animals from the deep
snows that covered the surrounding areas. (When ice and hardpack
snow blanket the Plains, bison push through with their mouths and

noses, leaving behind pools of blood; they will starve to death if they cannot reach the grass below.)

The same conditions that made the region hospitable for bison also made it so for horses. Without winter shelter for their mounts, native peoples had to fell, cut, transport, and thaw cottonwood trees, and then peel and soften the bark to feed and sustain the animals. Finding grass in the winter was "a toilsome and starvation task for women and horses respectively," said one observer. No wonder the Lakotas called the Black Hills their "meat pack."[28]

Circumstantial evidence suggests that the Black Hills may have been especially valuable to the Lakotas in the 1770s. According to one tree-ring reconstruction, in 1772 the Lakotas' traditional homeland along the Minnesota–South Dakota border experienced one of its worst single-year droughts over the previous three centuries and the single worst in the 1700s. That calamity struck after a series of dry years in the 1750s, whose length surpassed even the Dust Bowl drought of the 1930s. The Black Hills region appears largely to have avoided the 1772 drought, though not that of the 1750s. If that was the case, then in 1775–1776, Standing Bull would have encountered numerous bison in the area at a time when the animals were scarce east of the Missouri River.[29]

The most spectacular evidence of the Black Hills' bounty is found in a circular gypsum sinkhole that measures about one hundred feet across at its mouth and descends roughly fifty feet. Archaeologists estimate that the remains of between ten thousand and twenty thousand bison line the bottom. The bones are over twelve feet deep in some places. The Vore Site, as it is known, sits in the northwestern section of the Red Valley, in present-day Wyoming. An open grassy expanse that is several miles wide, the Red Valley receives more rainfall than the neighboring plains and, with running water and sheltered and timbered slopes, is prime bison country. For three hundred years beginning in 1500, Indians (but presumably not the Sioux, who did not yet live in the area) used the sinkhole to trap the animals, driving them from at least a quarter mile away, and perhaps much farther. As much as ten million pounds of meat may have been retrieved from the site—an astonishing figure, especially considering that most of the bison were culled during only two centuries of operation.[30]

To local residents, bison seemed to materialize from the soil itself—a perception that gave rise to the belief that as winter receded, the animals emerged from underground caves. One such place of origin was Ludlow Cave, located about seventy miles due north of the Black Hills. The cave overlooks a valley and faces an ancient rock carving of a seven-foot-long bison cow and calf, representing fecundity. (Ludlow Cave was once covered with carvings and filled with offerings, but Custer's men visited and desecrated the site in 1874. The ancient carvings have since been destroyed.) In the cave-riddled Black Hills there are numerous petroglyphs of animal tracks and human vulvae, linking women's fertility and bison abundance. The art dates from 500 CE to 1800 CE and often appears next to communal bison-hunting sites.[31]

Yet even the most dedicated Plains hunters relied on game for only 80–90 percent of their sustenance, undeniably a large share of their diet but still one that necessarily had to be supplemented. It is a surprising fact that humans can starve to death on a diet composed only of lean meat, as Plains Indians might have encountered during the coldest winters. In such situations, humans must augment their diet with plants. The Cheyennes ate some forty wild plant species, raided rodent seed caches, and cultivated small plots of corn. The Lakotas could obtain those necessary foods in trade with Missouri River farmers, but they also surely exploited the diverse plant resources of the Black Hills. The mountain uplift marks the intersection of several different ecozones, making for a region rich in plant diversity. By one count, the Black Hills and the nearby Powder River basin contain roughly six hundred plant species—producing an abundance of seeds, tubers, pollen, pods, petals, and other edible parts—which may have been utilized by native peoples. By comparison, the surrounding plains are ecologically homogeneous and support grasses that are inedible to humans.[32] With their towering spires, sheer cliffs, deep caves, and numerous springs, the Black Hills inspired awe in the Lakotas, but the mountains also offered material advantages to equestrian hunters.

• • •

According to one acquaintance, American Horse was "shrewd, "sagacious," and "slippery." "He could say very sharp things of the duplicity of the whites," said another, who recalled American Horse's acerbic response to a popular spiritual of the time. "If you have got to wear golden slippers to enter the white man's heaven," American Horse reportedly said, "no Indian will ever get there, as the whites have got the Black Hills and with them all the gold."[33]

Those qualities may explain why he placed the Sioux discovery of the Black Hills and American independence in the same celebrated year. The chronological coincidence perhaps was a clever ploy on the part of the Sioux leader to put the Lakota Nation and the United States on an equal footing. (The precise date of the event cannot be verified and may well have occurred in one of the surrounding decades.) Likewise, he may have deliberately spoken of "discovery" (as the word was translated) to imply that Lakota and US land claims rested on the same right, established by Standing Bull in one case, by Christopher Columbus in the other. William Corbusier, the army officer who copied the winter count, could not let the presumption stand. The Sioux "have of late years claimed the Black Hills, probably by right of discovery in 1775–76," he commented on the first entry, "but the Crows were the former possessors."[34]

Corbusier had a point, even if he failed to recognize that every land title in the United States was based on a similar fallacy. The Black Hills have been known to humans for at least ten thousand years. In the 1770s, the Crows, Kiowas, Kiowa-Apaches, Arapahos, and Cheyennes probably all visited the hills seasonally. It also appears that villagers from the Missouri River occasionally used the hills for hunting and procuring tool materials. The Lakotas called the Black Hills' ancient inhabitants the "Island Hill people" and made their predecessors' sacred traditions their own. Bears' Lodge Butte (now also known as Devils Tower), for example, was sacred to the Kiowas, Cheyennes, Arikaras, and Arapahos before the Lakotas associated it with their own culture hero, Fallen Star, and began performing the annual sun dance at the iconic rock formation.[35]

The surviving Black Hills rock art that is inscribed and painted on sandstone cliffs suggests that the Lakotas and other denizens of the mountain uplift shared and borrowed artistic and cultural traditions. Images of animal tracks and human vulvae appear not only throughout the Black Hills but also range from the northern Great Plains to the southern shores of Lake Erie. They are associated with Algonquian and Siouan peoples and reflect shared beliefs about the link between women's fertility and abundant game. Some cliff walls contain pictures of stylized shield-bearing warriors—often no more than circles with stick legs and arms and a small head—a tradition that may originate with Shoshone peoples from the Great Basin, west of the Rockies. Different shields bear heraldry that is distinctly Sioux, Crow, Cheyenne, and perhaps Blackfoot, illustrating how widely the artistic convention was shared.[36]

There also exists a five-thousand-year-old Black Hills tradition of memorializing sacred visions on their limestone walls. The first vision seekers recorded abstract designs—arcs, waves, circles, dots, spirals, radials, and other patterns—that resemble the images humans see in altered states of consciousness. By the eighteenth century, the iconography had changed, but the tradition of memorializing visions persisted. One small sandstone rock shelter overlooking the Cheyenne River is inscribed with an image of an individual with raised hands and forked, thunderbolt eyes. The image may have been drawn by a Lakota or Crow person on a vision quest.[37]

Despite the sharing of traditions among Black Hills' residents, the Lakota arrival in the mountain uplift marked the onset of an invasion. The closest we can come to native accounts of that moment are the pictures of violence inscribed on the Black Hills and nearby bluffs. One rock art panel near the Cheyenne River portrays a man standing near an upside-down woman, who bears a spear-shaped icon on her chest. In Plains Indian iconography, the head-over-heels position often represents death.[38] Exactly who killed this woman and in what context is lost to history.

Seventy miles to the north, on a panel illustrating martial exploits in the north Cave Hills, a warrior touches the genitals of a woman, a form of coup counting (that is, demonstrating one's bravery by striking an enemy) and also, perhaps, a representation of sexual violence. A second image in the north Cave Hills captures the period after the arrival of horses but before the introduction of guns. Two mounted warriors bearing lances (or the same warrior pictured twice) attack a Crow woman, who is pierced through with an arrow. The horses are crudely drawn, and the riders sit awkwardly on their mounts, suggesting the still unfamiliar nature of equestrian warfare. The horses appear to be covered in leather armor, indicating that the attackers were probably Shoshone. One scholar dates the image to 1730–1760, just before the Lakotas arrived in the region.[39]

Among the early and most successful adopters of the horse in the northern plains, the Sioux possessed the advantages of speed and leverage over their pedestrian enemies. One skeletal report of an attack by mounted Shoshones on people who had never before seen a horse describes how they "dashed at" their foes and "knocked them on the head." Later, the survivors (in this case Blackfeet) sought out the exotic beasts, eventually locating and examining a dead horse.[40] But neither that account nor any rock art succeeds in capturing the terror that possessed individuals when equestrians bore down on them for the first time.

The violent moments inscribed on the Black Hills obviously meant different things to the perpetrators and the victims. On a rock face now in Custer County, Lakotas celebrated victories over their enemies. Five handprints in red paint probably signal triumph in hand-to-hand combat. A red spot on the same panel marks the death of an enemy, and two crosses commemorate rescuing friends in battle.[41] On this rock and on others, the Lakotas laid claim to the Black Hills.

In 1926, the 150th anniversary of the Lakota discovery of the Black Hills, three men hauled a winch to the summit of Mount Rushmore, fixed it into the granite, and began pulling tools up from the valley floor, four hundred feet below. They were preparing to sculpt four colossal figures onto the face of the mountain. "The stone will have to be drilled, hand-plugged and machine cut by what are known as air drills," explained the artist behind the project, Gutzon Borglum. "I shall use no explosives on any of the carving," he promised. A year later, workers began boring into the face of the mountain, loading the holes with dynamite, and blasting away four hundred thousand tons of rock.[42]

Borglum had a predilection for gargantuan art and grandiose declarations. "A monument's dimensions," he contended, "should be determined by the importance to civilization of the events commemorated." In the Black Hills, he found the perfect opportunity to realize his imperial ambitions. For one, the mountains were big and therefore suitable for subjects of worldwide significance, in this case the creation and westward expansion of the United States. For another, they were situated in the "center of this great Union, in the center of America, in the center of the territory which marked the first step from colonial conservation to continental dominion." And, as a final virtue, they were isolated enough to be protected from "selfish, coveting civilizations" that might arise in the future. "You know how vandalism in the name of Civilization raids the tombs of our ancestors and destroys the records of History," Borglum observed. "If this monument fails to become the first of our great memorials to the Anglo-Saxon in the Western Hemisphere," said the KKK sympathizer and professed anti-Semite, "it will be because we ourselves have failed."[43]

While Borglum blasted away at Black Hills granite, the Sioux were pursuing a lawsuit against the United States for the theft of the mountains. In the years since the Lakota migration, the Black Hills had become the mythic birthplace of their nation, the geographic equivalent of the Declaration of Independence. The Hills "hold their 'Mother's heart and pulse' with sustaining myth," says one tribal citizen; they are "the Heart of our home and the home of our Heart," states another; according to a third, they are "the heart of the earth, the center of our origin stories, spiritual history and sacred places." In 1980, the Supreme Court granted the Sioux a victory, ordering the federal government to pay $102 million for the theft of the Black Hills. The Sioux refuse to accept the money. The sum sits untouched in an interest-bearing account and had grown to $1.3 billion by 2011. Standing Bull's descendants are holding out for the return of the lands he discovered in 1776.[44]

. . .

Manhattan's most fashionable district in the 1760s surrounded Fort George, at the southern tip of the island. With broad streets and pleasing views of the water, the area was home to the city's wealthiest families, busiest commercial streets, and most respectable social institutions. Within a few blocks, residents could purchase goods at the Exchange, enjoy a coffee at the Merchant's Coffeehouse, and socialize with fellow elites at Fraunces Tavern. For a time, the slave market at the east end of Wall Street blocked the aristocracy's "agreeable prospect" of the East River, but a 1762 petition succeeded in having the "offensive" structure removed.[45]

At the end of Broadway in the heart of this desirable neighborhood stood the stone gray King's Arms Tavern, a "commodious house" with "genteel lodging apartments." Two days before Amherst departed on the *Weasel* in November 1763, Thomas Gage, Britain's new commander in chief for North America, arrived from Montreal and took up temporary residence in the tavern. Gage was a capable and honest administrator but irredeemably cautious. He would soon earn the moniker "Old Woman" from his soldiers, and it was quipped that his American-born and independent-minded wife, Margaret Keble Gage, was the man of the family.[46]

The King's Arms was surmounted by a cupola furnished with a table, seats, and a good telescope. From this vantage point, Gage could enjoy unobstructed views of the East River, northern Manhattan, and New York Harbor.[47] Turning to the west, Gage could look over the Hudson River into New Jersey, but not nearly far enough to see the troubled West—that is, the territory immediately to the east of the Mississippi. Along with unruly New England, the West was one of the two regions that consumed his attention in the late 1760s.

"There is little appearance that the advantages will arise from it,

which nations expect, when they send out colonies into foreign coun-
trys," Gage observed in 1770. The problem arose not from the intrinsic
value of the land but from the border defined by the Mississippi. On
paper, the river divided Spanish and English subjects, but in practice it drew them together, leading to economic conflict and political
intrigue. As long as the continent's largest thoroughfare separated the
two empires, Gage concluded, Spain and England would be "mutually endeavoring to cultivate the Friendship of every Indian Nation,
far and near."[48]

Gage was annoyed and perhaps surprised that local
residents—"savages," he called them—understood their political interests "extreamly well," for they knew it was to their advantage to "have
a door open to treat and trade with another power." It was even more
exasperating that European armies were no match for native peoples
in this part of the world. After considering these sobering facts, Gage
encouraged Britain to abandon its western outposts. "Let the savages
enjoy their desarts in quiet," he concluded.[49]

West of the Mississippi, Spain faced the same struggles. Imperial bluster—the determination to "exterminate" the Osage Indians,
for example—always gave way to reality. Spain had about five hundred troops to patrol the entirety of Louisiana, a region encompassing
some half a million square miles, almost twice the size of present-day
Texas. When not reduced by disease and desertion, twelve soldiers were
charged with policing all of Arkansas; thirty-eight others patrolled
everything to the north. The minuscule imperial footprint and porous
Mississippi border allowed native residents to evade Spanish authority
at will.[50]

The European diplomats who divided the continent down the Mississippi may have been far from the mind of Joseph de la Miranda when
he floated down the Arkansas River in late March 1776. Next to him lay
one severed head and the corpses of two of his companions. Miranda's
party of twenty hunters had been camped on a prairie along the banks
of the river when a band of Osage men attacked them. Residents of
the Missouri River, the Osages increasingly frequented the Arkansas

to their south in the 1770s. By Miranda's account, his party killed four Osages, wounded another ten, and took the head of one warrior as a prize. The grisly trophy and the pallid corpses must have made for an unpleasant journey downriver, but Miranda was determined to deprive the Osages of scalps by burying the bodies far from the encounter. It was small consolation for the fact that his own son had been gravely wounded in the attack.[51]

More than any other people in the region, the Osages profited from the Mississippi border. Numbering five thousand people, they controlled nearly a hundred thousand square miles in the center of the continent, including lands that would later become Missouri and Arkansas. By Spanish measure, the Osages were predisposed to "cruelty and evil inclinations" and devoted to "the most sanguinary hostilities and to incessant robberies."[52] But from the Osages' perspective, they were merely seizing the opportunity opened by the Treaty of Paris.

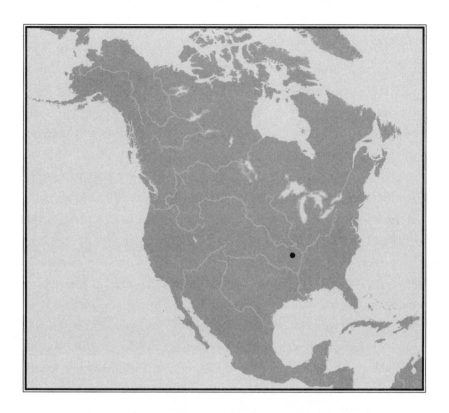

CHAPTER SEVEN

An Invasion of Malefactors:
Osage Country

Though Joseph Orieta commanded Arkansas Post in the name of the Most Serene and Potent Prince, Charles III, king of Spain and of the Indies, there was nothing glorious about the assignment. The fort, situated in a floodplain about ten miles above the mouth of the Arkansas River, was a ruin, with rotting palisades, roofless barracks, and useless cannons. When Joseph de la Miranda arrived in April 1776 to present Orieta with the head of an Osage man, the fort was knee-deep in stagnant floodwater. The grim gift could hardly have lightened the commandant's mood. As a final indignity, when Orieta died two months later, his corpse reeked so badly that it was hastily buried without ceremony. Arkansas Post, concluded one officer, was "the most disagreeable hole in the universe."[1]

From the perspective of imperial administrators, the middle Mississippi was in disarray after the Treaty of Paris. Several dozen soldiers and officers, scattered among a few isolated and undermanned forts, were charged with bringing order to the entire region. Though the forts were situated at strategic locations on the river, the distances between them made it impossible to impose on local residents.

Arkansas Post sat three hundred miles up the winding Mississippi River from the closest of Spanish Louisiana's tobacco and indigo plantations. North of Arkansas Post, it took another six hundred miles of arduous rowing to reach the next colonial outpost, Ste. Genevieve. The village shared Paris's patron saint, but the two locales had nothing else in common. Of the seven hundred residents of Ste. Genevieve, which was known as *Misère*, or "misery," 40 percent were enslaved. St. Louis stood fifty miles farther upriver on the same side. Though it was situated impressively on a tall limestone bank overlooking the Mississippi, it had earned its own disparaging nickname: *Paincourt*, or "Short of Bread."[2]

Britain's sole garrison in the area was Fort Chartres, across the river from Ste. Genevieve. One cheery visitor described it as "the most commodious and best built fort in North America," even though the British were in a losing battle to keep its two-foot-thick walls from washing into the Mississippi. Laboring in vain, soldiers reinforced the bank with earth and fascines. In the space of a year, however, the river eroded seventy-five yards, and in 1772 the British abandoned the post, just before the south wall collapsed.[3]

Even worse problems plagued the garrison at Fort Chartres. The fort was surrounded by "innumerable" stagnant pools of water, the ideal environment for producing deadly "Summer Exhalations." (Why would the French have chosen a place "so cursed with surrounding Evils," wondered one scornful British officer.) No colonist born there ever reached the age of fifty, it was claimed, and only a few survived into their forties.[4]

Newcomers, such as the British regiment that arrived at Fort Chartres in 1768, were hit especially hard. "The Groans & cries of the Sick Was the only Noise to be heard within the Fort," wrote a witness, who was fortunate enough to survive. The symptoms, as detailed by an officer named George Butricke, unmistakably characterize malaria. Seized by a "Hott fitt" one evening, Butricke awoke the next day with an intermittent fever. A day later, the fever returned "in such a Violent manner" that he was completely incapacitated. For six days he suffered through hot and cold spells until a final severe attack of shaking marked the end of the episode. (His malarial fevers would return periodically, as is typical of the illness.) Butricke was one of the lucky ones. Dozens of others were "at Deaths door . . . week, feable, emaciated poor Souls," and the regiment carted off four or five corpses a day. Perhaps over a hundred people succumbed to the epidemic.[5]

While isolated officials tried to bring order to their immense jurisdictions, one group of residents seized the opportunity born of the imperial upheaval in the 1760s and 1770s. Known as the Osages, they had moved into central and western Missouri by the late seventeenth century, perhaps migrating from the Ohio River. In their new homelands, they enjoyed a favored status with the French for a time, but in the 1740s, traders began arming native peoples to the west of the Osages, marking the start of a predictable sequence of events: as the Osages became expendable, Europeans would inevitably turn against them, and the Osages, now dependent on European manufactures, would be unable to defend themselves against either encroaching colonists or opportunistic native peoples.[6] Numerous nations along the continent's East Coast had already faced this predicament. Some of them took refuge with more powerful peoples, others eked out a living on the margins of the colonies, and still others disappeared altogether. As a result of the unintended consequences of the Treaty of Paris, the Osages would be spared such an unfortunate fate.

• • •

Back in 1725, when the Osages were profiting from the attention of French traders, one of their leaders had traveled to Paris with six other natives, including an Indian slave and a woman identified as the "Princess of the Missouris." The junket, organized by a French explorer and entrepreneur, was intended to win the admiration of the North Americans and attach them to France. Accordingly, they visited the most impressive sights of Paris, including the Opéra, the Comédie-Française, and Versailles. At the Hôtel des Invalides, a hospital and residence for injured soldiers, they were amazed by the crude prostheses. "You may lose an arm, a leg, an eye, a tooth, a breast, if you are in France," one of them reportedly told a skeptical crowd back home, "and they will supply you with others, so that it will not be noticed." At an audience with the king, they were perhaps surprised that the resplendent Louis XV was a callow youth of fifteen years, and they advised the recently married adolescent to father many children and keep his health. The king canceled the visitors' planned meeting with the queen on account of their "savage and bizarre manner of dress"—"that is to say," specified one report, they were "utterly nude," except for a loincloth.[7]

By the 1760s, those heady days had long since vanished. Early adopters of firearms, the Osages had once enjoyed an enormous advantage over their indigenous rivals, but they were no longer the sole possessors of European technologies in the region. Over the same period, as their exposure to Old World diseases increased, their population had plummeted, falling from a high of perhaps eighteen thousand at the beginning of the century to barely five thousand. In their diminished communities, stories still circulated about the marvels of Paris, where the French were said to be as abundant as the leaves in a forest. In disbelief, locals contended that the travelers must have been hoodwinked—perhaps they were shown the same individuals over and over again—and even one member of the delegation began to suspect as much as his memory faded with age.[8]

It was indeed true that the European empires were vastly more populous than Native America. About nine million people lived in Spain, the self-proclaimed sovereign of Louisiana after the Treaty of Paris; over six million people lived in England, which ruled over the Mississippi's east bank. With those numbers, the Osages might have been overwhelmed, had they not possessed a fortuitous advantage: it was extraordinarily difficult for the agents of empire to reach the heart of the continent.[9]

When Spanish and British officials strategized how to control the middle Mississippi, their list of difficulties began with the river itself. The journey from New Orleans to St. Louis could take three to five months, more than twice as long as a trans-Atlantic voyage, and soldiers who were sent upriver faced the exhausting and dangerous trial of rowing against the current for weeks on end. To avoid the powerful flow in the river's center, they hewed to one side or the other in search of countercurrents and eddies. There, they risked being engulfed by a collapsing bank. After a cave-in, wrote a later traveler, the "whole vast face" of the Mississippi turned "black with drifting dead logs, broken boughs, and great trees"—all obstacles that could stave in a boat.[10]

Each of the river's hundreds of bends posed a particular challenge. Because water runs faster on the outside bank, boats crossed over to the inside, slipping a half mile back at each traverse. Experienced pilots estimated that they crossed the Mississippi 390 times between New Orleans and St. Louis, adding almost three hundred miles to the journey. The river winds so tightly that along one stretch, troops rowed fifty-four miles to gain five, and along another, thirty miles to gain one and a half. "The Hardships and immense Difficulties," one officer insisted to his superior, are "beyond your Excellency's Conception."[11]

Even with an experienced guide, troops progressed with tremendous difficulty. Without one, they barely progressed at all. "As the Islands in this great River, form many different Channels," explained a newcomer, "We could not be Judge which was the most Convenient for Us." Fighting the current and skirting numerous fallen and half-submerged trees, one party of soldiers gained less than a mile every four hours, driving the commanding officer "almost mad." It was, said one, "the most dangerous and fatiguing journey I ever made."[12]

Winter ice and spring flood currents added to the colonists' woes by forcing them to travel in late summer, when mosquitoes were at their fiercest and the sun burned the hottest. Though one detachment began rowing at 3:00 a.m. and rested in the heat of the day, forty soldiers still succumbed to heatstroke, and one died. They perhaps could not force themselves to swallow the river water, said to be so muddy that it was "impossible to drink." The Mississippi, one sailor would later write, was the "great common sewer of the Western America."[13]

Exhausted troops especially dreaded Indian attacks, which put them in an impossible bind. If they dropped their oars to pick up arms, their boats were swept downriver, and the disoriented soldiers became easy targets for concealed gunmen. If they continued laboring upriver, their fate was equally unhappy. Rather than face those dangers, some 80 of 350 troops deserted when the British ordered them up the Mississippi to Fort Chartres in 1765.[14]

Though the region continued to be the object of various speculative ventures, it remained beyond imperial control. Only fourteen hundred free and enslaved residents lived in Spanish St. Louis, Ste. Genevieve, and Arkansas Post in the 1770s, and even fewer colonists trod on the banks of the British side of the Mississippi. In a letter to his superior, one British officer, charged with implementing imperial policy in Indian country, encapsulated his deep sense of isolation, writing about "the distance we are here from the world."[15]

· · ·

The distance between the middle Mississippi and the middle of New Spain ensured that the post–Treaty of Paris years were extraordinarily good ones for the Osages. Within the "Dominions of His Majesty," as the Spanish liked to call Louisiana, the Osages reigned over both natives and non-natives alike, not only dominating the region between the Missouri and the Arkansas but also expanding farther south to the Red River. (The Red River today defines the northern border of Texas.) They were "insolent" and haughty, charged one Spanish officer. "Execrable," said another, a "pernicious" race known for their "turbulence and ferocity."[16] In short, they were imperial.

From his post in Natchitoches on the lower Red River, Athanase de Mézières witnessed the expansion firsthand. With almost four decades of service in Louisiana behind him, he was outraged by Osage attacks in the neighborhood of his profitable tobacco plantation. "All at once," he wrote in 1770, "this district has become a pitiful theater of outrageous robberies and bloody encounters." Osages were stealing Indian women, kidnapping children, and rustling horses and mules.[17]

Though de Mézières begged Pedro Piernas, the commander in St. Louis, to put a halt to Osage attacks, Piernas had no means. In a 1772 letter to his commanding officer, Piernas was full of bluster, calling for a war of extermination, but in front of the Osages themselves he was humbler: "I formally remonstrated with them," he wrote, "for their lack of co-operation, their hostile attitude, overbearing procedure, and their failure to keep peace or submit to reason." At Arkansas Post, when Fernando de Leyba suggested rewarding Quapaws with bullets, powder, and six pesos for each dead Osage, Governor Luis de Unzaga rejected the proposal, instead ordering him to "reprimand" the Osages "kindly concerning their bad faith."[18] (The Quapaws, a small community of under a thousand people, lived next to Arkansas Post.)

In summer 1772, a party of Osage and Missouri men broke into Fort San Carlos on the Missouri River and overwhelmed the garrison of five soldiers. After stealing the fort's munitions and provisions, they stormed nearby St. Louis and planted a British flag in the heart of the settlement. The brazen attack prompted Unzaga to call for the "extermination" of the Osages. Admitting that he lacked the money, the troops, and the allies to support such an ambitious undertaking, he wondered if this "sad remedy" could be accomplished "without cost."[19]

De Mézières, writing with an air of authority, assured Unzaga that the goal was both "feasible" and "proper," and confidently outlined how it might be accomplished. Though Osage families decamped for the hunt every winter, in the summer they returned to their villages on the Missouri and Osage Rivers, where women tended immense cornfields. "Their towns hold more people in the same space of ground than any place I ever saw," said one native of Trenton, New Jersey, who visited in 1806. Osage houses, built of posts and reed mats and up to one hundred feet long, made "a very comfortable and pleasant summer habitation," he wrote. But these same admirable qualities, speculated de Mézières, were also vulnerabilities. Populous and compact, the villages could be easily besieged. While the attacking party lived on Osage corn from outlying fields, the villagers would be reduced "to the greatest extremes of thirst and hunger." Whether murderous fantasy or cunning design, the plan was never implemented. Instead, Unzaga recommended that the offenders pay for the damages.[20]

Under different conditions, Spanish officers would have compensated for their small numbers by cutting off Osage access to European manufactures. By the simple act of an embargo, observed one Louisiana governor, dependent Indians lived in danger of "being disarmed and dying of hunger." But when Piernas threatened to employ this tactic against the Osages, he reported that "they seemed confident they could get along very well without our aid and assistance."[21]

The problem, he observed, was that the Osages were "in close proximity" to the English, and the imperial border that separated the two was a fiction to just about everyone who lived next to it.[22] The Mississippi drains over a million square miles—a region more than twice the size of France, Spain, and Britain combined—and has for centuries served not to divide people but to draw them together. A treaty struck in the French capital by individuals who had never before set foot in North America was unlikely to reduce the river's attraction. Nor could such a treaty bring definition to the river's meandering and ever-changing course, captured in Figure 22. (It is worth noting that comparable rivers, such as the Nile, the Amazon, and the Yangtze, are national thoroughfares, not international borders.)

One Quapaw scoffed at the very idea of such a line. "An Indian makes everything that he wants one land by calumet," he said, referring

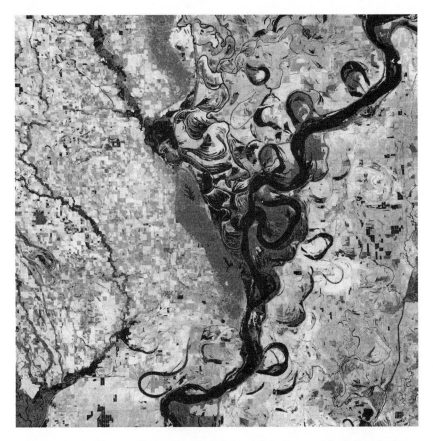

FIGURE 22 "A cut-off plays havoc with boundary lines and jurisdictions,"
Mark Twain would observe, exactly 120 years after European aristocrats
divided North America down the Mississippi. Twain, *Life on the Mississippi*, 24.
Image credit: NASA's Goddard Space Flight Center/USGS.

to a traditional peace pipe. Following native protocol, he suggested, he
could make alliances with whomever he pleased. Even a cursory visit to
the region revealed that a "Strong Connection" existed between native
residents "on His Majesty's side" of the Mississippi and the other side.[23]

Almost from the outset, the Osages took advantage of the English
presence on the east bank. In 1768, they passed through Spanish St.
Louis carrying British colors. Arriving at Fort Chartres, they promised
one hopeful merchant that "for the Future" they would "bring their
Trade to this Place." For "commercial ends," the British courted them

"lavishly" for several years—a policy that inspired the Osages to raise a British flag over one of their villages, in defiance of the Spanish Crown.[24]

Even without crossing the river, the Osages found that their homeland was swarming with smugglers who were willing to trade with anyone possessing a deerskin. To Spanish officers, the smugglers were "deserters" and "criminals"—"the most wicked persons, without a doubt in all the Indies." The "malefactors" were "depraved and wholly abominable," de Mézières wrote, under "no other rule than their own caprice." He was particularly scandalized by their sexual relations. They lived "in public concubinage" with enslaved Indian women, wrote the native Parisian, and loaned "those of whom they tire" to laborers, giving the workers "no other wage than the promise of quieting their lascivious passions." (De Mézières's own son would have seven children by one of his father's slaves, in violation of his father's ordinance curbing the "scandalous libertinage" of black women and punishing "whites base enough to addict themselves to their shameless prostitutions.")[25]

After purchasing furs, British traders had two options. They could spend weeks rowing their cumbersome cargoes up the Ohio to Fort Pitt and then haul them overland to Philadelphia—a route that was both toilsome and costly—or they could, with minimal labor, float down the Mississippi and sell them illegally but for a premium in Spanish New Orleans. They made the obvious choice. "Trade will go with the Stream," acknowledged Thomas Gage, the commander in chief of British forces in North America. By one account, some seven hundred thousand skins followed this "most expeditious Route to the Sea" in 1764. By 1776, it was estimated, over 97 percent of Louisiana's trade passed through illegitimate channels.[26]

Though it made little difference to the Osages whether their products were shipped up or down the Mississippi, the stream of smuggling in effect erased the international border that on paper gave Spain a trade monopoly west of the river. Not surprisingly, orders forbidding traders from "transgressing their Boundarys" were ineffectual. One frustrated Spanish official blamed the "proximity" of the Mississippi's two banks, an attribute of the river that European negotiators had somehow overlooked.[27]

It was not only the Mississippi proper that encouraged trafficking. Every feeder river invited traders to ascend in search of furs. In Britain's newly acquired territory, the Illinois, Kaskaskia, and Ohio Rivers were irresistible to French smugglers from Spanish Louisiana. The traders were, in the words of a British Indian agent, "Men of Spirit, Abilities, and a knowledge of the World," well liked by native peoples and tolerant of indigenous traditions. (The British, by contrast, were "a well meaning but Gloomy people.")[28] More important, the smugglers possessed the advantage of experience, having worked for decades in the region and having developed close ties with local residents.

The contraband trade in Illinois country was "Immense." "Coop'd up" in Fort Chartres, the British made "a foolish Figure" and hardly had "the Dominion of the Country," concluded a frustrated officer. Spanish and French smugglers reportedly passed back and forth "with Pleasure" under the fort's guns, often with the connivance of the commanding British officer. Though Gage ordered the garrison to "Scour" the rivers with armed boats to imprison interlopers, he had little hope of success. "There is no good Prospect that the Commerce of the Mississippi will prove of much Advantage to Great Britain," he concluded.[29]

Farther south, the British ran their own smuggling operation in Spanish territory, focusing on the Arkansas, White, and St. Francis Rivers. (These rivers drain the northern half of present-day Arkansas.) "You would not quite believe the brigandage, the insubordination, and the libertinage that reigns here," wrote the commandant of Arkansas Post. In the first few months of 1776 alone, smugglers reportedly harvested or purchased twelve thousand deerskins and six thousand pounds of beaver pelts. The region, de Mézières fulminated, was "infested" by deserters, robbers, rapists, and murderers. By trading with any and everyone, they freed native residents from Spanish dependence and underwrote Osage expansion toward the Red River.[30]

From his inundated fort on the Arkansas, Joseph Orieta speculated that sixty men and two artillery pieces stationed at the mouth of the

White River would be able to intercept the greater part of the illegal commerce, but he may as well have proposed damming the Mississippi. Arkansas Post itself housed only a dozen soldiers, and the garrison could barely maintain its own presence, let alone extend its reach. Instead, Orieta and his successor, Balthazar de Villiers, were forced to beg the Quapaws for assistance. Not surprisingly, the Quapaws had little interest in patrolling rivers on behalf of the Spanish. They "follow their caprice and not at all my will," confessed Villiers.[31]

. . .

Even among more reputable colonists, the remoteness of the middle Mississippi from imperial centers weakened ties to the mother country. Loyalty was stretched even thinner by the post-treaty shift from French Catholic to English Protestant rule on the east bank and from French to Spanish rule on the west bank.[32] Nowhere did the disruption benefit the Osages more than in St. Louis.

After the loss of France's possessions east of the Mississippi, French merchants had established the town in early 1764, imagining that it would become the gateway to a second New France, one based in the West and centered on the immense fur trade in the region. Construction on the first buildings had barely begun when word arrived that the settlement named for Louis XV actually belonged to Charles III. Thereafter, residents proved to be more loyal to their commerce than to the Crown.[33]

The fortunes of St. Louis depended on the Osages, who harvested more furs than any other people in the region. By 1776, the Osages accounted for somewhere between 40 and 60 percent of the town's trade, and every season its merchants extended huge sums of credit to native hunters. For good reason, creditors preferred to disregard Osage attacks on other Spanish posts rather than enforce an embargo that might jeopardize their profits, if not bankrupt them. Rumors even circulated, perhaps with some truth, that St. Louis merchants defended their market share by encouraging the Osages to attack Arkansas traders, who were fellow Spanish subjects, of French ancestry like themselves, but competitors nonetheless. There was "no lack of persons . . . overcome by greed," remarked de Mézières.[34]

Crown officers chased profits too, even if their actions were sometimes contrary to imperial policies. Postings on the middle Mississippi were both a curse and a prize. Remote and inhospitable, surrounded by unfriendly locals and malarial mosquitoes, the forts at least offered the advantage of the Indian trade. Fernando de Leyba had served as captain of an infantry company of one hundred soldiers before receiving command of the dozen troops at Arkansas Post. He arrived at the fort "so broken down in health" that he did not expect to survive, and so demoralized that he felt incapable of putting forth any effort to improve conditions. The fort, he said, had more holes than the garrison had fingers, and the cannons lacked carriages and platforms.[35]

Leyba sought to find some advantage in the misfortune by arriving with a large quantity of merchandise and plans to monopolize the Indian trade. Transferred to St. Louis in 1778, he cared so little for his former posting that he overlooked Osage raids on the Arkansas River in favor of maintaining the lucrative trade based in his new town. It was not right for the Osages to collect the king's gifts in St. Louis and then travel to Arkansas "to vent their cruelty against his vassals," observed Leyba's superior, but his only advice was consult with townspeople to find a way to prevent "such atrocities."[36]

Leyba's successor at Arkansas Post, Balthazar de Villiers, devised an ambitious plan of dubious legality to partner with a Swiss merchant from British Natchez. He also opened trade between Arkansas Post and the Osages, congratulating himself for impressing the "barbarians" with a ceremony full of "as much pomp as possible." The commerce was customarily reserved for St. Louis, however, and his initiative infuriated the commandants at both Natchitoches and St. Louis, earning him an official reprimand.[37]

Villiers frequently boasted about what he would do if only he had more forces and were not living in a decrepit fort, outnumbered by both the smugglers and the Quapaws. "I don't fear anything," he wrote his superior, "but I most urgently beg you and for the good of the king's service to put me in a position to impose on these rogues and even on the savages." If the English traders were not stopped, he warned, the security of Mexico itself would be at stake. Despite such dire warnings, the illicit commerce continued to expand. The governor of Louisiana looked forward to the day that the rebellion in the thirteen colonies would humble the British and put an end to their "haughtiness and arrogance."[38]

Bolstered by their access to smuggled goods, the Osages pushed west and south, driving the Wichitas deep into Texas and reducing the Caddos on the Red River to a shadow of their former selves. The Osages were "indomitable," wrote de Mézières in 1778, five years after suggesting that it was possible to exterminate them.[39] In the last half of the eighteenth century, they doubled the size of their empire, adding one hundred thousand square miles to their domain—a rate of expansion equal to that of the thirteen colonies and United States over the same period.

• • •

In May 1804, a few days after Lewis and Clark embarked from St. Louis on their epic journey to explore the West, a party of twelve Osage men and two boys struck out from the city in the opposite direction, heading to Washington, DC. Pawhuska (Figure 23), the senior member of the group, had fought against Arthur St. Clair in Ohio country in 1791 in the Battle of a Thousand Slain, which remains one of the single worst defeats in the history of the US Army. Out of thirteen hundred soldiers and officers, more than eight hundred were killed or wounded—a casualty rate of over 60 percent.[40] (By comparison, Custer's Seventh Cavalry lost roughly half its troops in the Battle of Little Bighorn.)

Traveling by barge and horseback, the delegation arrived in the US capital in mid-July. They were "certainly the most gigantic men we have ever seen," reported the six-foot-two-inch Thomas Jefferson (Figure 24) after greeting the delegation. One observer boasted that Europe could produce "no fat Englishman or meager Frenchman superior to these people." After formal discussions with Jefferson, the

FIGURE 23 Portrait of "Payouska" (Pawhuska), chief of the Great Osages in 1804, the year he met Thomas Jefferson. By Charles Balthazar Julien Févret de Saint-Mémin. Acc. no. 1860.92, Collection of the New-York Historical Society.

FIGURE 24 Portrait of Thomas Jefferson in 1804, shortly before meeting Pawhuska. By Charles Balthazar Julien Févret de Saint-Mémin. Worcester Art Museum, Worcester, MA, museum purchase.

Osages, accompanied by an Italian band, performed a war dance for the president, his cabinet officers, and "a large concourse of ladies and gentlemen."[41]

Like Louis XV before him, Jefferson wished to impress the Osages with "our populous cities." In Washington, the president's guests visited the Navy Yard and the cannon foundry. (One political partisan charged that while French and British frigates were molesting American shipping, the navy was snugly moored in the Potomac, "where it must remain until it rots to satisfy the curiosity of the Osage Indians.") They passed through the thriving port cities of Baltimore and Philadelphia before arriving in New York, which had just surpassed Philadelphia to become the republic's most populous metropolis. Their lodgings in the recently constructed City Hotel were only a few blocks north of the King's Arms Tavern, where Thomas Gage, Britain's commander in chief in North America, had spied on the West forty years earlier. The hotel, a massive brick structure with a grand ballroom, bars, stores, offices, and the largest lending library in the nation, was the meeting place for New York's political and economic elite.[42]

The westerners were treated to a cannonade on Governors Island and a military parade in the Battery, at the foot of Manhattan. But perhaps the most memorable event was organized by Jacques Delacroix, a confectioner and distiller turned impresario, who owned a pleasure garden—a space for public entertainment—just off Broadway. With Osage cooperation, he produced a "grand FETE," which included a torch-lit march behind US and Osage flags, Indian war dances (in which the Osages were accompanied by "their own savage instruments"), flaming arrows launched by the guests, and finally, a show of fireworks.[43]

As entertaining as the festivities were, one critic came away from the event convinced above all of US superiority. He pitied the Osages, who were ignorant of civilized life, of their own inevitable demise, and of the "principles and sentiments" that elevated white Americans to a "near relation" with God. While the audience beamed with intelligence, he wrote, the Osages possessed a "vacant stare and ruthless visage." Thank goodness he was not an Osage, he concluded.[44]

Yet this New Yorker had little sense of the state of affairs out west. "The truth is," Jefferson admitted in a letter to the secretary of the navy, the Osages "are the great nation South of the Missouri." Along with the Sioux, he explained, "we must stand well, because in their quarter we are miserably weak."[45] Forty years after aristocrats had devised the impractical Mississippi border in Paris in 1763, Jefferson grappled with the consequences.

Nonetheless, demographic trends soon brought an end to Osage ascendance. There were perhaps ten thousand colonists and six thousand Osages in Missouri when Pawhuska departed his homeland for Washington in 1804. Five years later, the colonial population had doubled; it would soon surpass sixty thousand. Shortly before dying in 1809, Pawhuska recognized that the tables had turned in Osage country. Jefferson "was strong and powerful," he said, reversing the president's earlier assessment, while "they were weak and pitiful."[46]

In 1865, the Osages traded the last of their homelands for just over twenty-three hundred square miles in Indian Territory (present-day Oklahoma). By a stroke of good luck, the reservation sits atop the Burbank, Avant, and Bartlesville-Dewey oil fields, for a time the most productive in the United States, but it took years for the Osages to profit from their holdings. In 1896, the Department of the Interior leased drilling rights on behalf of the Osages to a single company without entertaining any other bids. With powerful interests bribing both US officials and Osage politicians, it was difficult to rescind the ill-advised and improvident contract. Nonetheless, for twenty years Osages sustained a steady, if not unified, opposition to the "blanket lease," as it was called. At the same time, when the federal government broke up their reservation in 1906 (part of a larger effort to dissolve Indian nations once and for all), they were able to retain joint ownership of all subsurface mineral rights, creating an underground reservation that exists to this day—the only one of its kind in the United States.[47]

When the blanket lease finally expired in 1916, Osage royalties soared. Four times a year, oilmen crowded into the Constantine Theater in Pawhuska, Oklahoma, to bid against each other for the right to drill on Osage lands. The Osages sometimes netted as much as $6 million in a single day, and by one accounting they earned about $25 million in the first three years after expiration of the blanket lease.[48] Even after a hundred years of drilling, the Osage Mineral Estate produced $73 million in royalties in 2010.[49]

In the 1770s, the Osages had flourished because they maintained ties to multiple British and Spanish traders, thereby ensuring that no single empire monopolized their homelands. Now, with the corporation playing the role of the colonizer, Osages lobbied energetically in favor of competitive bidding, the modern-day equivalent of imperial competition. "The poor Indian, insofar as the Osage tribe of Oklahoma is concerned," frowned the *Wall Street Journal* in 1918, "exists in fiction only."[50] The Osages had not forgotten the lessons of the eighteenth century.

· · ·

François Ménard was almost certainly a more successful merchant than surgeon, judging from the contents of his medicine cabinet. Spanish fly, snake powder, and crawfish eyes were perhaps harmless, if not therapeutic; not so mercury, which drove at least one patient mad. By 1775, Ménard had abandoned the medical profession in favor of the more lucrative pursuit of trading and was the wealthiest resident of Arkansas Post. That year, he won a contract to supply ten thousand pounds of tallow to the naval shipyard in Havana, Cuba.[51]

Native peoples on the Mississippi had a long history of making tallow. In June and July, when bison bulls were "in their Fat," the animals would yield on average seventy-five pounds of tallow. (Fulfilling Ménard's contract would therefore have required roughly 150 bison.) After the hunt, the butchering and rendering fell to women. They skinned and carved up the animals, boiled the suet in copper kettles, and formed the resulting tallow into cakes. The product found a ready market among European traders, and in later years, if not in the 1770s, native peoples slaughtered bison solely for the tallow, leaving behind hundreds of carcasses to rot on the ground.[52]

Packed in boxes, the tallow was floated down the Mississippi—Ménard would lose nine thousand pounds of it to a boat wreck in 1780—and shipped across the Gulf of Mexico to Havana's naval shipyard. Sitting just outside the stone walls that enclosed the urban center, the shipyard was second to none in the Spanish Empire. In the 1760s it had undergone a major upgrade, with the construction of four new slipways and the rerouting of a freshwater canal to power an enormous state-of-the-art sawmill and its twin five-foot-long blades. The shipyard's four hundred workers produced twenty-two ships in the 1770s alone, including six ships of the line, the massive vessels that bristled with cannons and dominated naval warfare in the eighteenth century.[53]

The launching of a ship of the line was an extraordinary event that attracted large crowds. After the master shipwright gave the signal to knock out the chocks and cut the ropes, the new vessel began its three-minute passage down the slipway and into the water. The jubilation that accompanied the launching of a warship was indescribable, wrote one witness, who claimed that even the most impassive soul was moved by the celebration.[54] Underlying the entire operation was bison tallow, produced and sold by native peoples in the heart of North America. Slathered on slips, the substance made it possible for a two-thousand-ton ship, measuring more than half the length of a football field, to slide effortlessly into the waters of Havana Bay.

In early April 1775, a special delegation from the American Deep South was in Havana during the launching of the *San Ramón*, a 177-foot vessel with sixty cannons. Escuchape, the senior member of the contingent, hailed from Coweta, one of the two or three most important towns in the Creek Nation. (Coweta was situated on the Chattahoochee River, across from modern-day Columbus, Georgia.) Unlike the Osages, whose commercial options had multiplied after the Treaty of Paris, the Creeks found themselves in the opposite situation, reduced from having three European trading partners to having only one. Surrounded by the British, they had journeyed to Havana to break Britain's monopoly in the Southeast.

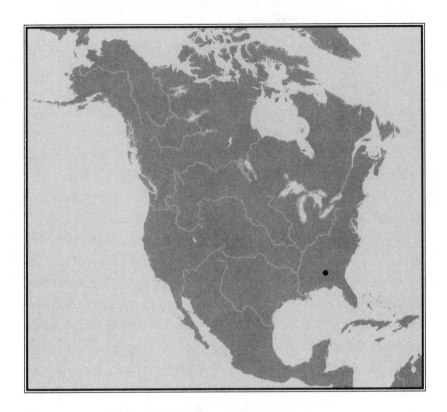

CHAPTER EIGHT

Surrounded: The Deep South Interior

Havana was perhaps the most heavily fortified city in the world when Escuchape, his wife, and twelve companions embarked from Tampa Bay for the Cuban port in February 1775. The travelers had gained passage on a Spanish fishing vessel. The first sight of their Caribbean destination was the Castillo de los Tres Reyes del Morro ("El Morro" for short), which looms over the harbor entrance from atop a rocky headland and is visible from a half mile out. Slipping by El Morro and entering the channel that separates the harbor from the open ocean, they passed under the enormous Castillo de San Carlos, popularly known as La Cabaña (see Figure 25). The citadel, fortified with 178 cannons, had only recently been completed as part of Spain's effort to strengthen the "Key to the New World" after the city's humiliating capitulation to British forces in 1762 during the Seven Years' War. The vessel carrying the Creeks turned to starboard and headed for a pier facing the recently constructed royal accounting house, where all fishing boats were by law required to dock.[1]

The Creeks stepped into a city of about forty thousand people, the third largest in New Spain (Figure 26). Including the immediate countryside, its population approached eighty thousand. (By contrast, Philadelphia, the most populous city in the mainland British colonies, had only about thirty thousand residents.) Havana proper, laid out on a grid bounded by walls six feet thick and fourteen feet high, contained numerous structures not found in Creek towns, including barracks, a jail, a customhouse, and three-story stone houses with tiled roofs. Yet the narrow, unpaved, and filthy streets erased any sense of order. "During my residence in Spanish America," wrote the Prussian scientist and traveler Alexander von Humboldt, "few of the cities presented a more disgusting appearance." Humboldt complained particularly about the "offensive odor of salted meat," known as *tasajo*, that "infected many of

FIGURE 25 Entering Havana Bay, with La Cabaña on the left. Joseph F. W. Des Barres, "The Harbour and Part of the Town of Havannah." Library of Congress, Prints & Photographs Division, reproduction no. LC-USZ62-46052.

FIGURE 26 On their arrival in Cuba, the Creeks stepped into a bustling city. "A view of the Market Place in the City of Havana," by Thomas Morris. Library of Congress, Prints & Photographs Division, reproduction no. LC-DIG-pga-03671.

the houses, and even some of the ill-ventilated streets." Another visitor, a British officer and veteran of the siege of 1762, objected not to the street smells but to Havana's "common people." They were "a low cunning, deceitful false and thieving sett, The Spanish joined indiscriminately in Marriage with Negroes, Mulattos &c, which produces as bad a Mongrel Crew, perhaps as any on Earth."[2]

Creek towns also accommodated diverse populations—including fugitive slaves and Scottish traders—but by comparison with the Cuban metropolis, the settlements were bucolic. Some thirty of them were situated in the Deep South, in the transition zone between rolling hills and the coastal plain, which is rich in flora, fauna, and fish. (Columbus, Georgia, and Montgomery, Alabama, now occupy this region.) Ranging in size from a few dozen individuals to close to one thousand, each town contained a central square, a council house, and numerous dwellings made of posts, wattle, and mud. Extensive cornfields lined the riverbanks, giving way to pine forests. The total number of Creeks was under fifteen thousand.[3]

From Havana's royal accounting house, where the Creeks disembarked, it was a short walk across the Plaza de Armas to the sixteenth-century Castillo de la Real Fuerza, the residence of the Marqués de la Torre, Cuba's captain general. Inside the thick-walled fortress, which overlooks the port and sits across the water from La Cabaña, the Creeks delivered a number of speeches to the Marqués. Surely the muddled translations did not do justice to the Creeks' eloquence, and the captain general deemed the orations "lengthy and tiresome."[4]

When another fishing vessel arrived two weeks after Escuchape's, the number of Creeks in Havana grew by three. Three days after that, ten more Creeks arrived, and two days later, still another ten disembarked in front of the royal accounting house, bringing the total number of visitors to thirty-seven. They were a costly annoyance to the Marqués, but he could ill afford to alienate them. For one, he did not want to put at risk the Cuban fishing trade off Florida. He also hoped that a continued friendship with the Creeks would serve the Crown if, at some later date, it repossessed Florida from the British. Consequently, he lavished gifts on his guests: shirts, scissors, knives, silk ribbon, cloth, tobacco, wine, and beaver felt hats, not to mention 525 pounds of beef, 775 pounds of rice, and over 1,000 pounds of corn. The Marqués also supplied the group with nearly 475 gallons of *aguardiente*, a potent sugarcane liquor. Escuchape and his companions enjoyed the captain general's largesse for twenty-seven days, living in the house of Antonio Lendian, the father of a fisherman who regularly worked off Tampa Bay.[5]

Despite the free-flowing liquor and valuable gifts, it was not the pleasure and excitement of travel that brought Escuchape and his companions to Cuba. The island's captain general summarized the purpose of the visit: "to complain about the English and plead for the protection of our sovereign, whether to wage war against them, form their settlements along the coast, or finally to ask for presents and gifts."[6] In the Treaty of Paris, Europe's imperial powers had bartered the Creeks' homelands. The British occupation of North America, and specifically of Florida, threatened the Creek Nation's independence and even its very existence.

. . .

The Creeks had nothing good to say about the Treaty of Paris. Creek leaders pointedly told the governor of Georgia, "they are surprized [*sic*] how People can give away Land that does not belong to them." The lands, which were only on loan to the Spanish and French, they insisted, should revert to the Creeks. The king of Spain may have conquered Florida lands by force of arms, they admitted, but "they in the same way took them back little by little from the beginning of the century." Therefore, Spain's monarch "could not freely cede them to another," except for the small tracts of land occupied by the settlements of Pensacola, St. Augustine, and, lying between them, Fort San Marcos. Even Thomas Gage, Amherst's replacement, had to admit, "The Indians say very true in Respect of what the Spaniards actually possessed at the Time of the Cession." But the British Crown had little patience for the argument. In the determination of Lord Hillsborough, secretary of state for the colonies, the Indians were "by the Spirit and Provisions of the Treaty of Paris, Subject to the Crown of Great Britain, and their Country [had] become a Part of its Possessions."[7]

Southeastern Indians found numerous reasons to object to Britain's newfound dominance in the region. When Britain assumed control of Florida and divided it into two provinces, the colonial populations were minimal. West Florida only had 120 white and 500 black residents at the end of 1763. Within two years, the population had risen to three thousand and continued to surge. Its counterpart, East Florida, peaked at three thousand. Those were small numbers in absolute terms, but nevertheless alarming, for southeastern Indians had already watched the similarly modest settlements in Georgia explode in the 1750s. In that decade, the Georgia population doubled, and then between 1760 and 1775 it more than tripled, reaching thirty-three thousand. Over that same period, the colony dispossessed Indians of more than 5.5 million acres of land. Georgians had agreed not to expand beyond Augusta,

one Creek recalled in 1763. But now that area was "settled all over
the Woods with People Cattle and Horses." As a result, Creek hunters
were unable to supply their families with provisions, the "Buffalo, Deer
and Bear being drove off the Land and killed." Creeks knew to remain
vigilant in Florida, lest they find themselves confronting an invasion of
land-hungry British colonists from the Gulf Coast as well.[8]

The departure of the Spanish and French presented an additional
problem. The Creeks were a trading people. "In former times," said
one Creek in 1765, "we were entirely unacquainted with the customs
of the white people, but since they have come among us, we have been
clothed as they are, and accustomed to their ways, which makes it at
this day absolutely necessary that we should be supplied with goods in
the nation." Each year, they exported close to two hundred thousand
deerskins, as well as smaller quantities of bear and hickory nut oil and
medicinal roots and herbs. In return, they imported cloth, kettles,
beads, thread, mirrors, and muskets, among other goods. The detritus
of the Creeks' import trade litter eighteenth-century archaeological
sites. Though Creeks may have been able to survive without European
manufactures, they did not wish to do so. And they understood that
their nation had no viable future without engaging in the regional and
Atlantic economy.[9]

For decades, they had benefited from simultaneous trade with Spain,
France, and Britain (see Figure 27). "They cannot countenance the state
of remaining traders with one nation only," wrote the Spanish governor of Pensacola shortly before evacuating the town. Their dissatisfaction stemmed from two concerns. First, the British were illiberal with
their possessions. The Spanish and French, by contrast, customarily
gave Indians generous gifts of tobacco, alcohol, food, and other trade
items. Spanish and French officials saw those presents as the necessary,
if vexing, cost of doing business and maintaining alliances in Native
America. The British arrogantly decided to curtail the practice. "It
will be difficult to break that Custom," observed the governor of British West Florida, "until they are convinced of Our Superiority and
their Dependence."[10]

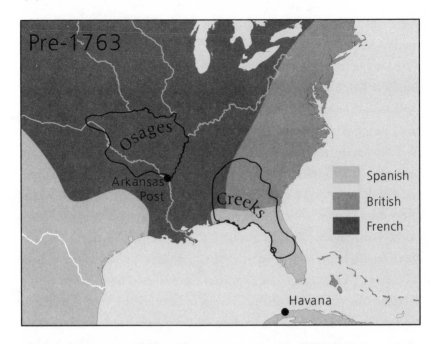

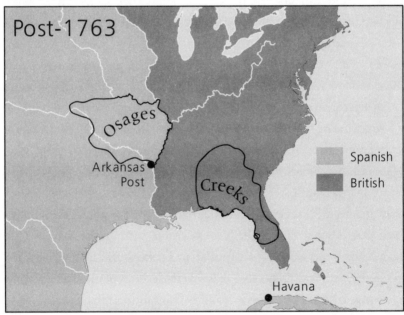

FIGURE 27 Imperial claims, before and after the Treaty of Paris.

The distrust occasioned by Britain's stinginess gave rise to a related concern: Britain's ability to cut off trade altogether. Soon after the British occupied East and West Florida, a frontier skirmish with the Creeks led a number of British officials to suggest that they do just that. General Gage observed that a trade embargo would be tantamount to declaring war, and the suggestions were wisely ignored. Instead, to the great displeasure of the Creeks, the British began funneling arms to the Choctaws and Chickasaws. With effective management, Gage reported, "other Nations can be Spirited up" against the Creeks.[11]

Relations deteriorated rapidly as the British pushed into Creek lands. In the early 1770s, Georgia and the Floridas did indeed embargo trade with the Creeks. The British were too ambitious, said the Creeks, who resolved to destroy them. One party of Creeks set out for New Orleans to secure weapons from the Spanish, but they were ambushed by British-armed Choctaws.[12] Perhaps a solution to their dilemma could be found in Havana.

· · ·

A prehistoric West Indian ax, recovered near Gainesville, Florida, suggests that contact between Cuba and Florida existed long before the Creeks began visiting in the 1760s, but the archaeological record is silent about its scale and frequency, in part because objects made of organic materials quickly disintegrate in the region's humid climate and acidic soils. It seems likely, however, that native peoples traveled occasionally, if not regularly, between Florida and Cuba in the enormous canoes that were common to the region. When Spain invaded Cuba in the sixteenth century, long-standing ties between the island and the Florida peninsula may have encouraged some Cubans to flee to the mainland in search of refuge. By the end of the first century of colonization, Spanish ships regularly plied the route between Havana and St. Augustine, and numerous Florida Indians lived in the Cuban capital, where they served as interpreters for expeditions to the mainland.[13]

Florida Indians, who covered the twenty-four-hour trip between the

Keys and Havana in large canoes, opened a profitable trade with Spanish Cuba, exchanging tree bark, fruit, and hides for scissors, knives, axes, hatchets, fishhooks, and tobacco. One traveler to Havana in 1698 described the arrival of a boat of Key natives in the port city. "Their chief commodity is fish; some little amber they find along the shore; tortoise-shells, and a sort of scarlet birds to keep in cages, for their colour call'd cardinals," the traveler wrote. He watched in amazement as sailors returning to Spain purchased over two thousand of the scarlet birds from one group of Indians, who earned an astonishing 18,000 pesos in the trade—enough to purchase over two thousand shirts or roughly seventeen hundred gallons of aguardiente.[14]

In the seventeenth century, there also existed a brisk trade between Havana and Apalachee, the area south and east of Tallahassee, where the Spanish had established a number of missions. Missionaries exported cattle, hides, deerskins, and other goods to the Cuban capital, at least until the Creeks and their onetime British allies destroyed the missions in the early eighteenth century. At the same time, Creeks began journeying down the peninsula to attack the Key Indians, interrupting that trade as well. Some of their victims sought refuge in Havana itself, where they accepted baptism and settled across the harbor from the walled city. Others remained in the Keys and survived by fishing, scavenging shipwrecks, and trading with Cuban fishermen. Still others, especially women and children, were captured and integrated into Creek families. Possessing firsthand knowledge of the Cuba trade, they may have facilitated contact between Creeks and Cubans.[15]

Between 1763 and the end of 1776, Creeks traveled to Havana at least nineteen times, in parties ranging in size from a single traveler to as many as twenty-four. The voyages usually embarked from Tampa Bay, where some thirty Spanish fishing vessels worked each year between August and March. From the Florida coast, Havana took its principal supply of fish, indispensable for feeding the city's growing population and supporting religious fasts such as Lent. After weaving nets and hauling out drum, pompano, and mullet, the fishermen went ashore to dry and salt their catch. Predictably, a small trade evolved between fishermen and local residents, just as had occurred in the Gulf of St. Lawrence two centuries earlier, at the outset of contact between Native Americans and Europeans.[16]

It was not difficult for the Creeks to talk their way onto the small Cuban sloops. Sometimes they showed the fishermen commissions from Florida governors—some as old as forty years—that they had carefully preserved over the decades. The letters impressed the unschooled if not illiterate skippers, who concluded that the embassies in question "could be of some importance." It probably worked to the Creeks' advantage that the two sides often could not understand each other. "He doesn't understand a word of their language nor do they know how to speak Castilian," wrote one official charged with debriefing a skipper named Francisco Pelaez. At other times the Creeks won passage by kindness, greeting the fishermen with cheer and presenting them with gifts of bear fat. In such cases, it seemed appropriate to concede to the Indians' request. Over the long term, Creeks had three factors working in their favor: the fishing crews were usually outnumbered, did not wish to jeopardize their livelihood by alienating local residents, and received reimbursement from the Spanish Crown for the expense of transporting Indian passengers.[17]

After visiting Havana, Creeks returned to their hometowns with "a thousand exclamations for the courtesies" extended to them. They described the temporary pleasures of alcohol, tobacco, and food offered to them in Cuba's capital, and they showed off the captain general's gifts. The travelers "look very gay in their Spanish Cloaths," noted one British trader, who took umbrage at their "rich loud" dress. (One observer stated, however, that the garments soon became so ragged and filthy that neither their material nor color could be discerned.)[18]

But Creek travelers also returned with descriptions of the sea voyage that were not always reassuring, especially for a people unaccustomed to the open ocean. Deer hunters and farmers, they were not at all like their Aleut counterparts in distant Alaska. Before his voyage, Escuchape learned from his son that "the sea is very Mountanious [*sic*] making the boat go from the Top of a high hill into a very Deep valley with great

Swiftnes." Nevertheless, "as some of their Women had gon[e] aCross these waters, he being a man was not affraid; besides he was now Old and in case he should be drowned all his Troubles would then be over." Other Creeks reported on the sea voyage's attractions. Passengers sometimes got their own berths and enjoyed breakfast, dinner, and supper at the skipper's table. The "cup of punch was always filled," one group gloated.[19]

Creeks visited Cuba sporadically in the 1760s to secure aid against Britain, but by 1773 the matter had become more pressing. In February of that year, Estimaslayche, a noted warrior, led a delegation to the Cuban capital. There, he explained that his men were charged with patrolling the entire Florida Gulf Coast, ready to attack any and all English fishermen and colonists. The Creeks intended to declare war against the British in the spring, he said, and to pursue it with such determination and persistence that they would not stop until they had destroyed them entirely. They needed arms, powder, and lead shot from the Spanish but instead received stacks of hats, mirrors, and thread and professions of "paternal affection." Any military assistance would destroy the "great peace and friendship" that reigned between Spain and Britain, Estimaslayche was told—though in fact Charles III wanted nothing better than to avenge his losses in the Seven Years' War.[20]

According to a remarkable account of Estimaslayche's visit, after hearing the disappointing response, the envoy rose to his feet and gave thanks for the hospitality and gifts he had received in Havana. Then, in words "both affectionate and arrogant," he praised "the great King of Spain":

As many Nations as walk the Earth tremble and surrender before his strength and power. The many Natives of the extensive Provinces of Montezuma's former empire say so, for they were conquered only by Spanish Arms.

If Carlos III so desired, Estimaslayche observed, it would not be difficult for him to throw the English out of Florida. The Creek emissary concluded by asking that his entreaty be forwarded to the king, for he was confident that His Majesty would "fulfill his many promises not to abandon them."[21]

Though Creeks traveled to Havana twice more in 1774, the Marqués de la Torre was tiring of the visits and began to suspect that his guests undertook the journey primarily to take advantage of his generosity. He strongly discouraged fishermen from transporting Indians and became stingier with his gifts, but to no effect.[22] Instead, the visits became more frequent and the requests for alliance more urgent.

• • •

By early 1775, the escalating conflict between the British colonies and George III was spilling into Creek country. As a result of the economic war waged by the two sides, the deerskin trade ground to a halt, and British manufactures became scarce in the Deep South.[23] Confronting the same situation a thousand miles to the northwest, the Dakota leader Wabasha set out for Montreal. The Creeks redoubled their efforts to find relief in Havana. Escuchape's was one of twelve different Creek parties to sail to the Cuban capital in the thirteen months between February 1775 and March 1776.

Though ocean travel was new to him, Escuchape had journeyed extensively in the South during his lengthy tenure as a Creek diplomat, and he enjoyed a long-standing relationship with the Spanish. In the 1740s, Manuel de Montiano, the governor of Florida, made him the "Captain of Indian Troops," an honorary commission marking his status among Spanish colonists. A decade later, Escuchape met with Montiano's successor to confirm the Creeks' alliance with Spain. Soon after, he had his son baptized in the Florida capital. The boy was given the name of Fernando, after the Spanish king, but two years later the teenager could no longer remember the name. In 1759, Escuchape visited the French in Mobile, the Cherokees in the Appalachians, the Catawbas in the South Carolina piedmont, and the British in Charleston and Augusta—a fifteen-hundred-mile journey that the British, about to embark on a campaign against the Cherokees, deemed "suspicious."

A few years later, shortly before the Spanish evacuated Florida, the governor of St. Augustine, in a letter sealed with his coat of arms, reconfirmed Escuchape's commission as "Captain of Indian Troops."[24]

Escuchape was one of several Creeks to sign a treaty with the British when they occupied Pensacola, but he quickly became frustrated with the new tenants. Five months after marking the treaty, he sent his son to Picolata (near St. Augustine) to voice his dissatisfaction to the British Indian agent: traders were not honoring the treaty's price schedule, and colonists were invading their lands. "If all the Country was settled up to their Towns," Escuchape's son observed, "they wou'd find nothing but rats and rabbits to kill for the skins of which the White people wou'd not give them goods." Deer were "turning very scarce," he said, and "the White people sold their goods, very dear." If Escuchape needed confirmation of the hostile intentions of the British, he got it in 1770. While inspecting a boundary line between Creek and Georgia lands near the upper Savannah River, he visited a frontier tavern. A crowd accosted and insulted him and attempted to wrest his gun away. As he fled, the settlers fired several shots.[25]

Even then, it was not until the 1773 Treaty of Augusta that Escuchape definitively broke ties with the British. Pressing relentlessly for more land, Georgia secured three thousand square miles of valuable Creek hunting grounds, nearly doubling the size of the forty-year-old colony. The land, "of the richest and best Quality," was supposed to be applied toward Creek debts. "We hope . . . that the traders will free us," Escuchape asserted. One southerner cogently observed in 1774 that the balance of trade inevitably favored merchants who possessed "both the opportunity to take our Commodities for what they please and send theirs to us at their own price."[26] Those were the words of soon-to-be revolutionary Landon Carter, complaining about British mercantile policies toward Virginia planters like himself. Escuchape and his fellow Creeks found themselves in the same unfavorable relationship with British merchants.

In late 1774, the Creek leader set out by canoe for Tampa Bay, where he and his thirteen companions secured passage to Havana on a fishing vessel. Meeting with Cuba's captain general, Escuchape described the dire situation in Creek country. The British had instituted an embargo and declared war on them, triggering an outbreak of violence between native peoples and colonists. Escuchape pledged loyalty to the Spanish Crown and asked for aid to fight the British. Those were familiar requests. More unusual and innovative was his proposal to form a new settlement on Tampa Bay to maintain "a reciprocal commerce of skins, horses, and other commodities" with Cuba—in essence, a free-trade zone. The Marqués was underwhelmed. He pledged to forward their petition to Spain, thanked them for their loyalty, and asked them not to visit again.[27]

Three weeks after departing Havana, they arrived once more in the Cuban capital, insisting on a positive resolution to their requests. The Marqués received them with displeasure, gave them minimal supplies, and told them they would bear the cost of their provisions if they returned. The Creeks would not be deterred. The fishing vessel that delivered Escuchape back to Florida returned to Havana carrying a single and evidently very persuasive emissary. With "great effectiveness," the envoy proposed that the captain general give the Creeks their own vessel to carry on a regular trade between the Deep South and Cuba. They would pay for the boat with profits from the commerce. The envoy also suggested that Spain allow Cuban merchants to trade without restriction with the Creeks.[28]

At the time, Charles III was in the midst of rationalizing Spain's burdensome commercial regulations by curbing monopolies, opening ports, and reforming tax policy—part of a broad effort to modernize the Spanish Empire.[29] Though in its scale Escuchape's proposal was dwarfed by the reforms being considered by Charles III's ministers, in spirit it was more rational and bolder—more enlightened, to use the language of the day—than anything they were prepared to adopt. It presumed that the Creek Nation was fully sovereign and capable of establishing foreign relations independent of Britain's claim to the Southeast. And it envisaged a mutually beneficial trade between the Creek Nation and Cuba, unrestricted by protectionist measures.

The notion of a crew of Indians navigating a schooner between Tampa and Havana must have struck the captain general as foolish, and he rejected the proposal out of hand. (Creeks thought it was a great idea; they presented it again in 1783.)[30] But he could not so easily dismiss the possibility of trading with the Creeks. His own colony was in desperate need of exactly the provisions that Creeks offered: beef, horses, corn, brined and salted fish, and deerskins.

In exchange for their products, Creeks desired textiles, axes, hoes, guns, powder, and lead balls. As they explained, they had no other way but through trade to provide themselves with clothing, tools, and arms. They had ample reason to expect that Havana merchants could meet their needs. Before the brief British occupation, an average of only five ships a year visited the harbor from Spain, but by the 1770s that number had risen fourteenfold, to seventy. Over the same period, the value of imported merchandise rose by a factor of five hundred. By comparison, British St. Augustine and Pensacola seemed sleepy. Of the southern cities that the Creeks knew, only the port of Charleston rivaled Havana's. Moreover, the urban settlements in the South were tiny compared with the Cuban capital.[31]

If Havana seemed a promising place to purchase consumer goods, the enormous military presence suggested that weapons and ammunition might be had as well. After England ceded its prize back to Spain in 1763, the city underwent a conspicuous buildup of armed forces. It quartered nearly four thousand regular troops and counted among its citizens another five thousand to six thousand militia, who drilled every Sunday, as Creeks witnessed during their stay. The massive fortresses, extensive barracks, city walls, and hundreds of cannons impressed all visitors.[32]

Every time the captain general regaled them, Creeks obtained samples of the variety of commodities available in Havana. Estimaslayche's group, for example, received shirts, silk handkerchiefs, hats, scissors, mirrors, knives, strike-a-lights (used with flint to spark a fire), ivory combs, horse bits, iron spurs, iron hoes, chisels, nails, locks, and dozens of other items.[33] That was a particularly generous array of gifts, and subsequent parties were received with less bounty. Nonetheless, the Creeks had seen enough to pursue a trading relationship.

. . .

It is easy but perhaps mistaken to assume that Creeks inadvertently chanced upon a fortunate combination of circumstances when they arrived in Cuba, that they did not understand the economy or Cuba well enough to think like market-savvy merchants. Yet, since Britain's retrocession of Havana to Spain in 1763, they had spent some two years in the city. They were on hand to witness the beginning of two historic and violent transformations.

The first was man-made. Cuba was just setting out on the path to becoming the world's most profitable and oppressive slave colony. Since Creeks had begun visiting Cuba in 1763, the population of Havana and the western half of the island had nearly doubled. During the same period, sugar production took root, doubling in the 1760s and nearly doubling again between 1770 and 1775. To grow and process that sugarcane, Cubans depended on forced labor. In the 25 years following 1763, Cuba imported fifty-nine thousand slaves, as many as it had over the previous 250.[34] The numbers were still small compared to what they would become in the nineteenth century, but the trend was unmistakable.

The growing population, the massive military garrison, and the expansion of sugar cultivation created a serious food shortage on the island. By the late 1760s, Cuba was importing *tasajo*, salted fish, corn, cowhides, and deerskins from Mexico—goods that were all readily available in the Creek Nation. Demand outpaced supply, especially since planters were busy replacing pasture with cane fields.[35]

The second transformation was natural. The Little Ice Age, the five-hundred-year cooling period that had begun in the fourteenth century, was coming to a turbulent end. Beginning in the 1760s, several decades of severe climatic instability struck the Caribbean, leading to a series of crippling droughts and destructive hurricanes. In October 1768, one massive hurricane hit Cuba's south coast and crossed over the island, laying waste to a swath three hundred miles wide. In Havana, a storm surge of fifteen feet inundated the city and destroyed fifty-three of the fifty-five ships in the harbor. The island's major crops were razed by the intense winds and heavy rains. In the ensuing years, one misfortune followed after another: hurricane (1771), drought (1772), hurricane (1772), hurricane (1773), drought (1773), hurricane (1774).[36]

"It seemed as if a total dissolution of nature was taking place," wrote a young Alexander Hamilton from St. Croix, after a hurricane leveled the island in 1772. The "horror and destruction" were impossible to describe or imagine. In the aftermath, mangled corpses were strewn about the streets, whole families searched desperately for shelter, and the sick lay exposed to the elements. Cuba was spared the worst of this particular hurricane, but Havana's houses, shops, and barracks were nonetheless badly damaged. Even worse, local food crops were entirely destroyed, and no relief could be found anywhere in the Caribbean. Famine threatened the entire region.[37]

In short, opportunity beckoned. Given the visibility of the natural disasters, Creeks may not have needed any help perceiving the favorable economic climate. If they did, they had the assistance of numerous friends in the Cuban capital who surely described the food shortages. Antonio and Juan Lendian hosted the visitors for weeks on end. Several Florida Indians were longtime residents of the city and also crossed paths with the Creeks.[38] We can only speculate on the content of their conversations, which took place out of earshot of Spanish officials.

Escuchape's tailored proposal thus spoke to the immediate needs of Cuba's population, and it carried with it one additional attraction. Not only could Creeks supply food to the plantation labor force, but they would also consume the by-product of those same plantations: molasses distilled into aguardiente. Sugarcane aguardiente competed with Spain's homegrown product, made from grapes, and the Spanish Crown therefore had prohibited its production for decades. But as early as the 1730s, Cuban sugar planters had pled with the Crown for permission to peddle sugarcane alcohol to Florida Indians, devising a number of resourceful arguments on the spirit's behalf: it was the best means yet discovered to conquer Indians; Indians thought aguardiente from Spain and the Canary Islands was distasteful; and perhaps most ingenious of all, prohibition hindered the recovery of shipwrecks in the Florida Keys, since without the aid of sugarcane liquor, Indian divers could not stay underwater long enough to reach the sunken cargoes. In 1751, the governor of Florida admitted that aguardiente was the greatest attraction his government possessed for the Indians. "I discuss this matter with horror—for on its own merits it is such," he wrote, "but at this moment I am transmitting my thoughts on its utility to the State."[39]

Despite such protests, the ban on the production of sugarcane aguardiente was not lifted until 1764. Even then, a prohibition on export remained in place, and Cubans began pressing for permission to sell the product in Yucatán and Louisiana, tying that privilege to their willingness to pay the *alcabala*, a tax meant to support the huge military presence in Havana. They finally won the right to ship aguardiente to Louisiana in 1768, giving them much-desired access to Indian consumers, but the nearby Florida market still remained frustratingly out of reach.[40]

In short, Escuchape's proposal had several advantages: the *tasajo* trade would feed a sometimes desperately hungry population, the new market for aguardiente would line the pockets of planters, and the commerce would end the costly Creek embassies that arrived on a regular basis.[41]

The captain general, slow to see the merits of Escuchape's proposal, at last seized on it with enthusiasm. He extolled its benefits and dismissed the fear, voiced by one official, that the traffic to Florida would provide cover for contraband trade with the British. There was no shortage of Habaneros who, learning of Escuchape's proposal, asked for permission to travel to the Florida Gulf Coast, the captain general wrote. In September 1775, he sent off a letter to learn the pleasure of Julián de Arriaga, the aged and conservative minister of the Indies, and then patiently awaited a response.[42]

Four more parties of Creeks arrived and departed, Arriaga died, and finally, in late July 1776, the new minister of the Indies, José de

Gálvez, an ardent reformer, granted the captain general and Escuchape's request to permit "a few boats" to trade between Cuba and the Creek Nation.[43] (This was the same Gálvez who had overseen the extension of Spain's frontier into Alta California.) But by then it was too late. The opportunity had slipped away.

. . .

Over the years, Juan Lendian had transported numerous Indians between Havana and Tampa Bay on his fishing schooner and had become fluent in the Creek language. In Havana, many of his passengers stayed at the house of his father, Antonio, known familiarly as *el Campechano*. In fall 1776, three Creek men and their wives boarded Lendian's schooner for the return trip to Florida. During the voyage, Lendian and his passengers began drinking aguardiente. A fight broke out—by one account, over a woman—and Lendian stabbed the three men to death. Arriving at Tampa Bay, Lendian placed the women ashore and then went into hiding in the Florida Keys.[44]

In the small, tightly knit Creek communities, a murder committed by an outsider was always in some sense an international incident. Family members clamored for revenge, and relations between nations could not be normalized until mourning relatives received some sort of satisfaction. At least, that is how the Spanish understood it, and they were not wrong. Cuban fishermen halted all voyages to Tampa Bay, afraid that they would fall victim to Creek anger. But the Creeks' perspective was not so circumscribed that they ignored their broader interests, for they understood the importance of a regular intercourse with Havana. Because of mutual distrust and fear on both sides, communication with Spanish officials was slow, but finally, in December 1777, a Creek delegation informed the captain general that the victims' families had pardoned Juan Lendian, in part because Lendian's father, Antonio, had hosted them many times over the years and was indeed hosting the present delegation itself.[45] Trade could be resumed.

With the war in the British colonies, however, the interests of the captain general had shifted. He was then drawing up plans to invade

East Florida and saw the Creeks as a potential source of intelligence rather than as trading partners.[46] Spain eventually entered the war in May 1779. Another Treaty of Paris brought the war to an end in 1783, and like its 1763 predecessor, this one partitioned North America but failed to mention the continent's native peoples. Pressured by both Georgia and the new US federal government, and deeply in debt to British and American merchants, Creeks rapidly lost large portions of their lands to the new sovereign powers in North America.

What if Creeks had become purveyors to the fastest-growing slave colony in the New World? Would they have had the economic clout to avoid removal in the 1830s and retain their homelands? Would their nation have become a part of the Confederacy in some form, perhaps as a member state that shared the Old South's deep investment in slavery? How might the South and American history have been transformed?

· · ·

On July 12, 1776, the *Resolution* weighed anchor and slipped from the Thames into the English Channel. That same day, from his headquarters in Manhattan, George Washington reported to Congress that two British gunships had sailed up the Hudson River, testing the ineffectual American defenses. The Continental troops' "heavy and incessant cannonade" fell harmlessly into the river, though one cannonball exploded in the barrel, killing six men. The corpses were buried in a single grave in Bowling Green, the small park at the south end of the island.[47]

The *Resolution*, commanded by James Cook, had a more pacific intent. The British admiralty was sending Cook to search America's Northwest Coast for signs of a fabled passage that might join the Atlantic and Pacific Oceans. The undertaking was "truly laudable in itself," Benjamin Franklin would write in 1779, when he ordered all American captains and commanders to grant safe passage, even in wartime, to the famous British navigator. The "Increase of Geographical Knowledge," Franklin observed, would redound "to the Benefit of Mankind in general."[48]

The *Resolution* and its companion ship, the *Discovery*, proceeded south around Africa's Cape of Good Hope, bore east toward New Zealand, and then sailed up and across the Pacific for "New Albion," the name that Francis Drake had given to the California coast almost two hundred years earlier. At dawn on January 18, 1778, when Cook was over twenty-five hundred miles north of Bora Bora, the last inhabited island he had visited, land suddenly appeared on the horizon. He had spotted Oahu, which rises four thousand feet above the ocean. Until that mid-January day, Hawaiians had lived for hundreds of years in near complete separation from the rest of the world. Their lives would soon be shattered.

EPILOGUE

It is not known who first noticed the two ships on the horizon. By one account, the vessels resembled sections of land that had broken through the sky, piercing the distant wall that supports the dome of the heavens. As the ships approached from the south, canoeists met them several miles out, eager to trade for nails and iron, materials they knew from Japanese shipwrecks that had washed ashore. Curious locals flocked to the water and gathered atop outlooks to observe the strangers. A day later, a few adventurous individuals boarded the vessels. "I never saw Indians so much astonished at the entering [of] a ship before," wrote James Cook, "their eyes were continually flying from object to object, the wildness of thier [sic] looks and actions fully express'd their surprise and astonishment at the several new o[b]jects before them."[1]

West of the Revolution, the lives of North Americans were upended by events that originated half a world away. Like Cook's ships, challenges and opportunities seemingly arrived out of nowhere. In Kyakhta, merchants sold furs destined for the Chinese court in Beijing—a transaction with implications stretching far and wide. To supply the market, promyshlenniki moved across the Bering Strait and up the Aleutian archipelago in search of sea otters, setting off a scramble among Spanish officials to colonize the California coast and blaze a route between Santa Fe and Monterey. Neither Russia nor Spain had a practical knowledge of the Pacific coastline; colonists, unable even to converse in local languages, understood little about the residents they encountered. Likewise, Aleuts, Kumeyaays, Costanoans, and Utes struggled to make sense of the Russian and Spanish newcomers and to respond confidently to the complex and rapidly evolving transformations unleashed by the newcomers.

Meanwhile, European aristocrats in Paris drew a boundary through the center of the continent, dividing North America in half. They were entirely ignorant of its impact both on native peoples and on their own nations. In the Canadian prairies, the new boundary flooded the region with enterprising fur traders. To the south, it sparked Pontiac's War; the conflict resounded as far west as the Black Hills. Still farther south, the boundary opened up new trading opportunities for the Osages, while in the Southeast it shut them down, with dire consequences for the Creek Nation.

Cook's landfall in Hawaii had a similarly profound impact. The archipelago's population of 275,000 began to plummet soon after the navigator's unexpected appearance from across the seas. One of his officers returned to the islands fifteen years later and found some areas "reduced at least two-thirds," others "entirely abandoned." Syphilis and gonorrhea killed directly and indirectly, reducing female fertility and increasing infant mortality. Influenza, tuberculosis, typhoid, measles, whooping cough, and dysentery destroyed thousands of others. Within fifty years, only half as many people lived on the archipelago. Fifty years after that, the population reached its historic low point of only 54,000 individuals—an astonishing collapse.[2]

After departing the Hawaiian archipelago and striking the North American mainland, the *Resolution* and the *Discovery* proceeded up the western edge of the continent, making contact with coastal residents along the way. In late June 1778, they anchored in Samgunuda Harbor (now English Bay), on the north side of Unalaska, where Solov'ev had abused local populations only a few years earlier. While carpenters ripped off the sheathing of both ships to repair their leaky seams, Thomas Edgar, the master of the *Discovery*, used the month-long respite to explore the island's interior and visit the Aleuts and the Russian newcomers. Edgar observed that the Russian traders denounced "the Americans" as "savages & sad fellows, for defending themselves & driving off the invader of their country and preserving their native freedom." He could not resist a gibe at his British compatriots: "By this you will see that efforts for liberty are not confined totally to the east side of the continent."[3]

From the Aleutian archipelago to the Mississippi River (as well as in

Britain's well-explored Atlantic colonies) eighteenth-century Americans confronted revolutionary challenges. Diffuse but powerful, unmanageable and often beyond the comprehension of participants, those challenges resonate powerfully in the twenty-first century. The founding fathers courageously declared their independence in 1776, but we recognize today that we are unavoidably and always interdependent, as were our North American forebears: our fortunes depend on distant markets, our health on a profusion of microscopic biota, our food security on climatic change. Those forces and a multitude of others shape our lives in profound and unpredictable ways. On a much larger scale, we face today what North Americans west of the Revolution faced in the 1770s. Their world has become ours.

ABBREVIATIONS FOR WORKS CITED

AGI   Archivo General de Indias, Seville, Spain.

CRNC   *Colonial Records of North Carolina*. Edited by William L.
          Saunders. 10 vols. Raleigh: Josephus Daniels, 1886–1890.

DEJ   Silvestre Vélez de Escalante. *The Domínguez-Escalante
          Journal: Their Expedition through Colorado, Utah, Arizona, and
          New Mexico in 1776*. Edited by Ted J. Warner. Translated
          by Fray Angelico Chavez. Salt Lake City: University of
          Utah Press, 1995.

HBCA   Hudson's Bay Company Archives, Archives of Manitoba.

HEB   Herbert Eugene Bolton Papers, Bancroft Library,
          University of California, Berkeley.

PapC   Papeles de Cuba.

PapSD   Papeles de Santo Domingo.

PKY   P. K. Yonge Library of Florida History, University of
          Florida, Gainesville.

WJS   *Writings of Junípero Serra*. Edited by Antonine Tibesar. 4
          vols. Washington, DC: Academy of American Franciscan
          History, 1955–1966.

NOTES

INTRODUCTION

1. Thomas Paine, *Common Sense*, 4th ed. (Lancaster, PA: Francis Bailey, 1776), 29, 21; James D. Drake, "Appropriating a Continent: Geographical Categories, Scientific Metaphors, and the Construction of Nationalism in British North America and Mexico," *Journal of World History* 15, no. 3 (2004): 346 ("a quarter of the globe").

2. By another account, Kuskov placed the marker in 1811. George P. Taylor, "Spanish-Russian Rivalry in the Pacific, 1769–1820," *Americas* 15, no. 2 (1958): 115, 115n16.

3. Adolph (Steve) Volk, *Culinary Olympics 1976/84/88: With Pulled and Blown Sugar* (Bloomington, IN: AuthorHouse, 2005), 2–3.

4. Readers interested in the debate over what the subject matter of early American history is may consult Michael Witgen, "The Native New World and Western North America," *Western Historical Quarterly* 43, no. 2 (2012): 292–99; Claudio Saunt, "Go West: Mapping Early American Historiography," *William and Mary Quarterly* 65, no. 4 (2008): 745–78; Peter H. Wood, "From Atlantic History to a Continental Approach," in *Atlantic History: A Critical Appraisal*, ed. Jack P. Greene and Philip D. Morgan (New York: Oxford University Press, 2008), 279–98; Elizabeth A. Fenn, "Whither the Rest of the Continent?" *Journal of the Early Republic* 24, no. 2 (2004): 167–75; Alan Taylor, "Continental Crossings," *Journal of the Early Republic* 24, no. 2 (2004): 182–88; Joyce E. Chaplin, "Expansion and Exceptionalism in Early American History," *Journal of American History* 89, no. 4 (2003): 1431–55; Nicholas Canny, "Writing Atlantic History; or, Reconfiguring the History of Colonial British America," *Journal of American History* 86, no. 3 (1999): 1093–1114; Ian Tyrrell, "Making Nations/Making States: American Historians in the Context of Empire," *Journal of American History* 86, no. 3 (1999): 1015–44; Gordon S. Wood, "A Century of Writing Early American History: Then and Now Compared; Or How Henry Adams Got It Wrong," *American Historical Review* 100, no. 3 (1995): 678–96; James A. Hijiya, "Why the West Is Lost," *William and Mary Quarterly* 51, no. 2 (1994): 266–92; Joyce Appleby, "A Different Kind of Independence: The Postwar Restructuring of the Historical Study of Early America," *William and Mary Quarterly* 50, no. 2 (1993): 245–67; Ian Tyrrell, "American Exceptionalism in an Age of International History," *American Historical Review* 96, no. 4 (1991): 1031–55; and James Axtell, "A North American Perspective for Colonial History," *History Teacher* 12, no. 4 (1979): 549–63. For a critical discussion of the idea of the continent, see Martin W. Lewis and Kären E. Wigen, *The Myth of Continents: A Critique of Metageography* (Berkeley: University of California Press, 1997).

5. Joan Evans, "The Embassy of the 4th Duke of Bedford to Paris, 1762–1763," *Archaeological Journal* 113 (1956): 141; Richard Neville to the Duke of Bedford, 16 February 1763, in *Correspondence of John, Fourth Duke of Bedford*, ed. Lord John Russell (London: Longman, Brown, Green, and Longmans, 1846), 3:200–203. On the Treaty of Paris in North America, see the excellent introduction by Colin G. Calloway: *The Scratch of a Pen: 1763 and the Transformation of North America* (New York: Oxford University Press, 2006).

PROLOGUE—WESTERN SPECULATION:
HENDERSON'S TRANSYLVANIA COLONY

1. Louisa Company, Draper Manuscripts, Wisconsin Historical Society, Madison, 1CC2 ("on the west side of the Mountains"); minutes of the Transylvania House of Delegates, 23–27 May 1775, in *CRNC* 9:1267–79. The awed admirer is J. F. D. Smyth: *A Tour in the United States of America* (London: G. Robinson, 1784), 1:126.

2. Thomas Walker, "Journal," in *First Explorations of Kentucky*, ed. J. Stoddard Johnston (Louisville, KY: John P. Morton, 1898), 49.

3. William Calk, "Journal," 3 April 1775, Digital Collections, Special Collections and Archives, Kentucky Historical Society; Richard Henderson, "Journal," 30 March 1775, Draper Manuscripts, 1CC21-130; deposition of William Cocke, in Samuel C. Williams, "Henderson and Company's Purchase within the Limits of Tennessee," *Tennessee Historical Magazine* 5, no. 1 (1919): 13n12.

4. Henderson, "Journal," 30 March 1775; Henderson to proprietors, 12 June 1775, in George W. Ranck, *Boonesborough*, Filson Club Publications 16 (Louisville, KY: John P. Morton, 1901), 186; Williams, "Henderson and Company's Purchase," 14.

5. Bethabara Diary, 1776, in *Records of the Moravians in North Carolina*, ed. Adelaide L. Fries (Raleigh, NC: Edwards and Broughton, 1922–1969), 3:1096 ("new land").

6. Sketch of the family of Richard Henderson, Draper Manuscripts, 2CC44, p. 19; Francis Nash, *Hillsboro, Colonial and Revolutionary* (Raleigh, NC: Edwards and Broughton, 1903), 7; William Few, "Autobiography of Col. William Few of Georgia," *Magazine of American History* 7 (1881): 344 ("metropolis").

7. Few, "Autobiography," 344 ("Those lands"); sketch of the family of Richard Henderson, Draper Manuscripts, 2CC44. In theory, all grants were limited to 650 acres, but it was easy to accumulate tracts by purchase from third parties. Thornton W. Mitchell, "The Granville District and Its Land Records," *North Carolina Historical Review* 70, no. 2 (1993): 103–29.

8. John Mack Faragher, *Daniel Boone: The Life and Legend of an American Pioneer* (New York: Holt, 1992), 68–72; Brent Altsheler, "The Long Hunters and James Knox Their Leader," *Filson Club History Quarterly* 5, no. 4 (1931): 173. The most complete account of the Regulator movement is Marjoleine Kars, *Breaking Loose Together: The Regulator Rebellion in Pre-Revolutionary North Carolina* (Chapel Hill: University of North Carolina Press, 2002).

9. Washington to William Crawford, 21 September 1767, in *Correspondence between George Washington and William Crawford from 1767 to 1781, concerning Western Lands*, ed. C. W. Butterfield (Cincinnati, OH: Robert Clark, 1877), 1–5.

10. William Hooper to James Iredell, 26 April 1774, in *CRNC* 9:983–86; Louisa Company, Draper Manuscripts, 1CC2; Hugh T. Lefler and William S. Powell, *Colonial North Carolina: A History* (New York: Scribner's, 1973), 259–63.

11. Nathaniel Hart to Wilkins Tannenhill, 27 April 1839, in *United States Commercial and Statistical Register* 3, no. 1 (1 July 1840): 10–12. The junior Hart's account sixty-five years after the event is based on records of the Transylvania Company then in his possession. Since his is the only account to state that his father Nathaniel journeyed to the Cherokees in the spring to broach the possibility of a land purchase, it seems likely that only the fall trip occurred. Bethabara Diary, 1774, in *Records of the Moravians in North Carolina*, 2:835–36; Bethabara Diary, 1775, in *Records of the Moravians*, 2:900; Bethania Diary, 1775, in *Records of the Moravians*, 2:908. By one account, the goods were purchased at Cross

Creek (Fayetteville, North Carolina), not in Williamsburg. Archibald Henderson, *The Star of Empire: Phases of the Westward Movement in the Old Southwest* (Durham, NC: Seeman, 1919), 53.

12. Proclamation by Josiah Martin, 10 February 1775, in *CRNC* 9:1122–25; advertisement by Richard Henderson and the Transylvania Company, 25 December 1774, in *CRNC* 9:1129–31; *Virginia Gazette*, supplement, 10 March 1775, p. 2; Diary of Salem Congregation, 1775, in *Records of the Moravians*, 2:863; Bethania Diary, 1775, in *Records of the Moravians*, 2:908 ("The whole Province"); "Sketches and Anecdotes of the Family of Brown," *American Historical Magazine* 7 (October 1902), 362–72 (party of emigrants); Felix Walker, "The First Settlement of Kentucky: Narrative of an Adventure in Kentucky in the Year 1775," *Debow's Review* 16, no. 2 (1854): 150 (one participant).

13. Though Lyman C. Draper wrote that the land cost £10,000, that figure is questionable. The contract itself stated that the Cherokees received £2,000. For a second smaller tract, known as the "Path Deed," the Cherokees received about £700. One other source claims that the Cherokees received £4,000 worth of goods. See Ranck, *Boonesborough*, 151 (£2,000); *Calendar of Virginia State Papers*, ed. William P. Palmer (Richmond: McRae, Sherwin, and others, 1875–1893), 1:287, 292, 306 (Path Deed); Bethabara Diary, 1774, in *Records of the Moravians in North Carolina*, 2:835–36 (£4,000); Lyman C. Draper, *The Life of Daniel Boone*, ed. Ted Franklin Belue (Mechanicsburg, PA: Stackpole), 333; and deposition of John Reid, 16 April 1777, in *Calendar of Virginia State Papers*, 1:285 (dissatisfied onlooker).

14. William Tryon to Wills Hill, 11 March 1771, *CRNC* 8:524–25; Archibald Neilson to Andrew Miller, 28 January 1775, *CRNC* 9:1116–17.

15. Thomas Perkins Abernethy, *Western Lands and the American Revolution* (New York: Russell and Russell, 1959); George E. Lewis, *The Indiana Company, 1763–1798: A Study in Eighteenth Century Frontier Land Speculation and Business Venture* (Glendale, CA: Arthur H. Clark, 1941); Clarence Walworth Alvord, *The Mississippi Valley in British Politics*, 2 vols. (Cleveland, OH: Arthur H. Clark, 1916).

16. Lewis, *Indiana Company*, 88.

17. Chad Wozniak, "The New Western Colony Schemes: A Preview of the United States Territorial System," *Indiana Magazine of History*, 68, no. 4 (1972): 291n30 ("not the fittest"); George Henry Alden, *New Governments West of the Alleghenies before 1780* (Madison: University of Wisconsin Press, 1897), 7–11 (quotation "humble Application" on p. 8).

18. Abernethy, *Western Lands*, 2.

19. Paul Semonin, *American Monster: How the Nation's First Prehistoric Creature Became a Symbol of National Identity* (New York: New York University Press, 2000), 84–161.

20. Barnet Schecter, *George Washington's America: A Biography through His Maps* (New York: Walker, 2010), 22, 24–25; John Mitchell, *A Map of the British and French Dominions in North America* ([London]: Andrew Millar, 1755); Thomas Hutchins, *A New Map of the Western Parts of Virginia, Pennsylvania, Maryland and North Carolina* (London: T. Hutchins, 1778). In late 1776, an unknown cartographer, probably linked to the Transylvania Company, produced an informative, hand-drawn map of "Transilvania." Elizabeth Fraas, "An Unusual Map of the Early West," *Register of the Kentucky Historical Society* 73, no. 1 (1975): 61–69.

21. Alden, *New Governments*, 7.

22. North Carolina Declaration of Rights, 17 December 1776, in *CRNC* 10:1004; charter granted by Charles II, 24 March 1663, in *CRNC* 1:21. The difficulties of surveying even a single parallel are described in Thornton W. Mitchell, "Granville District," 103–29.

23. Williams, "Henderson and Company's Purchase," 9; Charles C. Royce, "The Cherokee

Nation of Indians: A Narrative of Their Official Relations with the Colonial and Federal Governments," in *Fifth Annual Report of the Bureau of Ethnology* (Washington, DC: Government Printing Office, 1887), 148–49.

24. "John Williams' Report (January 3, 1776) of Transylvania Affairs to the Proprietors in North Carolina," in Ranck, *Boonesborough*, 234 ("abounded with land-mongers"); Richard Henderson, "Journal," 7 May 1775 ("every piece of land"); James Nourse, "Journey to Kentucky in 1775," *Journal of American History* 19, no. 4 (1925): 352; "James Nourse of Virginia," *Virginia Magazine of History and Biography* 8, no. 2 (1900): 199.

25. Henderson and John Luttrell to their partners, 18 July 1775, Draper Manuscripts, 1CC195-97.

26. Diaries of John Adams, 25 October 1775, Adams Family Papers: An Electronic Resource, Massachusetts Historical Society; Henry Stuart to John Stuart, 25 August 1776, in *CRNC* 10:778.

27. Jefferson to Edmund Pendleton, 13 August 1776, Founders Online, National Archives (http://founders.archives.gov/documents/Jefferson/01-01-02-0205, ver. 2013-06-26); William Hooper, Joseph Hewes, and John Penn to the North Carolina Council of Safety, 7 August 1776, in *CRNC* 10:730–32; Rutherford to the North Carolina Council of Safety, 5 July 1776, in *CRNC* 10:652; Rutherford to William Christian, 5 July 1776, in *CRNC* 10:651.

28. Thomas Cook, *Captain Thomas Cook (1752–1841) a Soldier of the Revolution*, ed. William M. Sweeny ([New York?]: n.p., 1909), 4.

29. Christian to Henry, 23 October 1776, in "Virginia Legislative Papers (Continued)," *Virginia Magazine of History and Biography*, 17, no. 1 (1909): 64; deposition of Arthur Campbell, October 1778, in *Calendar of Virginia State Papers*, 1:303–04 ("snug little purchase"); Jerry C. Cashion, "Griffith Rutherford," in *Dictionary of North Carolina Biography*, ed. William Stevens Powell (Chapel Hill: University of North Carolina Press, 1986), 5:275–76; A. P. Whitaker, "The Muscle Shoals Speculation, 1783–1789," *Mississippi Valley Historical Review* 13, no. 3 (1926): 365–86.

30. "Transylvania Purchase Declared Void," 4 November 1778, in Ranck, *Boonesborough*, 253; Treaty of Hopewell, 1785, in *American State Papers: Indian Affairs* (Washington, DC: Gales and Seaton, 1832), 1:42.

PART ONE: THE RUSSIANS ARE COMING—INTRODUCTION

1. Pedro Font, *With Anza to California, 1775–1776: The Journal of Pedro Font, O.F.M.*, trans. and ed. Alan K. Brown (Norman, OK: Arthur H. Clark, 2011), 293 ("greatest fear describable"); Juan Bautista de Anza, "Anza's Diary of the Second Anza Expedition, 1775–1776," in *Anza's California Expeditions*, ed. Herbert Eugene Bolton (New York: Russell and Russell, 1930), 3:136 ("lying prone" and "even a remote notice").

2. Anza, "Anza's Diary," 3:136.

3. Bill Mason, "The Garrisons of San Diego Presidio: 1770–1794," *Journal of San Diego History* 24 (Fall 1978). The precise layout of the fort remains unclear, but for a contemporary description see Francisco Palóu, *Historical Memoirs of New California*, ed. Herbert Eugene Bancroft (1926; reprint, New York: Russell and Russell, 1966), 3:214–15. The Kumeyaays are also known as the Kamias, Diegueños, Tipais, and Ipais, among other names. Today, all of these peoples call themselves Kumeyaays. M. Steven Shackley, "The Kumeyaay Paradise," in *The Early Ethnography of the Kumeyaay*, ed. Shackley (Berkeley, CA: Phoebe Hearst Museum of Anthropology, 2004), 2–4. See also Katharine Luomala,

"Tipai and Ipai," in *Handbook of North American Indians: California*, ed. Robert F. Heizer (Washington, DC: Smithsonian Institution, 1978), 8:592–610.

4. *DEJ*, 66–69.

5. Hans Jakob Fries, *A Siberian Journey: The Journal of Hans Jakob Fries, 1774–1776*, ed. and trans. Walther Kirchner (London: Frank Cass, 1974), 127.

CHAPTER ONE—SOFT GOLD: ALEUTS
AND RUSSIANS IN ALASKA

1. I have converted from the Julian to the Gregorian calendar. Roza G. Liapunova, *Essays on the Ethnography of the Aleuts*, trans. Jerry Shelest (1975; reprint, Fairbanks: University of Alaska Press, 1996), 88–89 (nestlings and newborn sea mammals); Ivan Solov'ev, "Report," fol. 259, file 539/4110, pp. 246v–47r, 248r–48v, Rossiiskii Gosudarstvennyi Arkhiv Drevnikh Aktov (RGADA) [Russian State Archive of Ancient Acts], Moscow. On the *St. Paul* (*Sv. Pavel* in Russian), see Vasilii Nikolaevich Berkh, *A Chronological History of the Discovery of the Aleutian Islands or the Exploits of Russian Merchants*, ed. Richard A. Pierce, trans. Dmitri Krenov (1823; reprint, Kingston, ON: Limestone Press, 1974), 42; and Thomas Edgar, "Journal," in *The Journals of Captain James Cook on His Voyages of Discovery*, ed. J. C. Beaglehole, vol. 3, pt. 2, *The Voyage of the* Resolution *and* Discovery*, 1776–1780* (Cambridge: Cambridge University Press, 1967), 1355 ("very strong & clumsy"). Though he did not mention the ship's name, Edgar described what must have been the *St. Paul* in detail in his journal. Cook met only two Russian captains in the Aleutians: Gerasim Izmailov, who succeeded Solov'ev as captain of the *St. Paul*, and Iakov Ivanov Sapozhnikov of the *Evpl* (called Jacob Ivanovich by the English who met him). The *Evpl* was then resting on Umnak Island, according to Charles Clerke. Clerke, "Remarks &c at Samgoonoodha, October 1778," in *Journals of Captain James Cook*, 3(pt. 2):1336; Johann Georg Gmelin, "Voyage de Gmelin en Sibérie," in *Abrégé de l'histoire générale des voyages*, ed. J. F. LaHarpe (Paris: Ménard et Desenne, 1825), 9:355–56 ("miserable wooden houses"); Martin Sauer, *An Account of a Geographical and Astronomical Expedition to the Northern Parts of Russia* (London: T. Cadell, 1802), 40–41; James R. Gibson, *Feeding the Russian Fur Trade: Provisionment of the Okhotsk Seaboard and the Kamchatka Peninsula, 1639–1856* (Madison: University of Wisconsin Press, 1969), 126–27.

2. William Coxe, *Account of the Russian Discoveries between Asia and America*, 3rd ed. (London: T. Cadell, 1787), 349–50; Gibson, *Feeding the Russian Fur Trade*, 120–22; Varlam Shalamov, *Kolyma Tales*, trans. John Glad (New York: Norton, 1982), 46.

3. Solov'ev, "Report," 237r–37v; John Ledyard, "Siberian Journal," in *The Last Voyage of Captain Cook: The Collected Writings of John Ledyard*, ed. James Zug (Washington, DC: National Geographic Adventure Classics, 2005), 172, 176 ("constantly charged with Snow"); Ian R. Christie, *The Benthams in Russia, 1780–1791* (Oxford: Berg, 1991), 84.

4. Sauer, *Account*, 14–15 (description of Irkutsk); "Report of the Sea Voyage . . . under the Command of Captain Krenitsin and Lieutenant Levashev," in *Bering's Successors, 1745–1780*, ed. James R. Masterson and Helen Brower (Seattle: University of Washington Press, 1948), 58; "Report of a Four-Year Voyage . . . under the Command of the Peredovshik Dmitri Bragin," in *Bering's Successors*, 68–71 (description of Aleutian communities). Before contact, Aleutian communities were somewhat larger but never had more than several hundred people. Brian W. Hoffman, "Agayadan Village: Household Archaeology on Unimak Island, Alaska," *Journal of Field Archaeology* 26, no. 2 (1999): 147–61. On the Aleutian population: Margaret Lantis, "Aleut," in *Handbook of North American Indians: Arctic*, ed.

David Damas and William C. Sturtevant (Washington, DC: Smithsonian Institution, 1984), 5:163. On Kyakhta trade: Coxe, *Account of the Russian Discoveries*, 347–50.

5. Clifford M. Foust, *Muscovite and Mandarin: Russia's Trade with China and Its Setting, 1727–1805* (Chapel Hill: University of North Carolina Press, 1969), 24–67, 164–84, 232; W. Bruce Lincoln, *The Conquest of a Continent: Siberia and the Russians* (New York: Random House, 1994), 143–49; Hans Jakob Fries, *A Siberian Journey: The Journal of Hans Jakob Fries, 1774–1776*, ed. and trans. Walther Kirchner (London: Frank Cass, 1974), 133; Peter Simon Pallas, *Voyages du Professeur Pallas* (Paris: Maradan, 1794), 5:319–24.

6. On Kyakhta and prices: Foust, *Muscovite and Mandarin*, 340, 350–51; James R. Gibson, "Russian Expansion in Siberia and America," *Geographical Review* 70, no. 2 (1980): 130; and Valery M. Garrett, *Chinese Dress: From the Qing Dynasty to the Present* (Tokyo: Tuttle, 2007), 12–14. Lydia T. Black notes that Alaskan black fox furs sold for twice as much in Kyakhta as sea otter pelts, but that contradicts the prices recorded in the late eighteenth century by Peter S. Pallas. Pallas, *Voyages*, 5:281–84; Black, *Russians in Alaska, 1732–1867* (Fairbanks: University of Alaska, 2004), 69. On otter: M. L. Riedman and J. A. Estes, *The Sea Otter (Enhydra lutris): Behavior, Ecology, and Natural History*, Biological Report 90-14 (Washington, DC: US Dept. of the Interior, Fish and Wildlife Service, 1990), 20; and Jeffrey P. Cohn, "Understanding Sea Otters," *BioScience* 48, no. 3 (1998): 151. Georg Wilhelm Steller, *Journal of a Voyage with Bering, 1741–1742*, ed. O. W. Frost, trans. Margritt A. Engel (Stanford, CA: Stanford University Press, 1993), 147 (quotation).

7. Coxe, *Account of the Russian Discoveries*, 337–38; Foust, *Muscovite and Mandarin*, 350; E. E. Rich, "Russia and the Colonial Fur Trade," *Economic History Review*, 7, no. 3 (1955): 307–28. On camels and oxen: M. S. Bentham, *The Life of Brigadier General Sir Samuel Bentham* (London: Longman, Green, Longman, and Roberts, 1862), 55.

8. On Aleut perceptions: Coxe, *Account of the Russian Discoveries*, 272. On the number of vessels: Raisa V. Makarova, *Russians on the Pacific, 1743–1799*, trans. Richard A. Pierce and Alton S. Donnelly (Kingston, ON: Limestone, 1975), 212–13. On Tobolsk: Lincoln, *Conquest of a Continent*, 59–60. Unless otherwise noted, the following account of the voyage of the *St. Paul* is based on Solov'ev, "Report." The document is a copy of a first-person account related by Ivan Solov'ev and is more detailed and extensive than Peter Simon Pallas's 1781 abstract of the voyage, published in translation in *Bering's Successors*, 77–85. Where the two accounts conflict, I have favored the older, unabstracted RGADA document (see note 1).

9. On *iasak* (tribute) and the taking of *amanaty* (hostages): Raymond H. Fisher, *The Russian Fur Trade, 1550–1700* (Berkeley: University of California Press, 1943), 53–61; James Forsyth, *A History of the Peoples of Siberia: Russia's North Asian colony, 1581–1990* (New York: Cambridge University Press, 1992), 38–42, 57–66, 75–79, 87–98, 131–39; Yuri Slezkine, *Arctic Mirrors: Russia and the Small Peoples of the North* (Ithaca, NY: Cornell University Press, 1994), 60–71; and Makarova, *Russians on the Pacific*, 140–44. Quotations: Mark Bassin, "Inventing Siberia: Visions of the Russian East in the Early Nineteenth Century," *American Historical Review* 96, no. 3 (1991): 768–70.

10. On early exploration of the Aleutian Islands: Gibson, "Russian Expansion," 127–36; A. I. Alekseev, *The Destiny of Russian America, 1741–1867*, trans. Marina Ramsay (Kingston, ON: Limestone, 1990); Makarova, *Russians on the Pacific*; and Coxe, *Account of the Russian Discoveries*.

11. A fifth ship, the *Nikolai*, visited Unimak in 1763. Aleuts killed most of the crew, but the ship returned to Okhotsk in 1766 with a small cargo. Berkh, *Chronological History*, 34–35. Quotations: "Report of Ivan Solov'ev to T. I. Shmalev," in *Russkie otkrytiia v Tikhom okeane i Severnoi Amerike v XVIII veke [Russian Discoveries in the Pacific Ocean and North*

America in the 18th Century], ed. A. I. Andreev (Moscow: Gosudarstvennoe izdatel'stvo geograficheskoi literatury, 1948), 149.

12. Coxe, *Account of the Russian Discoveries*, 90–100; Berkh, *Chronological History*, 32–34.

13. The fifty-four castaways included the seven survivors from the *Zacharias and Elizabeth.* "Report of Ivan Solov'ev to T. I. Shmalev," 148; Coxe, *Account of the Russian Discoveries*, 101–14. On discovery of the steam bath: William S. Laughlin, *Aleuts: Survivors of the Bering Land Bridge* (Fort Worth, TX: Harcourt Brace, 1980), 122–25.

14. "Report of Ivan Solov'ev to T. I. Shmalev," 163 (Solov'ev quotation). See also Coxe, *Account of the Russian Discoveries*, 157, 158, 162, 169. For a sympathetic assessment of Solov'ev see Black, *Russians in Alaska*, 89. Berkh, *Chronological History*, 40–42 ("on the spot"); Ivan Veniaminov, *Notes on the Islands of the Unalashka District*, trans. Lydia T. Black and R. H. Geoghegan (Kingston, ON: Limestone, 1984), 251 ("terrible"). When Russians first landed on Unalaska in 1759, they reported a population of only three hundred, but ten years later Aleuts said the population numbered a thousand and had been significantly larger before Solov'ev's incursion. A. I. Andreev, ed., *Russian Discoveries in the Pacific and in North America in the Eighteenth and Nineteenth Centuries* (Ann Arbor, MI: J. W. Edwards, 1952), 20; "Report of the Sea Voyage . . . under . . . Krenitsin and . . . Levashev," 58.

15. Veniaminov, *Notes on the Islands*, 248–49, 281.

16. "Complaints Made by Natives of the Unalaska District," in *Russian Penetration of the Northern Pacific Ocean, 1700–1799*, ed. Basil Dmytryshyn, E. A. P. Crownhart-Vaughn, and Thomas Vaughn (Portland: Oregon Historical Society, 1988), ("shot all the men" and cruel experiment); Veniaminov, *Notes on the Islands*, 248–49, 252 ("The slaughter").

17. The Russian manuscript has *Chaguzyak* and *Kalu.* The standard orthography is *Chagusix̂,* meaning "digging stick," and *Kaluu,* meaning "his shot." Knut Bergsland, *Ancient Aleut Personal Names* (Anchorage: Alaska Native Language Center, 1998), 192, 193. The word *toion* comes from Kamchatkan Russian and is ultimately of Chinese origin. See *tuyuuna-x̂* in Knut Bergsland, *Aleut Dictionary* (Fairbanks: University of Alaska, Alaska Native Language Center, 1994), 412. Lydia Black, working from an abstract of Solov'ev's journal, suggests that Vaska was the same person as Chutekh (*Chuutix̂*), "whom Solov'ev affectionately termed *Vas'ka.*" The complete journal in the Russian State Archive of Ancient Acts (RGADA), however, makes clear in numerous places that they were two different people. Black, "Sanak," in *The History and Ethnohistory of the Aleutians East Borough,* ed. Black et al. (Kingston, ON: Limestone, 1999), 62; Solov'ev, "Report," 238r.

18. Black, "Sanak," 59–78; James Cook, "Journal of Captain Cook," in *Journals of Captain James Cook,* 3(pt. 1):386.

19. Solov'ev, "Report," 238r–239v. Solov'ev reported, "The group consists of 51 persons," but by noting that "each of them has a small leather kayak," he revealed that he was only counting men. An 1880 report to Congress called Sanak and its immediate vicinity "the great sea-otter hunting-ground of Alaska Territory." Ivan Petroff, *A Preliminary Report upon the Population, Industry, and Resources of Alaska,* H. Exec. Doc. No. 40, 46th Cong., 3d sess. (1880), p. 19. See also Black, "Sanak," 71.

20. Solov'ev, "Report," 239v–240r.

21. Ibid., 242v.

22. Ibid., 240v–241r.

23. Ibid., 241v. On Aleut slavery, see Liapunova, *Essays*, 138–41.

24. Peter Simon Pallas, in his abstract of Solov'ev's journal, mistakenly wrote that Solov'ev left Sanak in July 1773. The 1772 date is made clear in Solov'ev, "Report." Pallas, "Abstract of the Diary of a Voyage Made by Ivan Soloviev," in *Bering's Successors,* 81–82.

25. "Complaints Made by Natives."

26. Solov'ev, "Report," 243v.

27. Coxe, *Account of the Russian Discoveries*, 215 ("They long"); description of trade goods from "A Report on the Voyage of Potap K. Zaikov," in *Russian Penetration of the Northern Pacific Ocean*, 263, 266; Cook, "Journal of Captain Cook," 383, 386, 390–92; David Samwell, "Some Account of a Voyage to the South Sea's," in *Journals of Captain James Cook*, 3(pt. 2):1119, 1121; James King, "King's Journal," in ibid., 3(pt. 2):1442 ("for the Natives have Phelgm").

28. The Unalaskans were reportedly "more friendly," but the assessment was relative. "Report of the Sea Voyage . . . under . . . Krenitsin and . . . Levashev," 59; King, "King's Journal," 1449 ("the Russians have cut"); Clerke, "Remarks &c at Samgoonoodha," 1336 ("by stabbing").

29. Russians had often justified the conquest of Siberian peoples by reference to their filth. Slezkine, *Arctic Mirrors*, 42, 56–57; "Explanation of the Cossack S. T. Ponomarev and the Foreman S. G. Glotov concerning the Islands Discovered by Them, 1762," in Andreyev, *Russian Discoveries in the Pacific*, 23 ("no cleanliness"); "A Report Dictated in St. Petersburg by Feder Afansevich Kulkov," in *Russian Penetration of the Northern Pacific Ocean*, 229 ("do not subscribe"); "Report of the Sea Voyage . . . under . . . Krenitsin and . . . Levashev," 57 ("In their persons").

30. Johann Gottlieb Georgi, *Russia: or, A Compleat Historical Account of All the Nations Which Compose That Empire* (London: J. Nichols, 1780), 3:214–15 ("descending into hell"); "Description of the Andreanof Islands, Composed on the Basis of the Reports of the Cossacks M. Lazarev and P. Vasiutinsky, 1764," in Andreyev, *Russian Discoveries in the Pacific*, 28 ("do not care"); Black, *Russians in Alaska*, 223–29.

31. "Description of the Andreanof Islands," 29 ("gentle and agreeable"); "Account of the Totma Merchant, Stepan Cherepanov," in *Russian Penetration of the Northern Pacific Ocean*, 210 ("very kind"); "Report Dictated in St. Petersburg," 229 ("peaceful").

32. Lydia Black writes that it is a "myth that the main aim of the Russians was to enslave the Aleuts to hunt sea otters," suggesting that they "hunted sea otters quite by themselves." Veniaminov, *Notes on the Islands*, 163n. But contemporary sources suggest that Russians hunted the animals at sea only with great difficulty. Coxe, *Account of the Russian Discoveries*, 59–60, 102–3; "Account of the Totma Merchant," 212; Riedman and Estes, *Sea Otter*, 24; James R. Gibson, "European Dependence upon American Natives: The Case of Russian America," *Ethnohistory* 25, no. 4 (1978): 359–85 (quotation "toilsome, and sometimes dangerous" on p. 361). On attacks: "Report of the Sea Voyage . . . under . . . Krenitsin and . . . Levashev," 61. On boats: Berkh, *Chronological History*, 11; and Black, *Russians in Alaska*, 68. On fog and tide rips: *United States Coast Pilot*, 38th ed. (Washington, DC: US Dept. of Commerce, 2008), 341–43.

33. Liapunova, *Essays*, 89–97, 102–3; Veniaminov, *Notes on the Islands*, 284; King, "King's Journal," 1444 (quotation).

34. On firearms: Miranda Wright, "The Sea Otter Industry in the Eastern Aleutians, 1867–1911," in *History and Ethnohistory of the Aleutians*, 256, 259, 260; and Joan B. Townsend, "Firearms against Native Arms: A Study in Comparative Efficiencies with an Alaskan Example," *Arctic Anthropology* 20:2 (1983): 1–34. On clothing: Svetlana G. Fedorova, *The Russian Population in Alaska and California: Late 18th Century—1867*, trans. and ed. Richard A. Pierce and Alton S. Donnelly (Kingston, ON: Limestone, 1973), 228–29; and Liapunova, *Essays*, 193–210. Veniaminov, *Notes on the Islands*, 266–67 ("indispensable," "suffered," and "In the worst"); Katherine B. Menz, *Russian Bishop's House, Sitka National Historical Park, Sitka Alaska*, Historic Furnishings Report ([Harpers Ferry, WV?]: Dept. of the Interior/National Park Service, 1986), 11–13 ("manly, athletic man");

Clerke, "Remarks &c at Samgoonoodha," 1337; Fedorova, *Russian Population*, 229 ("Take their productions").

35. Sauer, *Account*, 157.

36. Gavriil Sarycev ("infinite toil and trouble"), as quoted in George Dyson, *Baidarka: The Kayak* (Anchorage: Alaska Northwest Books, 1986), 29; Liapunova, *Essays*, 112–16, 134; George Dyson, "Form and Function of the Baidarka: The Framework of Design," in *Contributions to Kayak Studies*, ed. E. Y. Arima (Hull, QC: Canadian Museum of Civilization, 1991), 261–317.

37. Veniaminov, *Notes on the Islands*, 160; Sauer, *Account*, 158 ("more like amphibious animals"); G. H. von Langsdorff ("the best means"), as quoted in George Dyson, *Baidarka* (Edmonds, WA: Alaska Northwest, 1986).

38. Veniaminov, *Notes on the Islands*, 271.

39. Copy of order of Russian Senate, fol. 259 (fond Senata), file 539/4110, 315r, Rossiiskii Gosudarstvennyi Arkhiv Drevnikh Aktov [Russian State Archive of Ancient Acts], Moscow ("nothing worthy"); Berkh, *Chronological History*, 28 ("indescribable abuses"). Berkh describes the actions of the promyshlenniki on pp. 23–26.

40. Solov'ev, "Report," 244v.

41. Ibid., 246r; Slezkine, *Arctic Mirrors*, 18 (*inozemtsy*); Veniaminov, *Notes on the Islands*, 83 ("disobedient"), 251 ("exterminated").

42. Veniaminov, *Notes on the Islands*, 103; Petroff, *Preliminary Report*, 21; Lydia T. Black, "Akutanax̂: The Krenitzin Islands and Akutan from Prehistory to 1867," in *History and Ethnohistory of the Aleutians*, 33–44.

43. Lydia Black mistakenly writes that there is no record of Natrubin working for Solov'ev and concludes that Aleut memories as reported by Veniaminov were faulty. She, like other scholars, relied on Peter Simon Pallas's and N. N. Ogloblin's abstracts of Solov'ev's journal describing his second voyage. In fact, in the copy of the original housed in the RGADA, Solov'ev listed Natrubin as a crew member of the *St. Paul*. More often than not, Aleut recollections accord with the historical record. Veniaminov, *Notes on the Islands*, 102n, 252 ("henchman"); Black, "Sanak," 76n6; Black, "Akutanax̂," 37, 40; Samwell, "Some Account of a Voyage," 1139–40 ("extravagantly fond"). Regarding piety and alcohol, see also John Ledyard, *A Journal of Captain Cook's Last Voyage to the Pacific Ocean, and in Quest of a North-west Passage, between Asia & America* (Hartford, CT: Nathaniel Patten, 1783), 95. On Aleut place names: Bergsland, *Aleut Dictionary*, 601. Solov'ev, "Report," 245r ("invitation").

44. Hoffman, "Agayadan Village," 147–61; Allen P. McCartney and Douglas W. Veltre, "Aleutian Island Prehistory: Living in Insular Extremes," *World Archaeology* 30, no. 3 (1999): 503–15; Solov'ev, "Report," 245r.

45. David Nordlander, "Innokentii Veniaminov and the Expansion of Orthodoxy in Russian America," *Pacific Historical Review* 64, no. 1 (1995): 28–31; Veniaminov, *Notes on the Islands*, 102, 252.

46. Description of rifles: Edgar, "Journal," 1355; Veniaminov, *Notes on the Islands*, 103 (quotation).

47. A tally of the figures compiled by A. S. Polonskii in the 1860s indicates that just under 342,000 otter and fox pelts were imported into Okhotsk in the second half of the eighteenth century. The number of fur seal pelts approached 700,000, reflecting the discovery of the Pribilof Islands in 1786. Polonskii, "Perechen' puteshestvii russkikh promyshlennykh v Vostochnom Okeane s 1743 po 1800 god," Arkhiv Russkogo geograficheskogo obshchestva ["List of Voyages of Russian Promyshlenniki on the East Ocean from 1743 to 1800," Archive of the Russian Geographical Society], St. Petersburg.

48. Makarova, *Russians on the Pacific*, 5 ("Russian might"); Lydia T. Black, "The Question of Maps: Exploration of the Bering Sea, Eighteenth Century," in *The Sea in Alaska's Past: First Conference Proceedings* (Anchorage: Alaska Division of Parks, 1979), 6–50.

49. Solov'ev, "Report," 246r–47; Lincoln, *Conquest of a Continent*, 147–48. On two survivors: Fries, *Siberian Journey*, 118–19.

50. Vladimir Platonovich Sukachev, *Irkutsk. Ego mesto i znachenie v istorii i kul'turnom razvitii vostochnoi Sibiri. Ocherk* [*Irkutsk. Its Place and Meaning in History and the Cultural Development of Eastern Siberia. A Study*] (Moscow: Tipolit. I. N. Kushnerev, 1891), 14; Nemtsov to the Senate, 27 November 1776, fol. 259, file 539/4110, p. 254, Rossiiskii Gosudarstvennyi Arkhiv Drevnikh Aktov [Russian State Archive of Ancient Acts], Moscow (quotation).

51. José Torrubia, *I Moscoviti nella California* (Rome: Generoso Salomoni, 1759), 2–3, 32–40. A translation was published as Torrubia, *The Muscovites in California* (Fairfield, WA: Galleon, 1996). Translations here are the author's own.

52. Torrubia, *I Moscoviti nella California*, 11–12, 32.

53. The recipient of the instruction to spy on the Russians, the Marqués de Almodóvar, concluded that Russia was not a major threat to Spanish interests in the Pacific, but his successors thought otherwise. "De la instrucción que llevó el Marqués de Almodóvar," March 9, 1761, in *Colección de documentos inéditos para la historia de España*, ed. Feliciano Ramírez de Arellano (Madrid: José Perales y Martínez, 1893), 108:13–14.

CHAPTER TWO—A WAR FOR INDEPENDENCE:
THE SAN DIEGO UPRISING

1. Warren L. Cook, *Flood Tide of Empire: Spain and the Pacific Northwest, 1543–1819* (New Haven, CT: Yale University Press, 1973), 1–20. The first reference to "Alta California" occurred in 1546. Dora Beale Polk, *The Island of California: A History of the Myth* (Spokane, WA: Arthur H. Clark, 1991), 157–59.

2. Marqués de Almodóvar to Ricardo Wall, 7 October 1761, Estado, leg. 86B, no. 100, doc. 1, AGI.

3. G. Malcolm Lewis, "La Grande Rivière et Fleuve de l'Ouest: The Realities and Reasons behind a Major Mistake in the 18th-Century Geography of North America," *Cartographica* 28, no. 1 (1991): 80–81.

4. Lucie Lagarde, "Le Passage du Nord-Ouest et la Mer de l'Ouest dans la Cartographie française du 18e Siècle, Contribution à l'Etude de l'Ouevre des Deslisle et Buache," *Imago Mundi* 41, no. 1 (1989): 19–43; G. Malcolm Lewis, "Misinterpretation of Amerindian Information as a Source of Error on Euro-American Maps," *Annals of the Association of American Geographers* 77, no. 4 (1987): 542–63; Miguel León-Portilla, *Cartografía y crónicas de la antigua California* (Mexico City: Universidad Nacional Autónoma de México, 2001), plate 38; "Relación del P. Velarde, 1716," in *La obra cartográfica de la Provincia Mexicana de la Compañía de Jesús*, ed. Ernest J. Burrus (Madrid: José Porrúa Turanzas, 1967), 186. The myth of a navigable river connecting the Gulf of California to the North Pacific had roots in the sixteenth century and was not entirely discredited until the nineteenth. Polk, *Island of California*, 158–69.

5. Eusebio Francisco Kino, "Kino's Historical Memoir of Pimería Alta," in *Spain in the West: A Series of Original Documents from Foreign Archives*, ed. Herbert Eugene Bolton (Cleveland, OH: Arthur H. Clark, 1919), 3:343–44 ("painful flux"); "Relación del P. Velarde," 187 (storm); Fernandez Sánchez Salvador to the king, 2 March 1751, *Documentos para la historia de México*, ed. Francisco García Figueroa (Mexico City: Vicente García Torres, 1856), 3rd series, 1:661–66 ("practically educated" and fork of the Colorado River); Donald C.

Cutter, "Plans for Occupation of Upper California: A New Look at the 'Dark Age' from 1602 to 1769," *Journal of San Diego History* 24, no. 1 (1978). In the 1770s, some Spaniards still believed that a part of the Colorado disgorged into the Pacific. Paul W. Mapp, *The Elusive West and the Contest for Empire, 1713–1763* (Chapel Hill: University of North Carolina Press, 2011), 74–75.

6. Miguel Venegas authored the book in question, but it was heavily edited by Burriel. Burriel himself was skeptical that a navigable river existed connecting the Southwest and the California coast, but few Spanish officials shared his doubts. Venegas, *Noticia de la California, y de su conquista temporal y espiritual hasta el tiempo presente* (Madrid: la Viuda de Manuel Fernández, 1757), 3:4–6, and 2:368 ("sorry canoes" in vol. 3, p. 4); Burriel to Ignacio de Hermosilla y de Sandoval, 3 February 1756, in *Obra cartográfica*, 211 ("those Parisian boys"). For examples of the persistent belief in a waterway between the West Coast and the interior of continent, see León-Portilla, *Cartografía y crónicas*, 144–49; and Cook, *Flood Tide of Empire*, 49.

7. Francisco de Ajofrin to Bernardo Prado, 8 May 1764, in *Noticias y documentos acerca de las Californias, 1764–1795*, ed. José Porrúa Turanzas (Madrid: José Porrúa Turanzas, 1959), 16; Henry R. Wagner and Pedro Calderón y Henríquez, "Memorial of Pedro Calderón y Henríquez: Recommending Monterey as a Port for the Philippine Galleons with a View to Preventing Russian Encroachment in California," *California Historical Society Quarterly* 23, no. 3 (1944): 219–25. Wagner seems to have assumed that Calderón's source of information was Gerard Fridrikh Miller, *Voyages et découvertes faites par les Russes* (Amsterdam: Marc-Michel Rey, 1766), since that text contained the most complete account of Russian exploration to date. It is clear from Calderón's errors, however, that Calderón was relying on Stepan Krasheninnikov, *Histoire de Kamtschatka, des Isles Kurilski, et des contrées voisines* (Lyon, France: Benoit Duplain, 1767). See pp. 91–93 for the passages that Calderón misunderstood.

8. Gálvez to Marqués de Croix, 10 June 1769, part 1, carton 13, item 189, folder 2, HEB ("of paramount importance"); Charles Edward Chapman, *The Founding of Spanish California: The Northwest Expansion of New Spain, 1687–1783* (New York: Macmillan, 1916), 82–83; Cook, *Flood Tide of Empire*, 48–49. Gálvez's role in New Spain's northward expansion is explored in detail in Luis Navarro García, *Don José de Gálvez y la comandancia general de la provincias internas del norte de Nueva España* (Seville, Spain: Consejo Superior de Investigaciones Científicas, 1964). On Gálvez's illness: "Breve noticia de las principales Expediciones y Providencias de visita de Real Hacienda que promovió Don Joseph de Gálvez," August 1773, Estado, leg. 34, doc. 36, AGI; and Juan Manuel de Viniegra, "Apuntamiento instructivo," in *Gaspar de Portolá: Crónicas del descubrimiento de la Alta California, 1769*, ed. Ángela Cano Sánchez, Neus Escandell Tur, and Elena Mampel González (Barcelona: Ediciones de la Universidad de Barcelona, 1984), 276.

9. Vicente Vila, "Diario de navegación," in *Gaspar de Portolá*, 251–54; Miguel Costansó, "Diario Histórico," in *Noticias y documentos acerca de las Californias*, 98; Hubert Howe Bancroft, *History of California, 1542–1800* (San Francisco: History Company, 1886), 18:131n10.

10. In fact, the Spanish killed as many as five Kumeyaay individuals during the August 1769 attack. Serra to Juan Andrés, 10 February 1770, in *WJS*, 1:151; Maynard Geiger, "Fray Rafael Verger, O.F.M., and the California Mission Enterprise," *Southern California Quarterly* 49, no. 2 (1967): 221. On the relief ship: Maynard J. Geiger, *The Life and Times of Fray Junípero Serra* (Washington, DC: Academy of American Franciscan History, 1959), 1:239–44.

11. In addition to the garrison population, there were eighteen or so missionaries. Pauline

Maier, *American Scripture: Making the Declaration of Independence* (New York: Knopf, 1997), 41 (quotation); Bill Mason, "The Garrisons of San Diego Presidio: 1770–1794," *Journal of San Diego History* 24, no. 4 (1978); Serra to Francisco Pangua, 10 January 1775, in *WJS*, 2:213–15; Sherburne F. Cook, *The Population of the California Indians, 1769–1970* (Berkeley: University of California Press, 1976), 1–43; Katharine Luomala, "Tipai and Ipai," in *Handbook of North American Indians: California*, ed. Robert F. Heizer (Washington, DC: Smithsonian Institution, 1978), 8:596.

12. Before the beginning of 1776, the Spanish baptized a minimum of 1,544 Indians from Alta California. In San Diego, the baptism, marriage, and death registers were destroyed in the uprising and later re-created by the missionaries from memory. The data therefore must be read with this important caveat in mind. Fernando de Rivera y Moncada, *Diario del Capitán Comandante Fernando de Rivera y Moncada*, ed. Ernest J. Burros (Madrid: Ediciones José Porrúa Turanzas, 1977), 232–33 (quotation); Huntington Library, Early California Population Project Database, 2006; Zephyrin Engelhardt, *San Diego Mission* (San Francisco: James H. Barry, 1920), 39. For a brief sketch of Rivera's life, see Ernest J. Burrus, "Rivera y Moncada, Explorer and Military Commander of Both Californias, in the Light of His Diary and Other Contemporary Documents," *Hispanic American Historical Review* 50, no. 4 (1970): 682–92.

13. Serra to Antonio María de Bucareli, 31 May 1773, in *WJS*, 1:367; Serra to Marqués de Croix, 18 June 1771, in *WJS*, 1:209 (quotation).

14. Steven W. Hackel, *Children of Coyote, Missionaries of Saint Francis: Indian-Spanish Relations in Colonial California, 1769–1850* (Chapel Hill: University of North Carolina Press, 2005), 65–80. Livestock were numerous in San Diego. See Serra to Bucareli, 5 February 1775, in *WJS*, 2:227; and Francisco Palóu, *Historical Memoirs of New California*, ed. Herbert Eugene Bolton (New York: Russell and Russell, 1966), 3:216–17. For a different take on Indian motives for joining Franciscan missions, see Robert H. Jackson and Edward Castillo, *Indians, Franciscans, and Spanish Colonization: The Impact of the Mission System on the California Indians* (Albuquerque: University of New Mexico Press, 1995), 107–8. On California Indian subsistence practices: M. Kat Anderson, *Tending the Wild: Native American Knowledge and the Management of California's Natural Resources* (Berkeley: University of California Press, 2005). On San Diego's food shortage: Luis Jayme to Serra, 3 April 1773, in Engelhardt, *San Diego Mission*, 54–56; Serra to Bucareli, 5 February 1775, in *WJS*, 2:229; Engelhardt, *San Diego Mission*, 43; Pedro Font, *With Anza to California, 1775–1776: The Journal of Pedro Font, O.F.M.*, trans. and ed. Alan K. Brown (Norman, OK: Arthur H. Clark, 2011), 181, 189.

15. Engelhardt, *San Diego Mission*, 49n8; Palóu, *Historical Memoirs*, 1:309–10.

16. The following account is based on Vicente Fuster to Serra, 28 November 1775, in *WJS*, 2:449–58; José Francisco Ortega to Juan Bautista de Anza, 30 November 1775, pp. 2–8, C-A 15, Archives of California, Bancroft Library, UC Berkeley; and Joseph Francisco de Ortega, "Diligencias," 1 February 1776, in Rivera, *Diario del Capitán*, 436–39. The mission buildings are described in Engelhardt, *San Diego Mission*, 56–57.

17. Ortega to Juan Bautista de Anza, 30 November 1775, pp. 2–8, C-A 15, Archives of California, Bancroft Library, UC Berkeley; Francis F. Guest, *Fermín Francisco de Lasuén (1736–1803): A Biography* (Washington, DC: Academy of American Franciscan History, 1973), 89; Bancroft, *History of California*, 1:252.

18. Serra to Bucareli, 15 December 1775, in *WJS*, 2:405.

19. George Washington, "General Orders," 5 November 1775, in *The Papers of George Washington: Digital Edition*, ed. Theodore J. Crackel (Charlottesville: University Press of Virginia, 2008).

20. Ortega, "Diligencias," 441.
21. Ibid., 446.
22. Ibid., 446–47.
23. Ibid., 450–52.
24. Ibid., 460, 462.
25. Ibid., 463–72 (quotations on pp. 471–72); Francisco de Lasuén to Pangua, 1 January 1776, no. 307, part 1, carton 9, item 97, folder 2, HEB.
26. Ortega, "Diligencias," 475.
27. Ibid., 478–79.
28. Lasuén to Pangua, 1 January 1776, no. 307, part 1, carton 9, item 97, folder 2, HEB.
29. Rivera, *Diario del Capitán*, 216. The "ley de Bayona" was used in California missions on more than one occasion. See Eulalia Pérez, "An Old Woman and Her Recollections," in *Testimonios: Early California through the Eyes of Women, 1815–1848*, trans. Rose Marie Beebe and Robert M. Senkewicz (Berkeley, CA: Heyday, 2006), 109. The connection between campaign stocks and the "ley de bayona" is made in Martín Alonso, *Enciclopedia del idioma: Diccionario histórico y moderno de la Lengua Española (siglos XII al XX) etimológico, tecnológico, regional e hispanoamericano* (Madrid: Aguilar, 1982).
30. Florence Shipek, "California Indian Reactions to the Franciscans," *Americas* 41, no. 4 (1985): 480–92.
31. Lasuén to Pangua, 1 January 1776, no. 307, part 1, carton 9, item 97, folder 2, HEB.
32. The face-to-face confrontation, known as the *careo*, was a common procedure and is still used in Spanish courts. Charles R. Cutter, *The Legal Culture of Northern New Spain, 1700–1810* (Albuquerque: University of New Mexico Press, 1995), 128; Ortega, "Complot de Indios," 13 January 1776, pp. 216–20, C-A 1, Archives of California, Bancroft Library, UC Berkeley ("Good God!"); Lasuén to Pangua, 1 January 1776, no. 307, part 1, carton 9, item 97, folder 2, HEB ("unthinkable deception").
33. Ortega, "Complot de Indios."
34. Ibid.; Font, *With Anza to California*, 194; Geiger, *Life and Times of Fray Junípero Serra*, 2:73.
35. Lasuén to Pangua, 1 January 1776, no. 307, part 1, carton 9, item 97, folder 2, HEB ("I was the one"); Font, *With Anza to California*, 195 ("one could imagine").
36. Font, *With Anza to California*, 195 ("welcome"), 199 ("handed a serving"); Lasuén to Pangua, 1 January 1776, no. 307, part 1, carton 9, item 97, folder 2, HEB; Rivera, *Diario del Capitán*, 227–28; Juan Bautista de Anza, "Anza's Diary of the Second Anza Expedition, 1775–1776," in *Anza's California Expeditions*, ed. Herbert Eugene Bolton (New York: Russell and Russell, 1930), 3:90–91, 95.
37. Rivera, *Diario del Capitán*, 227–28 ("got a good dusting"), 230 ("Although heathens"), 298 ("got a scrubbing"). I am indebted to Oscar Chamosa and the late David J. Weber and Alan K. Brown for clarifying Rivera's obscure phrase "aunque salvajes, se curan."
38. Font, *With Anza to California*, 200.
39. Vicente Fuster to Pangua, 22 May 1776, no. 369, part 1, carton 9, item 97, folder 2, HEB; the story of Rivera's excommunication is narrated in Geiger, *Life and Times of Fray Junípero Serra*, 2:88–90.
40. Rivera, "Declaración de un indio," 5 June 1776, pp. 220–22, C-A 1, Archives of California, Bancroft Library, UC Berkeley.
41. Bucareli to Gálvez, 27 August 1776, in *Anza's California Expeditions*, 5:350–51; Rivera to Pangua, 18 May 1776, in *Diario del Capitán*, 2:418–19; Serra to Rivera, 5 October 1776, in *WJS*, 3:35–39; Bancroft, *History of California*, 1:302n8.
42. The register of burials reports that Diego was buried on September 24, 1778, but

according to Serra, he died on that day and was buried a day later. San Diego death register, no. 42, the Huntington Library, Early California Population Project Database, 2006; Serra to Bucareli, 4 October 1778, in *WJS*, 3:263.

43. Miguel Costansó, "Diary," *Publications of the Academy of Pacific Coast History* 2 (1911): 266.

CHAPTER THREE—FIRST CONTACT:
COLONIZING SAN FRANCISCO

1. Javier Portús, *The Spanish Portrait: From El Greco to Picasso* (Madrid: Museo Nacional del Prado, 2004), 246; *Trazos de las luces: Dibujos españoles del siglo XVIII* (Madrid: José Manuel de la Mano Galería de Arte, 2002), 51–52.

2. Lacy to Jerónimo Grimaldi, 22 October 1772, Estado, leg. 86B, no. 100, doc. 6, AGI.

3. Lacy to Grimaldi, 23 April 1773, Estado, leg. 86B, no. 100, doc. 7, AGI ("keep the deepest silence"); Lacy to Grimaldi, 11 May 1773, Estado, leg. 86B, no. 100, doc. 15, AGI ("because that country"); Lacy to Grimaldi, 23 April 1773, Estado, leg. 86B, no. 100, doc. 12, AGI ("The projects").

4. Lacy to Grimaldi, 23 April 1773, Estado, leg. 86B, no. 100, doc. 11, AGI; George Verne Blue, "A Rumor of an Anglo-Russian Raid on Japan, 1776," *Pacific Historical Review* 8, no. 4 (1939): 453–63. In 1781, a well-placed English merchant would, in fact, devise a "plan for an alliance with Russia, in order to carry on the American War." The plan, in short, was to divide the Americas between Russia and Britain, crippling Spain and France and ending the colonial rebellion on the Atlantic Coast. R. A. Humphreys, "Richard Oswald's Plan for an English and Russian Attack on Spanish America, 1781–1782," *Hispanic American Historical Review* 18, no. 1 (1938): 95–101.

5. Rafael Verger to the viceroy, 25 December 1772, in *Who Discovered the Golden Gate: The Explorers' Own Accounts*, ed. Frank M. Stanger and Alan K. Brown (San Mateo, CA: San Mateo County Historical Association, 1969), 129 ("We cannot but fear" and "possess themselves"); Juan Crespí to Verger, 23 December 1772, part 1, carton 9, item 97, folder 1, HEB; Alan K. Brown, introduction to Pedro Font, *With Anza to California, 1775–1776: The Journal of Pedro Font, O.F.M.*, ed. and trans. Alan K. Brown (Norman, OK: Arthur H. Clark, 2011), 21 ("prudent and zealous"), 25–26.

6. Font, *With Anza to California*, 176 ("YEAR 1776"); George Washington, "General Orders," 1 January 1776, in *The Papers of George Washington: Digital Edition*, ed. Theodore J. Crackel (Charlottesville: University Press of Virginia, 2008) ("in every point of View").

7. Font, *With Anza to California*, 243, 248 ("The whole thing," "very dirty," and "somewhat roomy"); Serra to Antonio María de Bucareli, 21 May 1773, in *WJS*, 1:353 ("an entrance"); Juan Bautista de Anza, "Anza's Diary of the Second Anza Expedition, 1775–1776," in *Anza's California Expeditions*, ed. Herbert Eugene Bolton (New York: Russell and Russell, 1930), 3:119 ("they like").

8. Font, *With Anza to California*, 259, 262 (quotation); Randall Milliken, *A Time of Little Choice: The Disintegration of Tribal Culture in the San Francisco Bay Area, 1769–1810* (Menlo Park, CA: Ballena, 1995), 3; Barbara Bocek, "Prehistoric Settlement Pattern and Social Organization on the San Francisco Peninsula, California," in *Between Bands and States*, ed. Susan A. Gregg (Carbondale: Southern Illinois University, 1991), 58–88; Catherine A. Callaghan, "The Riddle of Rumsen," *International Journal of American Linguistics* 58, no. 1 (1992): 36–48.

9. Font, *With Anza to California*, 262–63; Junípero Serra, "Memorandum," 22 June 1774, in *WJS*, 2:87 (quotation). See also Francisco Palóu, *Relación histórica de la vida y apostólicas*

tareas del Venerable Padre Fray Junípero Serra (Mexico City: Don Felipe de Zúñiga y Onit-veros, 1787), 105–7.

10. Font, *With Anza to California*, 264–67, 268 ("long-bearded chief"), 269 ("quite ugly" and "a good, developed mission").

11. Ibid., 274 (quotation); Milliken, *Time of Little Choice*, 19–20; Greg Gaar and Ryder W. Miller, *San Francisco: A Natural History* (Charleston, SC: Arcadia, 2006), 11–20.

12. Font, *With Anza to California*, 274 ("a wonder"), 285 ("quite attentive" and "They would be easy to convert"), 286–87 ("saddened," "quiet and attentive," and "struck with wonder"); Anza, "Anza's Diary," 129 ("numerous and docile" and "with great pleasure"), 131–32 ("very friendly").

13. Font, *With Anza to California*, 287–90 ("a great deal"); Anza, "Anza's Diary," 135–36 ("fled").

14. Font, *With Anza to California*, 298–99 (quotation), 302–3.

15. Ibid., 309–11.

16. Ibid., 313 ("boundless"), 320–24, 326 ("like a deer"), 328.

17. George Ezra Dane and Francisco Palóu, "The Founding of the Presidio and Mission of Our Father Saint Francis," *California Historical Society Quarterly* 14, no. 2 (1935): 104; Francisco Palóu, "Palóu's Account of the Founding of San Francisco, 1776," in *Anza's California Expeditions*, ed. Herbert Eugene Bolton (New York: Russell and Russell, 1930), 3:387–89.

18. Miguel Costansó, "Diary," *Publications of the Academy of Pacific Coast History* 2 (1911): 257 ("with great affability"), 259 ("best disposition"); Juan Crespí, *A Description of Distant Roads: Original Journals of the First Expedition into California, 1769–1770*, ed. and trans. Alan K. Brown (San Diego, CA: San Diego State University Press, 2001), 521R ("very friendly" and "they had always"), 581M ("a great deal"), 585M ("anxious"), 593R ("a great many").

19. Vicente de Santa María, *The First Spanish Entry into San Francisco Bay*, ed. John Galvin (San Francisco: J. Howell, 1971), 41 ("We summoned"), 57 ("in great delight"), 59 ("Give me a light" and "marvelling"). Randall Milliken suggests that the *San Carlos* made contact with the Huimens, who spoke Coast Miwok but communicated with the Spanish in Costanoan. Milliken, *Time of Little Choice*, 46.

20. Crespí, *Description of Distant Roads*, 535M ("not in the mood"); Costansó, "Diary," 245 ("amazed" and "had no notice"), 273 ("evil disposition" and "very badly").

21. Crespí, *Description of Distant Roads*, 545M, 551M; Costansó, "Diary," 261–63; Crespí to Palóu, 6 February 1770, part 1, carton 7, item 90, folder 18, HEB.

22. Eric Brandan Blind et al., "El Presidio de San Francisco: At the Edge of Empire," *Historical Archaeology* 38, no. 3 (2004): 140.

23. Palóu, "Palóu's Account," 393–95 ("joy and happiness"), 401 ("The only ones").

24. Fernando de Rivera y Moncada, *Diario del Capitán Comandante Fernando de Rivera y Moncada*, ed. Ernest J. Burros (Madrid: Ediciones José Porrúa Turanzas, 1977), 102 (quotation), 114–15, 124–25, 219; Font, *With Anza to California*, 313–14, 321–22.

25. Francisco Tomás Hermenegildo Garcés, *On the Trail of a Spanish Pioneer*, ed. and trans. Elliot Coues (New York: F. P. Harper, 1900), 1:287.

26. Steven W. Hackel, *Children of Coyote, Missionaries of Saint Francis: Indian-Spanish Relations in Colonial California, 1769–1850* (Chapel Hill: University of North Carolina Press, 2005), 99–101, 113–18; Susan E. Klepp, "Seasoning and Society: Racial Differences in Mortality in Eighteenth-Century Philadelphia," *William and Mary Quarterly* 51, no. 3 (1994): 504.

27. Buenaventura Sitjar, *Vocabulario de la lengua de los naturales de la misión de San Antonio,*

Alta California (New York: Cramoisy, 1861), 23, 34; Rivera, *Diario del Capitán*, 180–83 (quotation).

28. Palóu stated that the Yelamus moved across the bay to escape their traditional enemies down the peninsula, but it seems likely that the Spanish were equally if not more responsible for the flight. Until the arrival of the Spanish, the Yelamus had presumably successfully fended off their enemies for decades. Palóu, "Palóu's Account," 402–5; Rivera, *Diario del Capitán*, 332–33; Milliken, *Time of Little Choice*, 68–69; Francisco Moraga, 24 June 1777, no. 7, San Francisco de Asis Mission, Libros de Bautismos. Original in the Chancery Archives, Archdiocese of San Francisco.

29. Font, *With Anza to California*, 180 (quotation); Terry L. Jones and L. Mark Raab, "The Rediscovery of California Prehistory," in *Prehistoric California: Archaeology and the Myth of Paradise*, ed. L. Mark Raab and Terry L. Jones (Salt Lake City: University of Utah Press, 2004), 1–11; Jack M. Broughton, "Prehistoric Human Impacts on California Birds: Evidence from the Emeryville Shellmound Avifauna," *Ornithological Monographs* 56 (2004): iii–90; Jack M. Broughton, "Declines in Mammalian Foraging Efficiency during the Late Holocene, San Francisco Bay, California," *Journal of Anthropological Archaeology* 13, no. 4 (1994): 371–401; Jack M. Broughton, "Widening Diet Breadth, Declining Foraging Efficiency, and Prehistoric Harvest Pressure: Ichthyofaunal Evidence from the Emeryville Shellmound, California," *Antiquity* 71, no. 274 (1997): 845–62; Dwight D. Simons, "Prehistoric Mammal Exploitation in the San Francisco Bay Area," in *Essays on the Prehistory of Maritime California*, ed. Terry L. Jones (Davis, CA: Center for Archaeological Research, 1992), 73–102.

30. Resource intensification occurred over several thousand years, and there is some evidence that population pressure moderated in the sixteenth century, perhaps because of the introduction of Old World epidemics. Any improvements in recent centuries, however, were more than offset by the destruction of local food sources by Spanish livestock. Mark E. Basgall, "Resource Intensification among Hunter-Gatherers: Acorn Economies in Prehistoric California," *Research in Economic Anthropology* 9 (1987): 21–52; E. Breck Parkman, "The Bedrock Milling Station," in *The Ohlone Past and Present: Native Americans of the San Francisco Bay Region*, ed. Lowell John Bean (Menlo Park, CA: Ballena, 1994), 43–63; Francis Ivanhoe and Philip W. Chu, "Cranioskeletal Size Variation in San Francisco Bay Prehistory: Relation to Calcium Deficit in the Reconstructed High-Seafoods Diet and Demographic Stress," *International Journal of Osteoarchaeology* 6, no. 4 (1996): 346–81; Broughton, "Prehistoric Human Impacts"; Terry L. Jones and Jennifer A. Ferneau, "Deintensification along the Central Coast," in *Catalysts to Complexity: Late Holocene Societies of the California Coast*, ed. Jon M. Erlandson and Terry L. Jones (Los Angeles: Cotsen Institute of Archaeology, University of California, 2002), 205–32. For circumstantial evidence of epidemics in sixteenth-century California, see William Preston, "Serpent in Eden: Dispersal of Foreign Diseases into Pre-mission California," *Journal of California and Great Basin Anthropology* 18, no. 1 (1996): 2–37; and Jon M. Erlandson and Kevin Bartoy, "Cabrillo, the Chumash, and Old World Diseases," *Journal of California and Great Basin Anthropology* 17, no. 2 (1995): 153–73. For a view that the California environment was more bountiful than suggested by the literature on resource intensification, see Kent G. Lightfoot and Otis Parrish, *California Indians and Their Environment: An Introduction* (Berkeley: University of California Press, 2009); and, especially, M. Kat Anderson, *Tending the Wild: Native American Knowledge and the Management of California's Natural Resources* (Berkeley: University of California Press, 2005). For a criticism of that position, see Jones and Raab, "Rediscovery of California Prehistory."

31. Robert Jurmain, "Paleoepidemiology of a Central California Prehistoric Population from

CA-Ala-329: Dental Disease," *American Journal of Physical Anthropology* 81, no. 3 (1990): 333–42; Robert Jurmain, "Paleoepidemiology of a Central California Prehistoric Population from CA-Ala-329: Degenerative Disease," *American Journal of Physical Anthropology* 83, no. 1 (1990): 83–94; Phillip L. Walker, Patricia Lambert, and Michael J. DeNiro, "The Effects of European Contact on the Health of Alta California Indians," in *Columbian Consequences: Archaeological and Historical Perspectives on the Spanish Borderlands West*, ed. David Hurst Thomas (Washington, DC: Smithsonian Institution Press, 1989), 1:349–64; Gary D. Richards, "Human Osteological Remains from CA-SCL-294, a Late Period and Protohistoric Site, San Jose, Santa Clara County, California," in *Human Skeletal Biology: Contributions to the Understanding of California's Prehistoric Populations*, ed. Gary D. Richards (Salinas, CA: Coyote, 1988), 97–178; Irina Nechayev, "A Bioarchaeological Study of Health in the Prehistoric Population from CA-ALA-329" (master's thesis, San Jose State University, 2007); Phillip L. Walker et al., "The Causes of Porotic Hyperostosis and Cribra Orbitalia: A Reappraisal of the Iron-Deficiency-Anemia Hypothesis," *American Journal of Physical Anthropology* 139, no. 2 (2009): 109–25.

32. Anderson, *Tending the Wild*, 135; Dane and Palóu, "Founding of the Presidio," 109.

33. Anza, "Anza's Diary," 129 ("a step outside"); Font, *With Anza to California*, 265, 268 ("very fierce"), 269, 306 ("smelled like warfare").

34. Richards, "Human Osteological Remains"; Randall Milliken et al., "Punctuated Culture Change in the San Francisco Bay Area," in *California Prehistory: Colonization, Culture, and Complexity*, ed. Terry L. Jones and Kathryn A. Klar (Lanham, MD: AltaMira, 2007), 113–14; Robert Jurmain et al., "Paleoepidemiology Patterns of Interpersonal Aggression in a Prehistoric Central California Population from CA-ALA-329," *American Journal of Physical Anthropology* 139, no. 4 (2009): 462–73.

35. Francisco Moraga, 24 June 1777, no. 7, San Francisco de Asis Mission, Libros de Bautismos. Original in the Chancery Archives, Archdiocese of San Francisco.

36. Catherine A. Callaghan, *Plains Miwok Dictionary* (Berkeley: University of California Press, 1984), 20 (*beeswax*), 28 (*dog*), 43 (*iron*), 80 (*ax*), 82 (*orange*), 100 (*mule*), 32 (*chicken*), 51 (*drunkard*), 54 (*devil*), 61 (*fever*), 147 (*work*); Howard Berman, review of *Plains Miwok Dictionary*, by Catherine A. Callaghan, *International Journal of American Linguistics* 52, no. 3 (1986): 307 (*rifle* and *soldiers*). At least one Costanoan word entered Spanish and eventually English. *Abalone* is derived from the Costanoan language of Rumsen. *Spanish Word Histories and Mysteries: English Words That Come from Spanish* (New York: Houghton Mifflin, 2007), 1–2. See also Paul V. Kroskrity and Gregory A. Reinhardt, "On Spanish Loans in Western Mono," *International Journal of American Linguistics* 51, no. 2 (1985): 231–37.

37. The missions in the San Francisco Bay Area were even more deadly than their counterparts elsewhere in Alta and Baja California. Robert H. Jackson, "The Dynamic of Indian Demographic Collapse in the San Francisco Bay Missions, Alta California, 1776–1840," *American Indian Quarterly* 16, no. 2 (1992): 141–56; Adele Ogden, "Russian Sea-Otter and Seal Hunting on the California Coast," *California Historical Society Quarterly* 12, no. 3 (1933): 221.

38. Statistics from Milliken, *Time of Little Choice*, 266.

39. Bernard E. Bobb, *The Viceregency of Antonio María Bucareli in New Spain, 1771–1779* (Austin: University of Texas Press, 1962), 9–10.

40. Maynard J. Geiger, *The Life and Times of Fray Junípero Serra* (Washington, DC: Academy of American Franciscan History, 1959), 1:356–57.

41. Michael E. Thurman, "The Establishment of the Department of San Blas and Its Initial Naval Fleet: 1767–1770," *Hispanic American Historical Review* 43, no. 1 (1963): 76;

Herbert Eugene Bolton, *Outpost of Empire: The Story of the Founding of San Francisco* (New York: Knopf, 1931), 28. The history of the port is told in Michael E. Thurman, *The Naval Department of San Blas: New Spain's Bastion for Alta California and Nootka, 1767 to 1798* (Glendale, CA: Arthur H. Clark, 1967).

42. Crespí, *Description of Distant Roads*, 251; Maynard Geiger, "Fray Rafael Verger, O.F.M., and the California Mission Enterprise," *Southern California Quarterly* 49, no. 2 (1967): 223; Frank M. Stanger and Alan K. Brown, *Who Discovered the Golden Gate? The Explorers' Own Accounts, How They Discovered a Hidden Harbor and at Last Found Its Entrance* (San Mateo, CA: San Mateo County Historical Association, 1969), 30–31 ("sad ship"); Thurman, "Establishment of the Department of San Blas," 73–76 ("new and beautiful").

43. Missions became more self-reliant in the 1780s and 1790s. See Steven H. Hackel, "Land, Labor, and Production: The Colonial Economy of Spanish and Mexican California," *California History* 76, nos. 2–3 (1997): 111–46; Serra to Bucareli, 22 April 1773, in *WJS*, 1:333–35; Serra, "Memorandum," 20 June 1771, in *WJS*, 1:227–35; Mario Hernández Sánchez-Barba, *La última expansion Española en América* (Madrid: Instituto de estudios politicos, 1957), 273 ("condemned"); Serra to Bucareli, 22 April 1773, in *WJS*, 1:321 ("maggoty" and "the most basic").

44. Serra to Francisco Pangua, 13 April 1776, in *WJS*, 2:419 (quotation); Felipe de Neve to Bucareli, 6 June 1777, Archivo General de la Nación, Provincias Internas, vol. 121, exp. 11, Bancroft Library, UC Berkeley; Serra to Bucareli, 13 March 1773, in *WJS*, 1:323.

45. Serra to Bucareli, 13 March 1773, in *WJS*, 1:299.

CHAPTER FOUR—ACROSS THE COLORADO PLATEAU

1. Bernard E. Bobb, *The Viceregency of Antonio María Bucareli in New Spain* (Austin: University of Texas Press, 1962), 30 (quotation); Charles E. Chapman, *The Founding of Spanish California: The Northwestward Expansion of New Spain, 1687–1783* (New York: Macmillan, 1916), 237; David J. Weber, *The Spanish Frontier in North America* (New Haven, CT: Yale University Press, 1992), 204–35. See also Pekka Hämäläinen, *The Comanche Empire* (New Haven, CT: Yale University Press, 2008).

2. One of Spain's foremost military strategists had successfully employed the cordon in Portugal and Sardinia. Mary Lu Moore, Delmar L. Beene, and Hugo O'Conor, "The Interior Provinces of New Spain: The Report of Hugo O'Conor, January 30, 1776," *Arizona and the West* 13, no. 3 (1971): 278 ("sea to sea"); Bobb, *Viceregency*, 31 ("Not everything"); Luis Arnal, "El sistema presidial en el septentrión novohispano, evolución y estrategias de poblamiento," *Scripta Nova: Revista Electrónica de Geografía y Ciencias Sociales* 10, no. 218 (1 August 2006).

3. The College of San Fernando supervised missions in Baja California until they were turned over to Dominicans in 1772. Verger was guardian of the college from 1770 to 1774 and again from 1777 to 1780. Maynard Geiger, "The Internal Organization and Activities of San Fernando College, Mexico (1734–1858)," *Americas* 6, no. 1 (1949): 3–31; Maynard Geiger, "Fray Rafael Verger, O.F.M., and the California Mission Enterprise," *Southern California Quarterly* 49, no. 2 (1967): 205–31; Chapman, *Founding of Spanish California*, 104, 127.

4. Marion A. Habig, "The Franciscan Provinces of Spanish North America [Continued]," *Americas* 1, no. 2 (1944): 215–30; Ramón A. Gutiérrez, *When Jesus Came, the Corn Mothers Went Away: Marriage, Sexuality, and Power in New Mexico, 1500–1846* (Stanford, CA: Stanford University, 1991), 39–142; Jim Norris, *After "The Year Eighty": The Demise of*

Franciscan Power in Spanish New Mexico (Albuquerque: University of New Mexico Press, 2000), 145, 152.

5. It was even suggested that Chinese goods could be imported to New Mexico through California. Chapman, *Founding of Spanish California*, 265–66, 271, 284, 366; Francisco Atanasio Domínguez, "Instructions," in *The Missions of New Mexico, 1776: A Description by Fray Francisco Atanasio Domínguez*, trans. Eleanor B. Adams and Angelico Chavez (Albuquerque: University of New Mexico Press, 1956), xxi ("both Majesties"); Serra to Antonio María Bucareli, 13 March 1773, in *Writings of Junípero Serra*, ed. Antonine Tibesar (Washington, DC: Academy of American Franciscan History, 1955–1966), 1:299 ("assuring a harvest").

6. Francisco Atanasio Domínguez to Isidro Murillo, 4 November 1775, in *Missions of New Mexico*, 270.

7. I am excluding the population of El Paso, though it was administratively part of New Mexico. Domínguez, "A Description of New Mexico," in *Missions of New Mexico*, 39–40 ("quasi-street" and "mournful"); Bernardo de Miera, "Plano geographico de la tierra descubierta nuevamente," Additional Manuscripts, 17661-D, British Library ("destroyed many Nations"); Alicia V. Tjarks, "Demographic, Ethnic and Occupational Structure of New Mexico, 1790," *Americas* 35, no. 1 (1978): 61. The Comanche expansion is described in Hämäläinen, *Comanche Empire*. For a concise introduction to the Pueblo Revolt of 1680, see Andrew L. Knaut, *The Pueblo Revolt of 1680: Conquest and Resistance in Seventeenth-Century New Mexico* (Norman: University of Oklahoma Press, 1995).

8. Domínguez to Murillo, 29 July 1776, in *Missions of New Mexico*, 282.

9. Francisco Silvestre Vélez de Escalante's proper last name is Vélez, but place names and books in the United States use Escalante, as I do here. Martín González de la Vara, "La visita eclesiástica de Francisco Atanasio Domínguez al Nuevo México y su relación," *Estudios de Historia Novohispana* 10 (1991): 267–88; Eleanor B. Adams, "Fray Francisco Atanasio Dominguez and Fray Silvestre Velez de Escalante," *Utah Historical Quarterly* 44, no. 1 (1976): 40–58.

10. Miera, "Mapa de esta Parta Interna de la Nueba Mexico," negative no. 135340, photo archives, Palace of the Governors, Santa Fe, New Mexico (quotation). On myths: Richard V. Francaviglia, *Mapping and Imagination in the Great Basin: A Cartographic History* (Reno: University of Nevada Press, 2005), 32–33; for Quivira, see Joseph P. Sánchez, *Explorers, Traders, and Slavers: Forging the Old Spanish Trail, 1678–1850* (Salt Lake City: University of Utah Press, 1997), 7–12; José M. Espinosa, "The Legend of Sierra Azul," *New Mexico Historical Review* 9, no. 2 (1934): 113–58; and George P. Hammond, "The Search for the Fabulous in the Settlement of the Southwest," in *New Spain's Far Northern Frontier*, ed. David J. Weber (Albuquerque: University of New Mexico Press, 1979), 17–34.

11. Escalante to Fernando Antonio Gómez, 18 August 1775, in *Missions of New Mexico*, 302–5 ("paisano" and "clever enough"); Escalante to Murillo, 29 July 1776, in *Missions of New Mexico*, 307–8; Donna Pierce, "The Life of an Artist: The Case of Captain Bernardo Miera y Pacheco," in *Transforming Images: New Mexican Santos in In-between Worlds*, ed. Claire Farago and Donna Pierce (University Park: Pennsylvania State University Press, 2006), 134–37; Mary Montano, *Tradiciones Nuevomexicanos: Hispano Arts and Culture of New Mexico* (Albuquerque: University of New Mexico Press, 2001), 33. On Miera's and Escalante's birthplaces: *Missions of New Mexico*, 345; and Adams, "Fray Francisco Atanasio Dominguez and Fray Silvestre Velez de Escalante," 40–46. Miera's life is chronicled in John L. Kessell, *Miera y Pacheco: A Renaissance Spaniard in Eighteenth-Century New Mexico* (Norman: University of Oklahoma Press, 2013).

12. Domínguez, "Description of New Mexico," 160 ("gossipy vulgar herd" and "not at all prepossessing"), 198 ("as seemly").

13. Peter Barber and Tom Harper, *Magnificent Maps: Power, Propaganda, and Art* (London: British Library, 2010), 14 (quotation). Miera's map exists in multiple copies and in three major variants or types, as outlined in Carl I. Wheat, *Mapping the Transmississipi West* (San Francisco: Institute of Historical Cartography, 1957–1963), 1:94–116. Since the publication of Wheat's book in 1957, another variant was discovered in the Beinecke Library, Yale University. Wheat suggests that type A is the earliest version and may be in Miera's hand, but Michael Frederick Weber shows convincingly that only the type C version in the British Library is in fact in Miera's hand. That map is likely the earliest extant as well. See Weber, "Tierra Incognita: The Spanish Cartography of the American Southwest, 1540–1803" (PhD dissertation, University of New Mexico, 1986), 184. Unless otherwise noted, all references to Miera's map in this chapter are to the one in his hand that resides at the British Library, Additional Manuscripts, 17661-D.

14. Domínguez, "Description of New Mexico," 126 ("idleness becomes"), 252–53, 259 ("weak, gamblers, liars").

15. A. M. C. Şengör suggests that Miera represented mesas first on his maps of the Domínguez-Escalante expedition. In fact, he did so earlier, in a 1758 map of New Mexico. The original map is now lost, but a tracing, made from an inferior photograph, appears in John L. Kessell, *Kiva, Cross, and Crown: The Pecos Indians and New Mexico, 1540–1840* (Albuquerque: University of New Mexico Press, 1987), 510–11; Şengör, *The Large-Wavelength Deformations of the Lithosphere: Materials for a History of the Evolution of Thought from the Earliest Times to Plate Tectonics* (Boulder, CO: Geological Society of America, 2003), 141–46.

16. Nowhere does the journal state explicitly that Lucrecio Muñiz had traveled through the region before, but Escalante's reference to "guides" suggests he had. *DEJ*, 11 ("the experts" and "lost the trail"), 19 ("well-used"), 22 ("put [their] trust").

17. Ibid., 22–24.

18. Uravan, which once produced uranium and vanadium for the Cold War, is now a ghost town and Superfund site.

19. *DEJ*, 26–27.

20. Ibid., 28.

21. Ibid., 38, 72.

22. Ibid., 39 (quotation), 41–42.

23. Ibid., 45.

24. Miera, "Plano geographico" (quotations); Hämäläinen, *Comanche Empire*, 44–88; *DEJ*, 46–47.

25. *DEJ*, 50–51.

26. More precisely, Atanasio stated that rivers up to and including the Colorado flowed into the Dolores. Today, we say that the Dolores empties into the Colorado, instead of the other way around. Ibid., 77.

27. Francaviglia, *Mapping and Imagination*, 6–7.

28. *DEJ*, 70–73.

29. Ibid., 67.

30. Ibid., 66 ("salvation of souls" and "single true God"), 67 ("wonderful docility"), 68 ("unutterable joy"). Native peoples sometimes associated European technology with a diffuse power possessed by colonists. See Evan Haefeli, "On First Contact and Apotheosis: Manitou and Men in North America," *Ethnohistory* 54, no. 3 (2007): 407–43; and Bruce M. White, "Encounters with Spirits: Ojibwa and Dakota Theories about the French and Their Merchandise," *Ethnohistory* 41, no. 3 (1994): 369–405.

31. Contrary to Miera's claim, Oñate was not the first European to discover the Río del Tizón, a name that the Spanish gave to the Colorado in the 1540s. *DEJ*, 71 ("narrow passage"); Miera to the king, 26 October 1777, in *Pageant in the Wilderness: The Story of the Escalante Expedition to the Interior Basin, 1776*, ed. Herbert Eugene Bolton (Salt Lake City: Utah State Historical Society, 1972), 245 ("very large and navigable" and "If it is as they say"); Miera, "Plano geographico" ("great width and depth").

32. Along the spine of the Rockies on his map, Miera wrote, "In the many rivers that arise from it, its waters empty into the two oceans, the South Sea and Gulf of Mexico." Perhaps he believed, as did some of his contemporaries, that the continent was shaped like a pyramid, with waters draining off the four sides. Miera, "Plano geographico" ("South Sea"); Miera to the king, 26 October 1777, in *Pageant in the Wilderness*, 245 ("In a short time"); Francaviglia, *Mapping and Imagination*, 56–58.

33. *DEJ*, 75 ("great heat"); Miera, "Plano geographico" ("Miera Lagoon"); Stephen Trimble, *The Sagebrush Ocean: A Natural History of the Great Basin* (Reno: University of Nevada Press, 1989), 50–51, 83.

34. *DEJ*, 78; C. Gregory Crampton and Gloria G. Griffen, "The San Buenaventura, Mythical River of the West," *Pacific Historical Review* 25, no. 2 (1956): 163–71.

35. Zuni blue may appear in the rivers in Miera, "Mapa de esta Parta Interna." William Wroth, *Christian Images in Hispanic New Mexico: The Taylor Museum Collection of Santos* (Colorado Springs, CO: Taylor Museum, 1982), 51–52 (quotation); Pierce, "Life of an Artist," 134–37; and Charles M. Carrillo, "A Saint Maker's Palette," *Tradición Revista* 3, no. 1 (1998): 23–27. Regarding Miera's employment as a *santero* ("saint maker"), see Donna Pierce, "From New Spain to New Mexico: Art and Culture on the Northern Frontier," in *Converging Cultures: Art and Identity in Spanish America*, ed. Diana Fane (New York: Harry N. Abrams, 1996), 59–68.

36. *DEJ*, 108.

37. Bare-breasted women appear occasionally on eighteenth-century maps as symbolic representations of America, but ethnographic representations of nude women, especially those as carefully rendered as Miera's, are less common. Ibid., 91 ("what one cannot"), 100–101, 109 ("go after the flesh").

38. Ibid., 80 (quotation), 120.

39. Ibid., 83–85.

40. In a letter, Escalante had estimated that it was "at the very least" four hundred leagues, or one thousand miles, from Santa Fe to Monterey. Escalante to Gómez, 18 August 1775, in *Missions of New Mexico*, 302–5.

41. Domínguez to Murillo, 29 July 1776, in *Missions of New Mexico*, 281–86; Adams, "Fray Francisco Atanasio Dominguez and Fray Silvestre Velez de Escalante," 53 ("never seemed attainable"); *DEJ*, 87–89 ("grandiose dreams" and "very peevishly").

42. *DEJ*, 89–90.

43. As Ned Blackhawk recounts, the Southern Paiutes suffered tremendously at the hands of the Utes because of the Utes' equestrian advantage. Blackhawk, *Violence over the Land: Indians and Empires in the Early American West* (Cambridge, MA: Harvard University Press, 2006); *DEJ*, 91–93 ("ancient individual" on p. 93)

44. Miera, "Plano geographico" ("On the Mesa"); *DEJ*, 101 ("San Ángel").

45. *DEJ*, 102 ("begged"), 103 ("vague directions").

46. Miera placed the nightly camps on his map but did not draw the route itself. Miera, "Plano geographico" (quotation); *DEJ*, 112–21.

47. From the beginning, Escalante was skeptical that the expedition could reach Monterey. *DEJ*, 127 (quotation), 128; Domínguez to Murillo, 29 July 1776, in *Missions of New*

Mexico, 281–86; Adams, "Fray Francisco Atanasio Dominguez and Fray Silvestre Velez de Escalante," 53.

48. *DEJ,* 136–37.

49. Thomas Paine, *The American Crisis. Number I* (Norwich, CT: John Trumbull, 1776), 1.

50. Humboldt did not list Miera's map among his sources, but some details on his map—"el rastrillo" (which should be "el Castillo") on the Colorado, or "R. de las Piramides Sulfureas," for example—suggest he must have seen it. Regardless, he consulted the map of Miguel Costansó and Manuel Mascaró, which itself incorporated Miera's. Alexander von Humboldt, *Political Essay on the Kingdom of New Spain* (New York: I. Riley, 1811), 1:xvii–xviv; Pike, *Map of the Internal Provinces of New Spain* (n.p., 1807) (quotation). On Miera's influence, see Crampton and Griffen, "San Buenaventura"; and Francaviglia, *Mapping and Imagination.*

51. John Melish, *Map of the United States of America* (Philadelphia: J. Melish, 1816) ("Supposed Course"); Melish, *Map of the United States* (Philadelphia: James Finlayson, 1823) ("improved to 1823" and "Unexplored Country").

52. John Bidwell, "The First Emigrant Train to California," *Century Illustrated Magazine* 41, no. 1 (1890): 106–30.

53. Donald K. Grayson, *The Desert's Past: A Natural Prehistory of the Great Basin* (Washington, DC: Smithsonian Institution Press, 1993), 6–8 (quotations); Francaviglia, *Mapping and Imagination,* 82.

54. Drawing boundaries around Indian nations might be understood to reflect the recognition of native sovereignty, but Barbara Belyea sees them as "assertions of imperial and scientific authority." Belyea, "Inland Journeys, Native Maps," in *Cartographic Encounters: Perspectives on Native American Mapmaking and Map Use,* ed. G. Malcolm Lewis (Chicago: University of Chicago Press, 1998), 137–38; *DEJ,* 122 (quotation).

55. Wheat, *Mapping the Transmississippi West,* 1:121–24 (Spanish maps); Alexander von Humboldt, *A Map of New Spain* ([London]: Longman, Hurst, Rees, 1804); Melish, *Map of the United States* (1816).

56. K. T. Khlebnikov, *Colonial Russian America: Kyrill T. Khlebnikov's Reports, 1817–1832,* ed. and trans. Basil Dmytryshyn and E. A. P. Crownhart-Vaughan (Portland: Oregon Historical Society, 1976), 77, 116–17; K. T. Khlebnikov, *The Khlebnikov Archive: Unpublished Journals (1800–1837) and Travel Notes (1820, 1822, and 1824),* ed. Leonid Shur, trans. John Bisk (Anchorage: University of Alaska Press), 132, 151.

57. Khlebnikov, *Khlebnikov Archive,* 27–30; Khlebnikov, *Colonial Russian America,* 53.

PART TWO: THE CONTINENTAL DIVIDE—INTRODUCTION

1. Edward Gibbon wrote that the Treaty of Paris "regulates the fate of Europe." It did so for North America as well. Gibbon to his stepmother, 12 February 1763, in *Private Letters of Edward Gibbon, 1753–1794,* ed. Rowland E. Prothero (London: John Murray, 1896), 1:28–30.

2. The North American component of the Seven Years' War is narrated in Fred Anderson, *The Crucible of War: The Seven Years' War and the Fate of Empire in British North America, 1754–1766* (New York: Knopf, 2000).

3. Choiseul to Voltaire, 14 January 1760, and Choiseul to Voltaire, 22 April 1760, in *Choiseul et Voltaire,* ed. Pierre Calmettes (Paris: Plon-Nourrit, 1902), 55 ("I like my pleasure"), 71 ("delicious"); C. Port, *Le train de Maison du duc de Choiseul, 1763–1766* (Paris: Édouard Champion, [1920]), 18, 24, 61.

4. Didier Ozanam, "Política y Amistad: Choiseul y Grimaldi. Correspondencia Particular

Entre Ambos Ministros (1763–1770)," in *Actas del Congreso Internacional Sobre Carlos III y La Ilustración*, ed. Pablo Fernández Albaladejo (Madrid: Ministerio de Cultura, 1988), 1:213–37; William Coxe, *Memoirs of the Kings of Spain of the House of Bourbon*, 2nd ed. (London: Longman, Hurst, Rees, Orme, and Brown, 1815), 4:299 ("elegance"); Henry Swinburne, *Travels through Spain in the Years 1775 and 1776*, 2nd ed. (London: J. Davis, 1787), 2:136 ("meeting with numerous"); Gibbon to his stepmother, 12 February 1763, in *Private Letters of Edward Gibbon*, 1:28–30 ("magnificence" and "politeness & elegance").

5. Gibbon to his stepmother, 12 February 1763, in *Private Letters of Edward Gibbon*, 1:28–30 (quotations); Joan Evans, "The Embassy of the 4th Duke of Bedford to Paris, 1762–1763," *Archaeological Journal* 113 (1956): 137–56.

6. Choiseul to Caspar Joseph Solar de Breille, 25 May 1762, and the Earl of Egremont's memoir of 26 June 1762, in *Anglo-French Boundary Disputes in the West, 1749–1763*, ed. Theodore Calvin Pease (Springfield: Illinois State Historical Library, 1936), 432 ("indispensable"), 435 ("worth absolutely nothing"). The complex diplomatic process that led to a treaty in 1763 is summarized in Matt Schumann and Karl Schweizer, *The Seven Years War: A Transatlantic History* (London: Routledge, 2008), 187–226. It should be noted that preliminary terms had already been settled before Bedford set out for Paris to finalize the treaty. For a preeminent example of deception, see Theodore C. Pease, "The Mississippi Boundary of 1763: A Reappraisal of Responsibility," *American Historical Review* 40, no. 2 (1935): 278–286.

7. Memoir on the limits to assign to Louisiana, 10 August 1761, in *Anglo-French Boundary Disputes*, 354–56 (quotations); J. H. Parry, *The Age of Reconnaissance: Discovery, Exploration, and Settlement, 1450 to 1650* (Berkeley: University of California Press, 1963), 159–62.

8. Egremont's memoir of 26 June 1762, in *Anglo-French Boundary Disputes*, 436–37 ("keeping to its side" and "forestall all disputes"); Pease, "Mississippi Boundary of 1763," 280 ("mix'd and complicated"); Arthur S. Alton, "The Diplomacy of the Louisiana Cession," *American Historical Review* 36, no. 4 (1931): 718–19 ("I say, no"). On the cession of Louisiana, see also Paul W. Mapp, *The Elusive West and the Contest for Empire, 1713–1763* (Chapel Hill: University of North Carolina Press, 2011), 359–412.

9. Richard Neville to the Duke of Bedford, 16 February 1763, in *Correspondence of John, Fourth Duke of Bedford*, ed. Lord John Russell (London: Longman, Brown, Green, and Longmans, 1864), 3:199–203; Evans, "Embassy of the 4th Duke," 143–44.

10. Pease, *Anglo-French Boundary Disputes*, clvi.

11. *The Expediency of Securing Our American Colonies* (Edinburgh: n.p., 1763), 55.

12. Silas Deane to James Hogg, 2 November 1775, in *CRNC*, 10:300–304.

CHAPTER FIVE—A FOREST TRANSFORMED:
THE HUDSON'S BAY COMPANY AND CUMBERLAND HOUSE

1. Bryant Lillywhite, *London Coffee Houses* (London: Allen and Unwin, 1963), 9, 46 (quotation), 223, 369, 531, 619, 1473–75 (numbers refer to coffeehouse entries, not pages); John Feltham, *Picture of London for 1803* (London: R. Phillips, 1802), 349–56.

2. Marjorie Gordon Jackson, "The Beginning of British Trade at Michilimackinac," *Minnesota History* 11, no. 3 (1930): 237–39, 249.

3. Watson followed the path of Alexander Henry (the elder), who was in the business of furnishing the British army at Oswego and Montreal and smoothly transitioned to the Indian trade. "Watson, Sir Brook," *Appleton's Cyclopaedia of American Biography*, ed. James Grant Wilson and John Fiske (New York: Appleton, 1889), 6:390 (quotation); *Oxford Dictionary of National Biography*, "Watson, Sir Brook" http://www.oxforddnb.com/templates/

article.jsp?articleid=28829&back=, accessed September 2013; E. E. Rich, *History of the Hudson's Bay Company* (London: Hudson's Bay Record Society, 1959), 2:8.

4. R. M. Breckenridge, "Paper Currencies of New France," *Journal of Political Economy* 1, no. 3 (1893): 423–31; Phillip Lawson, *The Imperial Challenge: Quebec and Britain in the Age of the American Revolution* (Montreal: McGill-Queen's University Press, 1989), 93; Jackson, "Beginning of British Trade," 237–70.

5. On the "rush of the English into Rupert's Land," see Rich, *History of the Hudson's Bay Company*, 2:1–43.

6. Extract from a letter of Andrew Graham to the governor and committee of the Hudson's Bay Company, 26 August 1772, in *Documents Relating to the North West Company*, ed. W. S. Stewart (Toronto: Champlain Society, 1934), 42 (quotation). Rich describes the operation and impact of the "pedlers" in detail in *History of the Hudson's Bay Company*, vol. 2. See also Wayne Edson Stevens, *The Northwest Fur Trade, 1763–1800*, University of Illinois Studies in the Social Sciences, vol. 14, no. 3 (Urbana: University of Illinois, 1926).

7. Anthony Henday, *A Year Inland: The Journal of a Hudson's Bay Company Winterer*, ed. Barbara Belyea (Waterloo, ON: Wilfrid Laurier University Press, 2000), E.2/11, 30 May 1755, 189 ("are masters"); Keith R. Widder, "The French Connection: The Interior French and Their Role in French-British Relations in the Western Great Lakes Region, 1760–1775," in *The Sixty Years' War for the Great Lakes, 1754–1814*, ed. David Curtis Skaggs and Larry L. Nelson (East Lansing: Michigan State University Press, 2001), 134 ("adopted the very Principles").

8. Henley House was established inland on the Albany River in 1743 but had a sporadic existence and, as E. E. Rich explains, was founded for different reasons than those that spawned Cumberland House. Rich, *History of the Hudson's Bay Company*, 1:589 (quotation), 2:17–41; Introduction to E. E. Rich, ed., *Cumberland House Journals and Inland Journal, 1775–82* (London: Hudson's Bay Record Society, 1951–1952), 1:xxiv–xxv. Part of the drop in beaver purchases may have been due to the declining beaver population. Ann M. Carlos and Frank D. Lewis, "Indians, the Beaver, and the Bay: The Economics of Depletion in the Lands of the Hudson's Bay Company," *Journal of Economic History* 53, no. 3 (1993): 481.

9. Samuel Hearne, "Journal of a Journey Inland," in *Journals of Samuel Hearne and Philip Turnor*, ed. J. B. Tyrrell (Toronto: Champlain Society, 1934), 113–15.

10. Georges-Louis LeClerc, Comte de Buffon, *Natural History, General and Particular* (Edinburgh: William Creech, 1780–1785), 5:129–30 ("shrink and diminish," "timid and cowardly," "no vivacity," "organs of generation," and "small and feeble"); Buffon, *Barr's Buffon* (London: J. S. Barr, 1792), 6:291 ("dispersed, forlorn"), 6:292–93 ("state of nature," "prison," and "gloomy and melancholy"), 6:294 ("superior").

11. Andrew Graham, *Andrew Graham's Observations on Hudson's Bay, 1767–91*, ed. Glyndwr Williams (London: Hudson's Bay Record Society, 1969), 9–10; James Isham, *James Isham's Observations on Hudsons Bay, 1743*, ed. E. E. Rich (Toronto: Champlain Society, 1949), 148 ("woud puzle"); *The Wonders of Nature and Art* (Reading, England: C. Corbett, 1750), 4:173 ("Sagacity and Beauty" and "little Cities").

12. Graham, *Andrew Graham's Observations*, 9–10; Robert Beverley, *The History and Present State of Virginia* (London: R. Parker, 1705), 74–75.

13. Samuel Hearne, *A Journey from Prince of Wales's Fort, in Hudson's Bay, to the Northern Ocean* (London: A. Strahan and T. Cadell, 1795), 231.

14. Horace T. Martin, *Castorologia, or the History and Traditions of the Canadian Beaver* (Montreal: Drysdale, 1892), 2.

15. A. Radclyffe Dugmore, *The Romance of the Beaver, Being the History of the Beaver in the*

Western Hemisphere (Philadelphia: J. B. Lippincott, 1914), 1 ("to provide a book"), 8 ("afternoon tea"), 13 ("animated"), 66 ("in his lowest form").

16. Dugmore, *Romance of the Beaver*, 138.

17. Robert J. Naiman, Carol A. Johnston, and James C. Kelley, "Alteration of North American Streams by Beaver," *BioScience* 38, no. 11 (1988): 753.

18. Invoice to Robert Cary and Company, 10 July 1773, Founders Online, National Archives (http://founders.archives.gov/documents/Washington/02-09-02-0204-0002, ver. 2013-08-02) (quotation); Murray G. Lawson, *Fur: A Study in English Mercantilism* (Toronto: University of Toronto Press, 1943), appendices A, B, and G; Rich, *History of the Hudson's Bay Company*, 1:531; Madeleine Ginsburg, *The Hat: Trends and Traditions* (London: Barron's, 1990), 70–71.

19. Ginsburg, *The Hat*, 44.

20. William Shakespeare, *Henry IV*, Part 1, ed. M. A. Shaaber, in *William Shakespeare: The Complete Works*, ed. Alfred Harbage (1969; reprint, New York: Viking, 1986), 694.

21. Murray G. Lawson, *Fur*, 5; Samuel Pepys, 29 November 1763, in *The Diary of Samuel Pepys*, ed. Robert Latham and William Matthews (Berkeley: University of California Press, 1971), 4:400 (quotations).

22. Ginsburg, *The Hat*, 66; Barbara E. Lacey, *From Sacred to Secular: Visual Images in Early American Publications* (Newark: University of Delaware Press, 2007), 137.

23. Hearne, "Journal of a Journey Inland," 105.

24. Dale R. Russell, *Eighteenth-Century Western Cree and Their Neighbours*, Archaeological Survey of Canada, Mercury Series Paper 143 (Hull, QC: Canadian Museum of Civilization, 1991), 12–13; Arthur J. Ray, *Indians in the Fur Trade: Their Role as Trappers, Hunters, and Middlemen in the Lands Southwest of Hudson Bay, 1660–1870* (Toronto: University of Toronto Press, 1974), 87. In the hundred years before 1775, the HBC on average shipped only 480 trade guns annually to its posts. M. L. Brown, *Firearms in Colonial America: The Impact on History and Technology, 1492–1792* (Washington, DC: Smithsonian Institution Press, 1980), 156–57; Ray, *Indians in the Fur Trade*, 72–79; Henday, *Year Inland*, B.239/a/40, 16 October 1754, p. 108 (quotation). Belyea is rightly skeptical of drawing any firm conclusions from Anthony Henday's journal, given the contradictions among the four extant copies.

25. 11 July 1776, "A Journal of the Most Remarkable Transactions and Occurrences at York Fort from 27th August 1775 to 31st August 1776," B239/a/73, HBCA, reel 1M159.

26. Christopher Middleton, "The Effects of Cold," *Philosophical Transactions* 42 (1742–1743): 159–60.

27. Copy of a letter from Humphrey Marten to Thomas Hutchins, 19 March 1776, B239/b/36, HBCA, reel 1M255 ("shockingly cold"); copy of a letter from Samuel Hearne to Humphrey Marten, 20 March 1777, B239/b/37, HBCA, reel 1M255 ("pureness of the Air" and "Some of us"); copy of a letter from Hearne to Marten, 18 January 1778, B239/b/38, HBCA, reel 1M255 ("a foul ulcer," "very alarming," and "we may be greatly mistaken"); copy of a letter from Hearne to Marten, 6 March 1778, B239/b/38, HBCA, reel 1M255 ("spitting out").

28. Graham, *Andrew Graham's Observations*, 300 ("We think nothing"); Stuart Houston, Tim Ball, and Mary Houston, eds., *Eighteenth-Century Naturalists of Hudson Bay* (Montreal: McGill-Queen's University Press, 2003), 61; Hearne, "Journal of a Journey Inland," 139 ("froze to the Bone"), 144 ("lay open"); William Walker et al., "Journal of the Most Remarkable Transactions and Occurrences," in *Cumberland House Journals*, 223.

29. Walker et al., "Journal," 202–3; Alexander Henry, *Travels and Adventures in Canada and the Indian Territories* (New York: I. Riley, 1809), 266–71.

30. Copy of a letter from Marten to Hutchins, 19 March 1776, B239/b/36, HBCA, reel 1M255; Graham, *Andrew Graham's Observations*, 315; copy of a letter from Hutchins to Marten, 13 June 1776, B239/b/36, HBCA, reel 1M255; Isham, *James Isham's Observations*, 66 (quotation).

31. Copy of a letter from Hutchins to Marten, 23 June 1777, B239/b/37, HBCA, reel 1M255.

32. Hearne, "Journal of a Journey Inland," 136–37 ("entire famine"), 159; Samuel Hearne, "Journal of the Most Remarkable Transactions and Occurrences on a Journey from and to York Fort and at Cumberland House from 8th July 1775 to 26th October 1775," in *Journals of Samuel Hearne and Philip Turnor*, 190 (moose skins); Walker et al., "Journal," 110 ("having been almost Starved").

33. Walker et al., "Journal," 88 (quotation); copy of a letter from Marten to Hearne, 4 January 1777, B239/b/37, HBCA, reel 1M255 (provisions market); Ray, *Indians in the Fur Trade*, 133 (fire).

34. 8 and 11 July 1776, "A Journal of the Most Remarkable Transactions and Occurrences at York Fort from 27th August 1775 to 31st August 1776," B239/a/73, HBCA, reel 1M159 ("This I think"); Hearne, "Journal of the Most Remarkable Transactions," 193 ("very great dependance"); copy of instructions given by Marten to Joseph Hanson on his going to Cumberland House, n.d., B239/b/37, HBCA, reel 1M255 ("a Manly firmness").

35. Cocking, 6 July 1774 ("incessant requests"), 12 July 1774 ("obliged to dissemble"), 2 August 1774 ("It was their own choice"), 29 July 1774 ("It gives me much uneasiness"), 2 August 1774 ("We have indeed"), "A Journal of a Journey Inland with the Natives, Commencing 4th July, and Ending the 27th June 1775," B239/a/72, HBCA, reel 1M159.

36. Cocking, 10 August 1774 ("I am obliged," "where we may," and "If the Natives") and 8 June 1775 ("There will be" and "a Trader will be"), "A Journal of a Journey Inland with the Natives, Commencing 4th July, and Ending the 27th June 1775," B239/a/72, HBCA, reel 1M159.

37. Hearne, "Journal of the Most Remarkable Transactions," 171 ("private drinking bouts"); copy of a letter from Cocking to Marten, 3 September 1775, B239/b/36, HBCA, reel 1M255; copy of a letter from Hansom to Marten, 6 August 1777, B239/b/38, HBCA, reel 1M255 ("privately"); 14 September 1775 and 29 September 1775, "A Journal of the Most Remarkable Transactions and Occurrences at York Fort from 27th August 1775 to 31st August 1776," B239/a/73, HBCA, reel 1M159 ("starve by himself").

38. 29 September 1775 ("We, for want of strength," "and use him kindly," and "he hath much sway") and 14 June 1776 ("a fine parcel of Furs" and "This plainly shews"), "Journal of the Most Remarkable Transactions and Occurrences at York Fort from 27th August 1775 to 31st August 1776," B239/a/73, HBCA, reel 1M159.

39. John Entick, *A New and Accurate History and Survey of London, Westminster, Southwark, and Places Adjacent* (London: Edward and Charles Dilly, 1766), 4:297–98 ("a very fine brick building"); Shepard Krech, *The Ecological Indian: Myth and History* (New York: Norton, 1999), 174 ("The English have no sense").

40. Ray, *Indians in the Fur Trade*, chap. 3; Rich, *History of the Hudson's Bay Company, 1670–1870*, 2:47; Henday, *Year Inland*, E.2/11, 26 March 1755, p. 165, E.2/4, 16 May 1755, p. 182, and E.2/6, 8 April 1755, p. 168 (quotation); ibid., E.2/4, 24 April 1755, pp. 172–73.

41. Isham, *James Isham's Observations*, 131 ("tilterkin"); Henday, *Year Inland*, E.2/6, 27 April 1755, p. 173 ("worse than cold weather"), B.239/1/40, 1 May 1755, p. 175; C. Douglas Ellis, ed., *Cree Legends and Narratives from the West Coast of James Bay* (Winnipeg: University of Manitoba Press, 1995), 151–53.

42. Henday, *Year Inland*, E.2/6, 12 May 1755, p. 179, E.2/4, 15 May 1755, p. 181, and E.2/4,

1 June 1775, p. 191; Graham, *Andrew Graham's Observations*, 256–57; Ray, *Indians in the Fur Trade*, 69.

43. Cocking, 27 March 1773 ("troublesome"), 26–27 May 1773 ("through fear" and "as they had got"), 27 August 1774, 29 August 1774 ("obliged"), 28 September 1774, and 1 April 1775, "A Journal of a Journey Inland with the Natives, Commencing 4th July, and Ending the 27th June 1775," B239/a/72, HBCA, reel 1M159; Henry, *Travels and Adventures*, 259 ("curbed their indignation").

44. Henday, *Year Inland*, B.239/a/40, 19 and 20 June 1755, p. 197.

45. Graham, *Andrew Graham's Observations*, 315–24.

46. Extract from a letter of Andrew Graham to the governor and committee of the Hudson's Bay Company, 26 August 1772, in *Documents Relating to the North West Company*, 42; Isham, *James Isham's Observations*, 48 ("This tobacco has a bad taste" and "I will ope'n another"), 54 ("Your tobacco is bad"); Rich, *History of the Hudson's Bay Company*, 1:512 ("so Nice and Difficul").

47. Hearne, "Journal of a Journey Inland," 122, 160; Hearne, "Journal of the Most Remarkable Transactions," 188.

48. The beaver population around York Fort declined significantly in the first half of the eighteenth century, as Ann M. Carlos and Frank D. Lewis show. But it is not clear how far that decline reached into the York Fort hinterlands. Indians may have been reassured by plentiful beaver populations farther west. Carlos and Lewis, "Indians, the Beaver, and the Bay," 465–94; Hearne, "Journal of a Journey Inland," 156–57 (quotation); Rich, *History of the Hudson's Bay Company*, 1:547–49.

49. The York Fort account books list 1,647 Made Beaver from inland in 1774–1775, and 2,901 Made Beaver "from Basquea" (actually Cumberland House) in 1775–1776. Introduction to *Cumberland House Journals*, xciii, n1.

50. The American revolutionaries never reached Hudson Bay, but their French allies did. In August 1782, three French ships under command of the Comte de Lapérouse entered Hudson Bay and destroyed both Fort Prince of Wales at Churchill and York Fort. Copy of instructions given by Marten to Cocking on his going to Cumberland House, n.d., B239/b/37, HBCA, reel 1M255 ("in a state," "strict watch," and "on the most"); Walker et al., "Journal," 94 ("Pedlers are all"); Rich, *History of the Hudson's Bay Company*, 2:83–89.

51. Walker et al., "Journal," 129, 152; Robert Longmoor, "Journal of a Journey Inland," in *Cumberland House Journals*; copy of a letter from Cocking to Marten, 13 June 1777, B239/b/37, HBCA, reel 1M255; Harold Adams Innis, *The Fur Trade in Canada: An Introduction to Canadian Economic History* (1930; reprint, Toronto: University of Toronto Press, 1999), 267–68.

52. Ronald L. Ives, "The Beaver-Meadow Complex," *Journal of Geomorphology* 5, no. 3 (1942): 194 (quotation); Frank Rosell et al., "Ecological Impact of Beavers *Castor fiber* and *Castor canadensis* and Their Ability to Modify Ecosystems," *Mammal Revue* 35, nos. 3–4 (2005): 252.

53. Ming-Ko Woo and James M. Waddington, "Effects of Beaver Dams on Subarctic Wetland Hydrology," *Arctic* 43, no. 3 (1990): 225–26; Robert J. Naiman, Jerry M. Melillo, and John E. Hobbie, "Ecosystem Alteration of Boreal Forest Streams by Beaver (*Castor canadensis*)," *Ecology* 67, no. 5 (1986): 1254; Rosell et al., "Ecological Impact of Beavers," 256.

54. Angela M. Gurnell, "The Hydrogeomorphological Effects of Beaver Dam-Building Activity," *Progress in Physical Geography* 22, no. 2 (1998): 181; Naiman, Johnston, and Kelley, "Alteration of North American Streams," 754.

55. Robert J. Naiman et al., "Beaver Influences on the Long-Term Biogeochemical Characteristics of Boreal Forest Drainage Networks," *Ecology* 75, no. 4 (1994): 905–21; C. A. Johnson et al., "Effects of Beaver and Moose on Boreal Forest Landscapes," in *Landscape Ecology and Geographic Information Systems*, ed. R. Haines-Young and David R. Green (London: Taylor and Francis, 1993), 255; Rosell et al., "Ecological Impact of Beavers," 252; Glynnis A. Hood and Suzanne E. Bayley, "Beaver (*Castor canadensis*) Mitigate the Effects of Climate on the Area of Open Water in Boreal Wetlands in Western Canada," *Biological Conservation* 141, no. 2 (2008): 556–67.

56. Justin P. Wright, Clive G. Jones, and Alexander S. Flecker, "An Ecosystem Engineer, the Beaver, Increases Species Richness at the Landscape Level," *Oecologia* 132, no. 1 (2002): 96–101; Glenn W. Bradt, "A Study of Beaver Colonies in Michigan," *Journal of Mammalogy* 19, no. 2 (1938): 153–56; Naiman, Johnston, and Kelley, "Alteration of North American Streams," 756; Rosell et al., "Ecological Impact of Beavers," 258.

57. Naiman, Johnston, and Kelley, "Alteration of North American Streams," 755; William M. Samuel, Margo J. Pybus, and A. Alan Kocan, eds., *Parasitic Diseases of Wild Mammals*, 2nd ed. (Ames: Iowa State University Press, 2001), 25–27; John L. Capinera, ed., *Encyclopedia of Entomology*, 2nd ed. (New York: Springer, 2008), 525–29; Isham, *James Isham's Observations*, 131 (quotations); Henry, *Travels and Adventures*, 29. Isham refers to "sand flies," a term often used to encompass blackflies as well.

58. Isaac J. Schlosser and Larry W. Kallemyn, "Spatial Variation in Fish Assemblages across a Beaver-Influenced Successional Landscape," *Ecology* 81, no. 5 (2000): 1371–82; Rosell et al., "Ecological Impact of Beavers," 261, 264, 265–66, 267.

59. On the ultimate causes of overhunting, see Ann M. Carlos and Frank D. Lewis, "Property Rights, Competition, and Depletion in the Eighteenth-Century Canadian Fur Trade: The Role of the European Market," *Canadian Journal of Economics/Revue canadienne d'Economique* 32, no. 3 (May 1999): 705–28. The approximate figure of six million beaver pelts is derived from the numbers given in Innis, *Fur Trade in Canada*, 268. David Thompson, *Writings of David Thompson*, ed. William E. Moreau (Montreal: McGill-Queen's University Press, 2009), 196–97 (quotations); Krech, *Ecological Indian*, 175.

60. Daniel Abramson, "C. R. Cockerell's 'Architectural Progress of the Bank of England,'" *Architectural History* 37 (1994): 117; Thomas Mortimer, *Every Man His Own Broker* (London: S. Hooper, 1761), x; Alice Clare Carter, *The English Public Debt in the Eighteenth Century* (London: Historical Association, 1968), 10–11; Reed Browning, "The Duke of Newcastle and the Financing of the Seven Years' War," *Journal of Economic History* 31, no. 2 (1971): 346–48; Larry Neal, "Interpreting Power and Profit in Economic History: A Case Study of the Seven Years War," *Journal of Economic History* 37, no. 1 (1977): 31.

61. Browning, "Duke of Newcastle," 346, 369–71, 374–75n128 ("The real cause"); Richard Middleton, *The Bells of Victory: The Pitt-Newcastle Ministry and the Conduct of the Seven Years' War, 1757–1762* (Cambridge: Cambridge University Press, 1985), 171 ("mony'd men").

62. John L. Bullion, "Security and Economy: The Bute Administration's Plan for the American Army and Revenue, 1762–1763," *William and Mary Quarterly* 45, no. 3 (1988): 499–509; John Shy, *Toward Lexington: The Role of the British Army in the Coming of the American Revolution* (Princeton, NJ: Princeton University Press, 1965), 110–11; Horace Walpole, as quoted in William R. Nester, *"Haughty Conquerors": Amherst and the Great Indian Uprising of 1763* (Westport, CT: Praeger, 2000), 8 (quotation).

63. Jeffery Amherst, *The Journal of Jeffery Amherst*, ed. J. Clarence Webster (Toronto: Ryerson, 1931), 185 ("To save" and "as idle good for nothing"); Gregory Evans Dowd, *War under Heaven: Pontiac, the Indian Nations and the British Empire* (Baltimore: Johns Hopkins University Press, 2002), 72–75 ("no end to it" on p. 73); Fred Anderson, *Crucible of War: The*

Seven Years' War and the Fate of Empire in British North America, 1754–1766 (New York: Knopf, 2000), 472–75; William Johnson, "Review of the Trade," in *Trade and Politics, 1767–1769,* ed. Clarence Walworth Alvord and Clarence Edwin Carter, Collections of the Illinois State Historical Library, vol. 16 (Springfield: Illinois State Historical Library, 1921), 36 ("This fell Severely").

64. Henry Bouquet to Thomas Gage, 30 November 1764, in *The Critical Period, 1763–1765,* ed. Clarence Walworth Alvord and Clarence Edwin Carter, Collections of the Illinois State Historical Library, vol. 10 (Springfield: Illinois State Historical Library, 1915), 366 ("fickle and Wavering"); Dowd, *War under Heaven,* 64 ("We can now talk"), 65 ("dogs"); J. C. Long, *Lord Jeffery Amherst, a Soldier of the King* (New York: MacMillan, 1933), 187 ("bastards"); Amherst to Bouquet, 16 July 1763, in *The Papers of Col. Henry Bouquet,* ed. Sylvester K. Stevens and Donald H. Kent (Harrisburg, PA: Pennsylvania Historical Commission, 1940–1943), series 21634, 219 ("Inhuman Villains").

65. Simeon Ecuyer to Bouquet, 30 May 1763, *Papers of Col. Henry Bouquet,* series 21649, part 1, pp. 115–17 ("means I think"); Amherst, *Journal of Jeffery Amherst,* 310, 314 ("ill-judged confidence").

66. Dowd, *War under Heaven,* 64 ("regard us as dogs"); copy of an embassy sent to the Illinois by the Indians at Detroit, in *The Gladwin Manuscripts,* ed. Charles Moore (Lansing, MI: Robert Smith, 1897), 644 ("to become Masters"); Long, *Lord Jeffery Amherst,* 185 ("more General).

67. Long, *Lord Jeffery Amherst,* 186 ("more nearly allied" and "no Prisoners"); Bouquet to Amherst, 13 July 1763, in *Papers of Col. Henry Bouquet,* series 21634, p. 215 ("the Vermin"); memorandum by Sir Jeffery Amherst, 4 May 1763, in *Papers of Col. Henry Bouquet,* series 21634, p. 161 ("Try Every other Method"). For a discussion of this incident of biological warfare and others in the eighteenth century, see Elizabeth A. Fenn, "Biological Warfare in Eighteenth-Century North America: Beyond Jeffery Amherst," *Journal of American History* 86, no. 4 (2000): 1552–80.

68. Dowd, *War under Heaven,* 213–33.

CHAPTER SIX—THE DISCOVERY: THE BLACK
HILLS AND THE LAKOTA NATION

1. Edward Patrick Hogan, *The Geography of South Dakota* (Sioux Falls, SD: Center for Western Studies, Augustana College, 1995), 9–29; Sven G. Froiland, *Natural History of the Black Hills and Badlands* (Sioux Falls, SD: Center for Western Studies, Augustana College, 1990); E. Steve Cassells, David B. Miller, and Paul V. Miller, *Paha Sapa: A Cultural Resource Overview of the Black Hills National Forest, South Dakota and Wyoming* (Custer, SD: US Department of Agriculture, Forest Service, 1984), 8–10; Alice M. Tratebas, "Black Hills Settlement Patterns Based on a Functional Approach" (PhD dissertation, Indiana University, 1986), 17–20.

2. Alexandra Witkin-New Holy, "Black Elk and the Spiritual Significance of *Paha Sapa* (the Black Hills)," in *The Black Elk Reader,* ed. Clyde Holler (Syracuse, NY: Syracuse University Press, 2000), 188–208; Linea Sundstrom, "Mirror of Heaven: Cross-Cultural Transference of the Sacred Geography of the Black Hills," *World Archaeology* 28, no. 2 (1996): 177–89; "Treaty of Fort Laramie," in *Indian Affairs: Laws and Treaties,* ed. Charles J. Kappler (Washington, DC: Government Printing Office, 1904), 2:998 ("for the absolute"); *Reports to the Proposed Division of the Great Sioux Reservation,* 51st Cong., 1st sess. (1890), S. Exec. Doc. 51, serial 2682, p. 99 ("The only place").

3. Thomas Powers, *The Killing of Crazy Horse* (New York: Knopf, 2010), 414–20, 434–35.

4. Christina E. Burke, "*Waniyetu Wówapi*: An Introduction to the Lakota Winter Count Tradition," in *The Years the Stars Fell: Lakota Winter Counts at the Smithsonian*, ed. Candace S. Greene and Russell Thornton (Washington, DC: Smithsonian Institution, 2007), 1–2 ("something that is marked"); William H. Corbusier, "The Corbusier Winter Counts," in Garrick Mallery, *Pictographs of the North American Indians* (Washington, DC: Smithsonian Institution, 1886), 128 ("counts back").

5. The American Horse winter count appears in *The Years the Stars Fell*. Jeffrey Ostler is skeptical of the authenticity of American Horse's winter count and suggests that the interpretation of the 1775–1776 illustration comes from the nineteenth-century ethnologist Garrick Mallery rather than from American Horse. Ostler, *The Lakotas and the Black Hills: The Struggle for Sacred Ground* (New York: Penguin, 2010), 9.

6. Peter Pond, "Narrative of Peter Pond," in *Five Fur Traders of the Northwest*, ed. Charles M. Gates (St. Paul: Minnesota Historical Society, 1965), 46 ("Hear was Sport"), 58; Pierre Antoine Tabeau, *Tabeau's Narrative of Loisel's Expedition to the Upper Missouri*, ed. Annie Heloise Abel (Norman: University of Oklahoma Press, 1939), 122 ("Each man brings"); Benjamin and Joseph Frobisher to General Haldimand, 4 October 1784, in *Report on Canadian Archives, 1890*, ed. Douglas Brymner (Ottawa: Maclean, Roger, 1891), 50 ("destitute of Goods"); Tabeau, *Tabeau's Narrative*, 121–23; Meriwether Lewis, "Affluents of the Missouri River," [Codex O], in *The Journals of the Lewis and Clark Expedition*, ed. Gary Moulton (Lincoln, NE: University of Nebraska Press / University of Nebraska-Lincoln Libraries-Electronic Text Center, 2005), http://lewisandclarkjournals.unl.edu/read/?_xmlsrc=1804-1805.winter.part1&_xslsrc=LCstyles.xsl; John C. Ewers, *Indian Life on the Upper Missouri* (Norman: University of Oklahoma Press, 1968), 28.

7. Baynton, Wharton, and Morgan [trading firm] to John Irwin, 21 September 1766, in *The New Régime, 1765–1767*, ed. Clarence Walworth Alvord and Clarence Edwin Carter, Collections of the Illinois State Historical Library, vol. 11 (Springfield: Illinois State Historical Library, 1916), 387 ("The Enormous *Expences*"); Jonathan Carver, *A Plan of Captain Carvers Travels in the Interior Parts of North America in 1766 and 1767*, 3rd ed. (London: C. Dilly, 1781) ("The Traders go"); Gordon's journal, 1766, in *New Régime*, 303–4 ("I fancy" and "free Navigation"); Douglas Stewart Brown, "The Iberville Canal Project: Its Relation to Anglo-French Commercial Rivalry in the Mississippi Valley, 1763–1775," *Mississippi Valley Historical Review* 32, no. 4 (1946): 501–3.

8. Alexander Henry, *Travels and Adventures in Canada and the Indian Territories* (New York: I. Riley, 1809), 86–87 ("Nothing could be"); Benjamin and Joseph Frobisher to Haldimand, 4 October 1784, in *Report on Canadian Archives*, 50 ("ungovernable and rapacious"); Marjorie Gordon Jackson, "The Beginning of British Trade at Michilimackinac," *Minnesota History* 11, no. 3 (1930): 240–41.

9. Jonathan Carver, *The Journals of Jonathan Carver and Related Documents, 1766–1770*, ed. John Parker (St. Paul: Minnesota Historical Society Press, 1976), 115 ("a lively aspiring genius"), 117 ("the necessity"); Paul L. Stevens, "Wabasha Visits Governor Carleton, 1776: New Light on a Legendary Episode of Dakota-British Diplomacy on the Great Lakes Frontier," *Michigan Historical Review* 16, no. 1 (1990): 28–29, 32–36.

10. Stevens, "Wabasha Visits Governor Carleton," 37–46.

11. William R. Swagerty, "Indian Trade in the Trans-Mississippi West to 1870," in *Handbook of North American Indians: History of Indian-White Relations*, ed. William C. Sturtevant and Wilcomb E. Washburn (Washington, DC: Smithsonian Institution: 1988), 4:352.

12. Francisco Atanasio Domínguez, "A Description of New Mexico," in *The Missions of New Mexico, 1776: A Description by Fray Francisco Atanasio Domínguez*, trans. Eleanor B. Adams and Angelico Chavez (Albuquerque: University of New Mexico Press, 1956), 112, 251–52.

13. Meriwether Lewis et al., 24 October 1805, in *Journals of the Lewis and Clark Expedition* (quotation); W. Raymond Wood, "Plains Trade in Prehistoric and Protohistoric Intertribal Relations," in *Anthropology on the Great Plains*, ed. W. Raymond Wood and Margot Liberty (Lincoln: University of Nebraska Press, 1980), 98–109; Ewers, *Indian Life on the Upper Missouri*, 14–33. Long-distance trade has deep roots along the Missouri River. See Charles E. Orser, Jr., "Trade Good Flow in Arikara Villages: Expanding Ray's Middleman Hypothesis," *Plains Anthropologist* 29, no. 103 (1984): 1–58; and John Ludwickson, James N. Gundersen, and Craig Johnson, "Select Exotic Artifacts from Cattle Oiler (39ST224): A Middle Missouri Tradition Site in Central South Dakota," *Plains Anthropologist* 38, no. 145 (1993): 151–68.

14. Donald J. Lehmer and David T. Jones, *Arikara Archeology: The Bad River Phase*, Publications in Salvage Archeology, no. 7 (Lincoln, NE: Smithsonian Institution, 1968), 88–89; Wood, "Plains Trade," 104–5; Dale R. Henning, "Continuity and Change in the Eastern Plains, A.D. 800–1700: An Examination of Exchange Patterns," in *Plains Village Archaeology: Bison-Hunting Farmers in the Central and Northern Plains*, ed. Stanley A. Ahler and Marvin Kay (Salt Lake City: University of Utah Press, 2007), 77–88; Alan M. Cvancara and Barrt C. Kent, "A Marine Shell-Pottery Find in North Dakota," *Plains Anthropologist* 8, no. 21 (1963): 170–73; W. Raymond Wood, "Northern Plains Village Cultures: Internal Stability and External Relationships," *Journal of Anthropological Research* 30, no. 1 (1974): 1–16; Ewers, *Indian Life on the Upper Missouri*, 14–33.

15. Meriwether Lewis et al., 19 September 1804, in *Journals of the Lewis and Clark Expedition*.

16. Jean Baptiste Truteau, "Journal of Truteau on the Missouri River, 1794–1795," in *Before Lewis and Clark: Documents Illustrating the History of the Missouri, 1785–1804*, ed. A. P. Nasatir (1952; reprint, Lincoln: University of Nebraska Press, 1990), 1:267–96. Quotations on 269 ("ferocious"), 296 ("feared and dreaded" and "Their very name").

17. Tabeau, *Tabeau's Narrative*, 130 ("a certain kind of serf"), 131 ("weakness and stupidity"), 144–45 ("However tenacious" and "at first caused murmuring").

18. Pierre Gaultier de Varennes de la Vérendrye, "Journal of the Chevalier de la Vérendrye," in *Journals and Letters of Pierre Gaultier de Varennes de la Vérendrye and His Sons*, ed. Lawrence J. Burpee (Toronto: Champlain Society, 1927), 339–40 (quotations). The construction of fortifications is more properly a reconstruction, following the "pax la Roche." W. W. Caldwell, "Fortified Villages in the Northern Plains," *Plains Anthropologist* 9, no. 23 (1964): 1–7. On the dating of fortifications in the eighteenth century: Lehmer and Jones, *Arikara Archeology*; J. J. Hoffman, review of Lehmer and Jones, *Arikara Archeology*, *American Antiquity* 35, no. 1 (1970): 113–15; J. J. Hoffman, "Seriation of Certain Arikara Villages," *Transactions of the Nebraska Academy of Sciences and Affiliated Societies* 1 (1972): 20–34; and Craig M. Johnson, *A Chronology of Middle Missouri Plains Village Sites*, Smithsonian Contributions to Anthropology, no. 47 (Washington, DC: Smithsonian Institution Scholarly Press, 2007), 148–54.

19. Douglas W. Owsley, Hugh E. Berryman, and William M. Bass, "Demographic and Osteological Evidence for Warfare at the Larson Site, South Dakota," *Plains Anthropologist* 22, no. 28, no. 2 (1977): 119–31.

20. Ibid.

21. Ibid.

22. The identification of the winter-count village as the Larson site is admittedly tentative. Linea Sundstrom, "The Destruction of Larson Village: A Possible Contemporary Lakota Account," *Newsletter of the South Dakota Archaeological Society* 26, no. 3 (1996): 1–3. I am indebted to Elizabeth Fenn for bringing Sundstrom's article to my attention.

23. "Trudeau's [Truteau's] Description of the Upper Missouri," in *Before Lewis and Clark*,

2:382; Tabeau, *Tabeau's Narrative*, 71 (quotation); Andrew C. Isenberg, *The Destruction of the Bison: An Environmental History, 1750–1920* (New York: Cambridge University Press, 2001), 22.

24. Scientists are still unraveling how genetic factors affect height, but over large populations, nutrition may be of primary importance. Joseph M. Prince and Richard H. Steckel, "Nutritional Success on the Great Plains: Nineteenth-Century Equestrian Nomads," *Journal of Interdisciplinary History* 33, no. 3 (2003): 353–84; Douglas W. Owsley, "Post-contact Period Nutritional Status and Cortical Bone Thickness of South Dakota Indians," in *Status, Structure, and Stratification: Current Archaeological Reconstructions: Proceedings of the Sixteenth Annual Conference*, ed. Marc Thompson, Maria Teresa Garcia, and Francois J. Kense (Calgary, AB: University of Calgary, Archaeological Association, 1985), 199–207; R. L. Jantz and Douglas W. Owsley, "Long Bone Growth Variation among Arikara Skeletal Populations," *American Journal of Physical Anthropology* 63, no. 1 (1984): 13–20; Douglas W. Owsley and Richard L. Jantz, "Long Bone Lengths and Gestational Age Distributions of Post-contact Arikara Indian Perinatal Infant Skeletons," *American Journal of Physical Anthropology* 68, no. 3 (1985): 321–28; Douglas W. Owsley, "Demography of Prehistoric and Early Historic Northern Plains Populations," in *Disease and Demography in the Americas*, ed. John W. Verano and Douglas H. Ubelaker (Washington, DC: Smithsonian Institution Press, 1992), 75–86.

25. Charles A. Reher and George C. Frison, "The Vore Site, 48CK302, a Stratified Buffalo Jump in the Wyoming Black Hills," *Plains Anthropologist* 25, no. 88, pt. 2 (1980): 42–43.

26. Douglas B. Bamforth, *Ecology and Human Organization on the Great Plains* (New York: Plenum, 1988), 33, 53–61, 74.

27. Paul Friggens, *Gold and Grass: The Black Hills Story* (Boulder, CO: Pruett, 1983), 64.

28. Alan J. Osborn, "Ecological Aspects of Equestrian Adaptations in Aboriginal North America," *Plains Anthropologist*, 85, no. 3 (1983): 567 ("a toilsome and starvation task"); Royal B. Hassrick, *The Sioux: Life and Customs of a Warrior Society* (Norman: University of Oklahoma Press, 1964), 189 ("meat pack").

29. Charles W. Stockton and David M. Meko, "Drought Recurrence in the Great Plains as Reconstructed from Long-Term Tree-Ring Records," *Journal of Applied Meteorology* 22, no. 1 (1983): 17–29; D. N. Duvick and T. J. Blasing, "A Dendroclimatic Reconstruction of Annual Precipitation Amounts in Iowa since 1860," *Water Resources Research* 17, no. 4 (1981): 1183–89; Scott St. George and Erik Nielsen, "Hydroclimatic Change in Southern Manitoba since A.D. 1409 Inferred from Tree Rings," *Quaternary Research* 58, no. 2 (2002): 103–11.

30. Reher and Frison, "Vore Site."

31. Shepard Krech, *The Ecological Indian: Myth And History* (New York: Norton, 1999), 148–49; Linea Sundstrom, *Storied Stone: Indian Rock Art in the Black Hills Country* (Norman: University of Oklahoma Press, 2004), 80–90, 132; James D. Keyser and Michael Klassen, *Plains Indian Rock Art* (Seattle: University of Washington Press, 2001), 176–89.

32. Reher and Frison, "Vore Site," 43; Bamforth, *Ecology and Human Organization*, 7–8; Marcel Kornfeld, *Affluent Foragers of the North American Plains: Landscape Archaeology of the Black Hills*, British Archaeological Reports International Series 1106 (Oxford: Hadrian, 2003), 38.

33. Philip F. Wells, in *Voices of the American West: The Indian Interviews of Eli S. Ricker, 1903–1919*, ed. Richard E. Jensen (Lincoln: University of Nebraska Press, 2005), 1:133 ("shrewd," "sagacious," and "slippery"); Charles A. Eastman, *Indian Heroes and Great Chieftains* (1918; reprint, Lincoln: University of Nebraska Press, 1991), 174–75 ("He could say" and "If you have").

34. American Horse witnessed the fireworks at the Fourth of July festivities at Camp Sheridan in 1879, the year he shared his winter count. He may very well have understood the significance of 1776 to white Americans. Fanny Dunbar Corbusier, *Recollections of Her Army Life, 1869–1908*, ed. Patricia Y. Stallard (Norman: University of Oklahoma Press, 2003), 92–93; William H. Corbusier, "Corbusier Winter Counts," 130 (quotations).

35. Stuart Banner, *How the Indians Lost Their Land: Law and Power on the Frontier* (Cambridge: Harvard University Press, 2005), 150–90; Linea Sundstrom, *Culture History of the Black Hills with Reference to Adjacent Areas of the Northern Great Plains* (Lincoln, NE: J and L Reprint, 1989); Tratebas, "Black Hills Settlement Patterns"; Cassells, Miller, and Miller, *Paha Sapa*; Robert Alex, "Village Sites off the Missouri River," in *The Future of South Dakota's Past*, ed. Larry J. Zimmerman and Lucille C. Stewart (Vermillion: University of South Dakota Archaeology Laboratory, 1981), 39–46; Linea Sundstrom, "The Sacred Black Hills: An Ethnohistorical Review," *Great Plains Quarterly* 17, nos. 3–4 (1997): 201–2 (quotation); Ronald Goodman, *Lakota Star Knowledge: Studies in Lakota Stellar Theology*, 2nd ed. (Rosebud, SD: Sinte Gleska University, 1992), 3–14; Sundstrom, "Mirror of Heaven," 177–89.

36. Sundstrom, *Storied Stone*, 78–98; Keyser and Klassen, *Plains Indian Rock Art*, 190–221.

37. Sundstrom, *Storied Stone*, 68–77, 165–73.

38. Ibid., 109.

39. James D. Keyser, *Rock Art of Western South Dakota: The North Cave Hills*, Special Publication of the South Dakota Archaeological Society, no. 9, sect. 1 (Sioux Falls: South Dakota Archaeological Society, 1984), 6, 10, 17–19; Sundstrom, *Storied Stone*, 106–9.

40. John C. Ewers, *The Horse in Blackfoot Indian Culture, with Comparative Materials from Other Western Tribes* (Washington: Smithsonian Institution Press, 1955), 16 ("dashed at" and "knocked them"); Pekka Hämäläinen, "The Rise and Fall of Plains Indian Horse Cultures," *Journal of American History* 90, no. 3 (2003), 859–62.

41. Linea Sundstrom, *Rock Art of Western South Dakota: The Southern Black Hills*, Special Publication of the South Dakota Archaeological Society, no. 9, sect. 2 (Sioux Falls: South Dakota Archaeological Society, 1984), 111–12.

42. Gutzon Borglum to the Harney Peak Memorial Association, 20 September 1926, Gilder Lehrman Collection, GLC06031, Gilder Lehrman Institute of American History, New York, http://www.gilderlehrman.org/collections/202bad1b-a1f1-439c-bc39-433806392100; Robert J. Dean, *Living Granite* (New York: Viking, 1949), 17 (quotations), 52–53, 63–64.

43. Dean, *Living Granite*, 17 ("A monument's dimensions"); Borglum to the Harney Peak Memorial Association, 20 September 1926, Gilder Lehrman Collection, GLC06031, Gilder Lehrman Institute of American History, New York, http://www.gilderlehrman .org/collections/202bad1b-a1f1-439c-bc39-433806392100 ("center of this great Union"); *Mount Rushmore National Memorial: A Monument Commemorating the Conception, Preservation, and Growth of the Great American Republic* (n.p.: Mount Rushmore National Memorial Commission, 1941), foreword ("selfish, coveting civilizations") and 6 ("You know how vandalism"); Matthew Glass, "Producing Patriotic Inspiration at Mount Rushmore," *Journal of the American Academy of Religion* 62, no. 2 (1994): 269 ("If this monument fails"). On anti-Semitism, the KKK, and Borglum's paternalistic relationship with native peoples, see Albert Boime, "Patriarchy Fixed in Stone: Gutzon Borglum's 'Mount Rushmore,'" *American Art* 5, nos. 1–2 (1991): 142–67; and John Taliaferro, *Great White Fathers: The Story of the Obsessive Quest to Create Mount Rushmore* (New York: PublicAffairs, 2002), 185–95.

44. Cassells, Miller, and Miller, *Paha Sapa*, 108–11; Frank Pommersheim, "The Black Hills Case: On the Cusp of History," *Wicazo Sa Review* 4, no. 1 (1988): 20 ("hold their 'Mother's

heart and pulse'"); Goodman, *Lakota Star Knowledge*, 50 ("the Heart of our home"); Don Doll, *Vision Quest: Men, Women and Sacred Sites of the Sioux Nation* (New York: Crown, 1994), 60 ("the heart of the earth"); Francine Uenuma and Mike Fritz, "Why the Sioux Are Refusing $1.3 Billion," *PBS NewsHour*, 24 August 2011, http://www.pbs.org/newshour/updates/north_america/july-dec11/blackhills_08-23.html. The origin and age of the Lakotas' attachment for the Black Hills is of some debate. David B. Miller, "Historian's View of S. 705—The Sioux Nation Black Hills Bill," *Wicazo Sa Review* 4, no. 1 (1988): 55–59; Donald Worster, *Under Western Skies: Nature and History in the American West* (New York: Oxford University Press, 1992), 106–53; Sundstrom, "Sacred Black Hills," 185–212.

45. Abram Wakeman, *History and Reminiscences of Lower Wall Street and Vicinity* (New York: Spice Mill, 1914), 21–22 (quotations); Carl Abbott, "The Neighborhoods of New York, 1760–1775," *New York History* 55, no. 1 (1974), 41–46.

46. Spencer Trask, *Bowling Green* (New York: Putnam, 1989), 47 ("commodious house" and "genteel"); *New-York Mercury*, 21 November 1763, p. 2; Mary Louise Booth, *History of the City of New York* (New York: W. R. C. Clark, 1860), 96; John Shy, "Thomas Gage: Weak Link of Empire," in *George Washington's Opponents: British Generals and Admirals in the American Revolution*, ed. George Athan Billias (New York: Morrow, 1969), 26 ("Old Woman"); John Richard Alden, *General Gage in America: Being Principally a History of His Role in the American Revolution* (Baton Rouge: Louisiana State University Press, 1948), 66–67.

47. Walter Barrett, *The Old Merchants of New York City* (New York: Knox, 1885), 4:274–77.

48. Clarence Walworth Alvord, *The Mississippi Valley in British Politics: A Study of the Trade, Land Speculation, and Experiments in Imperialism Culminating in the American Revolution* (Cleveland, OH: Arthur H. Clark, 1917), 2:48–49 ("There is little appearance"); Thomas Gage to Lord Hillsborough, 16 June 1768, in *Trade and Politics, 1767–1769*, ed. Clarence Walworth Alvord and Clarence Edwin Carter, Collections of the Illinois State Historical Library, vol. 16 (Springfield: Illinois State Historical Library, 1921), 318 ("mutually endeavoring").

49. Gage to Earl of Halifax, 13 July 1764, in *The Critical Period, 1763–1765*, ed. Clarence Walworth Alvord and Clarence Edwin Carter, Collections of the Illinois State Historical Library, vol. 10 (Springfield: Illinois State Historical Library, 1915), 284 ("savages," "extreamly well," and "have a door open"); William Johnson to the Lords of Trade, 30 August 1764, in *Critical Period*, 307; Alvord, *Mississippi Valley in British Politics*, 2:48–49 ("Let the savages").

50. In 1769, over two thousand soldiers sailed from Havana to New Orleans to put down an uprising, but their presence in the colony was localized and temporary. Athanase de Mézières to Unzaga, 10 February 1773, in *Athanase de Mézières and the Louisiana-Texas Frontier, 1768–1780*, ed. Herbert Eugene Bolton (Cleveland, OH: Arthur H. Clark, 1914), 2:24–25 (quotation); Pedro Piernas to Luis de Unzaga y Amezaga, 4 July 1772, in *Spain in the Mississippi Valley, 1765–1794*, ed. Lawrence Kinnaird, Annual Report of the American Historical Association, vol. 2 (Washington, DC: US Government Printing Office, 1945), pt. 1:204–5; M. Carmen González López-Briones, "Spain in the Mississippi Valley: Spanish Arkansas, 1762–1804" (PhD dissertation, Purdue University, 1983), 216; Gilbert C. Din, "Protecting the 'Barrera': Spain's Defenses in Louisiana, 1763–1779," *Louisiana History* 19, no. 2 (1978): 183–211; Gilbert C. Din, "Between a Rock and a Hard Place: The Indian Trade in Spanish Arkansas," in *Cultural Encounters in the Early South: Indians and Europeans in Arkansas*, ed. Jeannie Whayne (Fayetteville: University of Arkansas Press, 1995), 120.

51. Joseph Orieta to Unzaga, 14 April 1776, leg. 189-B, fol. 46, PapC, AGI.

52. Jeffrey K. Yelton, "The Depopulation of the Osage and Missouri Tribes," in Carl H. Chapman et al., *Osage and Missouri Indian Life, Cultural Change: 1675–1825* (Final Performance Report on National Endowment for the Humanities Research Grant RS-20296, 31 December 1985), 1:129–58; Piernas to Unzaga, 4 July 1772, in *Spain in the Mississippi Valley, 1765–1794*, pt. 1:204 (quotations); De Mézières to Unzaga y Amezaga, 10 February 1773, in *Athanase de Mézières*, 2:24.

<h3 style="text-align:center">CHAPTER SEVEN—AN INVASION OF
MALEFACTORS: OSAGE COUNTRY</h3>

1. Gilbert C. Din and A. P. Nasatir, *The Imperial Osages: Spanish-Indian Diplomacy in the Mississippi Valley* (Norman: University of Oklahoma Press, 1983), 77; Philip Pittman, *The Present State of the European Settlements on the Mississippi* (London: J. Nourse, 1770), 40; Balthazar de Villiers to Luis de Unzaga, 23 September 1776, leg. 189-B, fol. 58, PapC, AGI; Orieta to Unzaga, 3 January 1776, fol. 36, leg. 189-B, PapC, AGI; Orieta to Unzaga, 14 April 1776, fol. 46, leg. 189-B, PapC, AGI; Lucas García to Unzaga, 18 June 1776, leg. 189-B, fol. 53, PapC, AGI; Morris S. Arnold, "The Relocation of Arkansas Post to Ecores Rouges in 1779," *Arkansas Historical Quarterly* 42, no. 4 (1983): 317 (quotation).

2. Pedro Piernas to Unzaga, 1 April 1773, in Louis Houck, *The Spanish Régime in Missouri* (Chicago: R. R. Donnelley, 1909), 1:53–54; Patricia Cleary, *The World, the Flesh, and the Devil: A History of Colonial St. Louis* (Columbia: University of Missouri Press, 2011), 52.

3. Pittman, *Present State*, 45–46; Harry Gordon, "Gordon's Journal," in *The New Régime, 1765–1767*, ed. Clarence Walworth Alvord and Clarence Edwin Carter, Collections of the Illinois State Historical Library, vol. 11 (Springfield: Illinois State Historical Library, 1916), 298; Floyd Mansberger, *Archaeological Test Excavations at the Fort de Chartres Powder Magazine, Rural Randolph County, Illinois* (Springfield, IL: Fever River Research, 2004), 10.

4. John Wilkins to William Wildman Barrington, 5 December 1769, in *Trade and Politics, 1767–1769*, ed. Clarence Walworth Alvord and Clarence Edwin Carter, Collections of the Illinois State Historical Library, vol. 16 (Springfield: Illinois State Historical Library, 1921), 631–32 (quotations); George Morgan, "Voyage down the Mississippi," 21 November 1766, in *New Régime*, 439.

5. Morgan to Baynton, Wharton, and Morgan [trading firm], 30 October 1768, in *Trade and Politics*, 439–40 ("The Groans & cries"); Butricke to Thomas Barnsley, 30 October 1768, in *Trade and Politics*, 448–50 ("Hott fit" and "in such a Violent manner"); Butricke to Barnsley, 12 February 1769, in *Trade and Politics*, 499 ("at Deaths door"); Butricke to Barnsley, 27 June 1769, in *Trade and Politics*, 566.

6. Kathleen DuVal, *The Native Ground: Indians and Colonists in the Heart of the Continent* (Philadelphia: University of Pennsylvania Press, 2006), 116.

7. Mathurin le Petit to Père d'Avaugour, 12 July 1730, in *Jesuit Relations and Allied Documents*, ed. Reuben Gold Thwaites (Cleveland, OH: Burrows Brothers, 1900), 68:215 ("You may lose an arm"); Richard N. Ellis and Charlie R. Steen, "An Indian Delegation in France, 1725," *Journal of the Illinois State Historical Society* 67, no. 4 (1974): 387 ("Princess of the Missouris"), 390 ("that is to say"), 400–402 ("savage and bizarre").

8. I am including the Missouris in the population estimates. The Osages were early adopters of European technologies—so much so that their traditional material culture had largely vanished by the first decades of the eighteenth century. Dale R. Henning and Thomas D. Thiessen, "Regional Prehistory," *Plains Anthropologist* 49, no. 192 (2004): 395; Dale R.

Henning, "The Adaptive Patterning of the Dhegiha Sioux," *Plains Anthropologist* 38, no. 146 (1993): 257–62; M. Bossu, *Nouveaux Voyages aux Indes Occidentales*, 2nd ed. (Paris: Le Jay, 1768), 1:163.

9. J. H. Elliott, *Empires of the Atlantic World: Britain and Spain in America, 1492–1830* (New Haven, CT: Yale University Press, 2006), 260; Jacob M. Price, "The Imperial Economy, 1700–1776," in *The Oxford History of the British Empire: The Eighteenth Century*, ed. P. J. Marshall (Oxford: Oxford University Press, 1988), 100, table 4.1; Paul W. Mapp, *The Elusive West and the Contest for Empire, 1713–1763* (Chapel Hill: University of North Carolina, 2011); Gilbert C. Din, "Empires Too Far: The Demographic Limitations of Three Imperial Powers in the Eighteenth-Century Mississippi Valley," *Louisiana History* 50, no. 3 (2009): 261–92.

10. Mark Twain, *Life on the Mississippi* (Boston: James R. Osgood, 1883), 129.

11. Amos Stoddard, *Sketches, Historical and Descriptive, of Louisiana* (Philadelphia: Mathew Carey, 1812), 374–75; Robert Farmer to Thomas Gage, 16–19 December 1765, in *New Régime*, 133 (quotation).

12. Farmer to Gage, 16–19 December 1765, in *New Régime*, 131–32 ("As the Islands"); Butricke to Barnsley, 15 September 1768, in *Trade and Politics*, 410–11 ("almost mad" and "the most dangerous"); J. Frederick Fausz, *Founding St. Louis: First City of the New West* (Charleston, SC: History Press, 2011), 71–73; Jean-Jacques Blaise d'Abbadie to the minister, 10 January 1764, in *The Critical Period, 1763–1765*, ed. Clarence Walworth Alvord and Clarence Edwin Carter, Collections of the Illinois State Historical Library, vol. 10 (Springfield: Illinois State Historical Library, 1915), 210.

13. Fausz, *Founding St. Louis*, 73; Butricke to Barnsley, 15 September 1768, in *Trade and Politics*, 410 ("impossible to drink"); Twain, *Life on the Mississippi*, 295 ("great common sewer").

14. Farmer to the secretary of war, 24 November 1764, in *Critical Period*, 364; Fausz, *Founding St. Louis*, 73; "Loftus Attempts to Ascend the River," in *Critical Period*, 228.

15. Letter from the Illinois to Gage, [July?] 1768, in *Trade and Politics*, 340 (quotation); Morris S. Arnold, *Colonial Arkansas, 1686–1804: A Social and Cultural History* (Fayetteville: University of Arkansas Press, 1993), 181; "Census of Piernas for 1773," in *Spanish Régime in Missouri*, 1:61.

16. Orieta to Unzaga, 22 March 1776, leg. 189-B, fol. 43, PapC, AGI ("Dominions of His Majesty"); Piernas to Luis de Unzaga y Amezaga, 4 July 1772, in *Spain in the Mississippi Valley, 1765–1794*, ed. Lawrence Kinnaird, Annual Report of the American Historical Association for the Year 1945, vol. 2 (Washington, DC: US Government Printing Office, 1945), 205 ("insolent"); Athanase de Mézières to Unzaga, 10 February 1773, in *Athanase de Mézières and the Louisiana-Texas Frontier, 1768–1780*, ed. Herbert Eugene Bolton (Cleveland, OH: Arthur H. Clark, 1914), 2:24–25 ("Execrable," "pernicious," and "turbulence and ferocity").

17. De Mézières to Unzaga, 20 May 1770, in *Athanase de Mézières*, 1:167–68 (quotation); M. Carmen González López-Briones, "Spain in the Mississippi Valley: Spanish Arkansas, 1762–1804" (PhD dissertation, Purdue University, 1983), 176. De Mézières's biography is briefly sketched in the introduction to *Athanase de Mézières*, 1:79–85.

18. De Mézières to Unzaga, 20 May 1770, in *Athanase de Mézières*, 1:166–68; Piernas to Unzaga, 4 July 1772, in *Spain in the Mississippi Valley, 1765–1794*, 204–5 ("I formally remonstrated"); Din and Nasatir, *Imperial Osages*, 74–76 ("reprimand").

19. Din and Nasatir, *Imperial Osages*, 81–84.

20. De Mézières to Unzaga, 10 February 1773, in *Athanase de Mézières*, 2:24–26 ("feasible" and "proper"); Zebulon Pike, *Exploratory Travels through the Western Territories of North America*

(London: Longman, 1811), 175 ("Their towns" and "a very comfortable"); De Mézières to Unzaga, 10 February 1773, in *Athanase de Mézières*, 2:26 ("to the greatest extremes"); Din and Nasatir, *Imperial Osages*, 81–84.

21. González López-Briones, "Spain in the Mississippi Valley," 131n46 ("being disarmed"); Piernas to Unzaga, 12 April 1773, in *Spain in the Mississippi Valley, 1765–1794*, 214–18 ("they seemed confident").

22. Piernas to Unzaga, 4 July 1772, in *Spain in the Mississippi Valley, 1765–1794*, 204–5.

23. Morris S. Arnold, *The Rumble of a Distant Drum: The Quapaws and Old World Newcomers, 1673–1804* (Fayetteville: University of Arkansas Press, 2000), 111 ("An Indian makes"); George Croghan to Gage, 16 January 1767, in *New Régime*, 493 ("Strong Connection" and "on His Majesty's side").

24. Account of Baynton, Wharton, and Morgan, 13 September 1768, in *Trade and Politics*, 407 ("for the Future"); Piernas to Unzaga, 4 July 1772, in *Spain in the Mississippi Valley, 1765–1794*, 204–5 ("commercial ends" and "lavishly"); Din and Nasatir, *Imperial Osages*, 75.

25. Gilbert C. Din, "Between a Rock and a Hard Place: The Indian Trade in Spanish Arkansas," in *Cultural Encounters in the Early South: Indians and Europeans in Arkansas*, ed. Jeannie Whayne (Fayetteville: University of Arkansas Press, 1995), 113; De Mézières to Unzaga, 20 May 1770, in *Athanase de Mézières*, 1:166–68 (from "deserters" to "lascivious passions"); Elizabeth Shown Mills, "Quintanilla's Crusade, 1775–1783: 'Moral Reform' and Its Consequences on the Natchitoches Frontier," *Louisiana History* 42, no. 3 (2001): 289 ("scandalous libertinage"); Elizabeth Shown Mills, "(De) Mézières-Trichel-Grappe: A Study of a Tri-Caste Lineage in the Old South," *Genealogist* 6, no. 1 (1985): 17 ("whites base enough"), 23–25.

26. Gage to William Shelburne, 22 February 1767, in *New Régime*, 506 ("Trade will go"); Douglas Stewart Brown, "The Iberville Canal Project: Its Relation to Anglo-French Commercial Rivalry in the Mississippi Valley, 1763–1775," *Mississippi Valley Historical Review* 32, no. 4 (1946): 502–3; Gage to Lord Hillsborough, 3 February 1769, in *Trade and Politics*, 489 ("most expeditious"); Lawrence Kinnaird, ed., *Spain in the Mississippi Valley, 1765–1794*, xxiv.

27. Gage to William Johnson, 14 August 1768, in *The Papers of Sir William Johnson*, ed. Alexander C. Flick (Albany: University of the State of New York, 1928), 6:394 ("transgressing"); Ralph Lee Woodward, Jr., "Spanish Commercial Policy in Louisiana, 1763–1803," *Louisiana History* 44, no. 2 (2003): 144–47; Antonio de Ulloa to Jerónimo Grimaldi, 4 August 1768, in *Spain in the Mississippi Valley, 1765–1794*, 57–58 ("proximity").

28. "Review of the Trade and Affairs in the Northern District of America," 22 September 1767, in *Trade and Politics*, 53.

29. John Wilkins to Gage, 13 September 1768, in *Trade and Politics*, 389 ("Immense"); Gordon, "Gordon's Journal," 301 ("Coop'd up," "a foolish Figure," and "the Dominion"); Wilkins to Barrington, 5 December 1769, in *Trade and Politics*, 632 ("with Pleasure"); Morgan to Baynton and Wharton, 10 December 1767, in *Trade and Politics*, 130; Gage to Shelburne, 24 April 1768, in *Trade and Politics*, 267 ("Scour"); Gage to Hillsborough, 3 February 1769, in *Trade and Politics*, 489 ("There is no good Prospect").

30. Villiers to Unzaga, 3 February 1777, fol. 78, leg. 190, PapC, AGI; Villiers to Unzaga, 25 January 1777, fol. 77, leg. 190, PapC, AGI ("You would not quite believe"); Orieta to Unzaga, 22 March 1776, leg. 189-B, fol. 43, PapC, AGI; De Mézières to Unzaga, 20 May 1770, in *Athanase de Mézières*, 1:166–68 ("infested"); González López-Briones, "Spain in the Mississippi Valley," 176.

31. Orieta to Unzaga, 22 March 1776, leg. 189-B, fol. 43, PapC, AGI; Villiers to Unzaga,

26 October 1776, fol. 70, leg. 190, PapC, AGI; Villiers to Unzaga, 4 March 1777, leg. 190, fol. 84, PapC, AGI (quotation).

32. In his pathbreaking study, Daniel H. Usner characterized Louisiana as a "frontier-exchange economy," created by Indians, settlers, and slaves on the periphery of the empire. Usner, *Indians, Settlers and Slaves in a Frontier Exchange Economy: The Lower Mississippi Valley before 1783* (Chapel Hill: University of North Carolina Press, 1992).

33. Fausz, *Founding St. Louis*, 43–95.

34. Francisco Cruzat to Unzaga, 26 May 1775, leg. 81, fol. 636, PapC, AGI; Tanis C. Thorne, *The Many Hands of My Relations: French and Indians on the Lower Mississippi* (Columbia: University of Missouri Press, 1996), 86–91; Din and Nasatir, *Imperial Osages*, 94–98; Willard H. Rollings, *The Osage: An Ethnohistorical Study of Hegemony on the Prairie-Plains* (Columbia: University of Missouri Press, 1992), 137–38; Cruzat to Bernardo de Gálvez, 6 December 1777, in *Spanish Régime in Missouri*, 1:149–51; De Mézières to Gálvez, 14 September 1777, in *Athanase de Mézières*, 2:144 (quotation).

35. Morris S. Arnold suggests that imperial and personal interests were usually aligned. Morris, "The Significance of the Arkansas Colonial Experience," *Arkansas Historical Quarterly* 51, no. 1 (1992), 69–73; Stanley Faye, "The Arkansas Post of Louisiana: Spanish Domination," *Louisiana Historical Quarterly* 27, no. 3 (1944): 637–38; Din and Nasatir, *Imperial Osages*, 77; Ray H. Mattison, "Arkansas Post: Its Human Aspects," *Arkansas Historical Quarterly* 16, no. 2 (1957): 133 (quotation).

36. Din, "Between a Rock and a Hard Place," 116–17; Din and Nasatir, *Imperial Osages*, 118–19; Gálvez to Fernando de Leyba, 13 January 1779, in *Spanish Régime in Missouri*, 1:164–65 (quotations).

37. Din, "Between a Rock and a Hard Place," 116–17; Arnold, *Rumble of a Distant Drum*, 45–46, 49–51; Faye, "Arkansas Post of Louisiana," 649–52; Villiers to Gálvez, 7 April 1777, leg. 190, fol. 92, PapC, AGI (quotation); Villiers to Unzaga, 15 January 1777, fol. 76, leg. 190, PapC, AGI; Villiers to Unzaga, 4 March 1777, leg. 190, fol. 84, PapC, AGI; González López-Briones, "Spain in the Mississippi Valley," 184–85.

38. Villiers to Unzaga, 26 October 1776, fol. 70, leg. 190, PapC, AGI; Villiers to Unzaga, 12 December 1776, fol. 74, leg. 190, PapC, AGI; Villiers to Unzaga, 7 February 1777, fol. 80, leg. 190, PapC, AGI; Villiers to Unzaga, 1 March 1777, leg. 190, fol. 83, PapC, AGI ("I don't fear anything"); Gálvez to Villiers (draft), 6 March 1777, leg. 190, fol. 90, PapC, AGI ("haughtiness and arrogance").

39. F. Todd Smith, "Wichita Locations and Population, 1719–1901," *Plains Anthropologist* 53, no. 208 (2008): 409–10; Timothy K. Perttula, *The Caddo Nation: Archaeological and Ethnohistoric Perspectives* (Austin: University of Texas Press, 1992), 203; F. Todd Smith, "A Native Response to the Transfer of Louisiana: The Red River Caddos and Spain, 1762–1803," *Louisiana History* 37, no. 2 (1996): 178–83; Elizabeth A. H. John, *Storms Brewed in Other Men's Worlds: The Confrontation of Indians, Spanish, and French in the Southwest, 1540–1795* (1975; reprint, Norman: University of Oklahoma Press, 1996), 304–6, 338; De Mézières to the viceroy, 20 February 1778, in *Athanase de Mézières*, 2:176 (quotation).

40. Charles Sprague Sargent, "Winthrop Sargent's Diary While with General Arthur St. Clair's Expedition against the Indians," *Ohio Archaeological and Historical Quarterly* 33, no. 3 (1924): 256–69. I am indebted to Kurt Windisch for this reference.

41. Jefferson to Albert Gallatin, 12 July 1804, in *Thomas Jefferson Papers*, series 1, General Correspondence, http://hdl.loc.gov/loc.mss/mtj.mtjbib013621 ("certainly the most gigantic"); "Communication," *American Citizen* (New York) 5, no. 1343 (24 July 1804): 2 ("no fat Englishman"); *National Intelligencer* (New York) 20, no. 5563 (24 July 1804): 3 ("a large concourse").

42. Jefferson to Robert Smith, 13 July 1804, in *Thomas Jefferson Papers*, series 1, General Correspondence, http://hdl.loc.gov/loc.mss/mtj.mtjbib013624 ("our populous cities"); *Washington Federalist*, no. 689 (20 October 1804): 3; *Connecticut Centinel* (Norwich), 31, no. 1586 (14 August 1804): 2 ("where it must remain"); *Morning Chronicle* (New York), no. 573 (8 August 1804): 2; A. K. Sandoval-Strausz, *Hotel: An American History* (New Haven, CT: Yale University Press, 2007), 24.

43. *Daily Advertiser* (New York), vol. 20, no. 5576 (10 August 1804): 2, 3 (quotations); "Regimental Orders," *Evening Post* (New York), no. 848 (10 August 1804): 3; Thomas Myers Garrett, "A History of Pleasure Gardens in New York City, 1700–1865" (PhD dissertation, New York University, 1978), 177, 217–45.

44. *American Citizen* (New York) 5, no. 1362 (16 August 1804): 3.

45. Jefferson to Smith, 13 July 1804, in *Thomas Jefferson Papers*, series 1, General Correspondence, http://hdl.loc.gov/loc.mss/mtj.mtjbib013624.

46. Terry P. Wilson, *The Underground Reservation: Osage Oil* (Lincoln: University of Nebraska Press, 1985), 7 (quotation); *Historical Statistics of the United States*, Millennial Edition Online, table Aa4404; Din and Nasatir, *Imperial Osages*, 375.

47. It is unclear whether savvy Osage negotiators or avaricious oil lobbyists were responsible for the creation of the underground reservation. Wilson, *Underground Reservation*, 101–23; Jean Dennison, *Colonial Entanglement: Constituting a Twenty-First-Century Osage Nation* (Chapel Hill: University of North Carolina, 2012), 103–4.

48. Wilson, *Underground Reservation*, 121–25; Sherman Rogers, "Red Men in Gas Buggies: The Tale of an Auction with Million-Dollar Bids," *Outlook* 134 (22 August 1923): 629–32; Prentiss T. Moore, "Lo, the Poor Indian, Gets a Few More of the White Man's Millions," *Oil Trade Journal* 9, no. 12 (1918): 45.

49. Bob Jackman, "Model for Improving the Osage Nation Mineral Estate" (study presented to Department of the Interior's BIA Osage Negotiated Rulemaking Committee), 27 September 2012, http://www.bia.gov/cs/groups/mywcsp/documents/text/idc-022613.pdf.

50. "Millionaire Indians," *Wall Street Journal*, 7 March 1918, p. 2.

51. Arnold, *Colonial Arkansas*, 82–85, 168; Unzaga to Orieta, 22 April 1775, leg. 107, PapC, AGI.

52. Arnold, *Rumble of a Distant Drum*, 35; Morgan to Baynton and Wharton, 5 April 1768, in *Trade and Politics*, 223 (quotation); Joseph Patrick Key, "Indians and Ecological Conflict in Territorial Arkansas," *Arkansas Historical Quarterly* 59, no. 2 (2000): 134.

53. Arnold, *Rumble of a Distant Drum*, 36; Allan J. Kuethe and José Manuel Serrano, "El astillero de La Habana y Trafalgar," *Revista de Indias* 67, no. 241 (2007): 763–76; G. Douglas Inglis, "The Spanish Naval Shipyard at Havana in the Eighteenth Century," in *New Aspects of Naval History: Selected Papers from the Fifth Naval History Symposium*, ed. Craig L. Symonds (Baltimore: Nautical and Aviation Publishing Company of America, 1985), 47–58; Servicio Geográfico del Ejército, J-5-4-98, "Plano, y perfiles, de la casa, y Maquina construida dentro del R.l Arsenal de la Havana, situado extramuros de la ciudad," Havana, 5 October 1757, AGI. I am indebted to G. Douglas Inglis for sharing a copy of this illustration.

54. Antonio J. Valdes, *Historia de la isla de Cuba, y en especial de La Habana* (Havana: Oficina de La Cena, 1813), 1:322n; Inglis, "Spanish Naval Shipyard at Havana," 47.

CHAPTER EIGHT—SURROUNDED: THE DEEP SOUTH INTERIOR

1. [Declaration of Rafael de la Luz], 2 May 1775, leg. 1220, PapC, AGI. On the militarization of Havana following the British occupation: Allan J. Kuethe, *Cuba, 1753–1815:*

Crown, Military, and Society (Knoxville: University of Tennessee Press, 1986); Sherry Johnson, *The Social Transformation of Eighteenth-Century Cuba* (Gainesville: University Press of Florida, 2001); and Celia María Parcero Torre, *La Pérdida de la Habana y las reformas Borbónicas en Cuba (1763–1773)* (Valladolid, Spain: Junta de Castilla y León, 1998). Alexander von Humboldt describes entering the harbor in Humboldt, *The Island of Cuba: A Political Essay*, trans. Shelley L. Frisch (Princeton, NJ: Markus Wiener, 2001), 78–82. On law regarding fishing boats: Parcero Torre, *Pérdida de la Habana*, 254.

2. Johnson, *Social Transformation*, 19–24; Kuethe, *Cuba, 1753–1815*, 39–40; Humboldt, *Island of Cuba*, 79–80 ("During my residence" and "offensive odor"); "Diary of Major Joseph Gorman," in *Cinco Diarios del Sitio de la Habana*, ed. Amalia A. Rodríguez (Havana: Biblioteca Nacional José Martí, 1963), 198 ("common people" and "a low cunning").

3. The best overall description of eighteenth-century Creek country is Robbie Ethridge, *Creek Country: The Creek Indians and Their World* (Chapel Hill: University of North Carolina Press, 2003); but see also H. Thomas Foster II, *Archaeology of the Lower Muskogee Creek Indians, 1715–1836* (Tuscaloosa: University of Alabama Press, 2007). Population figures vary. Peter H. Wood conservatively estimates that there were fourteen thousand Creeks in 1775, though some documents suggest that there may have been as many as eighteen thousand. Peter H. Wood, "The Changing Population of the Colonial Southeast: An Overview by Race and Region, 1685–1790," in *Powhatan's Mantle: Indians in the Colonial Southeast*, ed. Gregory A. Waselkov, Peter H. Wood, and M. Thomas Hatley, rev. and exp. ed. (Lincoln: University of Nebraska Press, 2006), 57–132; "A List of Towns and Number of Gunmen in the Creek Nation," enclosed in Francis Ogilvie to Thomas Gage, 8 July 1764, Thomas Gage Papers, American series, reel 140F, PKY, original in the William L. Clements Library, University of Michigan.

4. Marqués de la Torre to Julián de Arriaga, no. 880, 4 May 1775, leg. 1524, PapSD, AGI.

5. Relación de los gastos, enclosed in Marqués de la Torre to Arriaga, no. 880, 4 May 1775, leg. 1524, PapSD, AGI.

6. Marqués de la Torre to Arriaga, no. 880, 4 May 1775, leg. 1524, PapSD, AGI.

7. "A Talk from the Mortar and the Gun Merchant," 8 May 1763, in *Colonial Records of the State of Georgia* (Atlanta: Franklin, 1904–), 9:73–74 ("they are surprized"); copy of a letter from John Stuart to Jeffery Amherst, 2 June 1763, Thomas Gage Papers, American series, reel 140F, PKY; *South Carolina Gazette*, 28 May–4 June 1763; Juan Joseph Elixio de la Puente to Antonio María de Bucareli y Ursúa, 12 September 1766, Stetson Collection, bnd. 6542, 87-1-5/2, PapSD 2595, PKY ("they in the same way" and "could not freely cede"); Gage to Earl of Halifax, 10 March 1764, in *The Correspondence of General Thomas Gage*, ed. Clarence Edwin Carter (New Haven, CT: Yale University Press, 1931), 1:19 ("The Indians say"); Hillsborough to Gage, 11 June 1768, in *Correspondence of General Thomas Gage*, 2:70–71 ("by the Spirit").

8. Steven C. Hann argues that the Treaty of Paris was a turning point in Creek politics. With only a sole remaining European empire in the Southeast, the balance of power no longer hinged on the Creek Nation. Hann, *The Invention of the Creek Nation, 1670–1763* (Lincoln: University of Nebraska Press, 2004), 1–4, 264–72; Robin F. A. Fabel, *The Economy of British West Florida, 1763–1783* (Tuscaloosa: University of Alabama Press, 1988), 18, 20–21; Charles Loch Mowat, *East Florida as a British Province, 1763–1784* (1943; reprint, Gainesville: University of Florida Press, 1964), 17; Wood, "Changing Population," 57–132; Colin G. Calloway, *The Scratch of a Pen: 1763 and the Transformation of North America* (Oxford: Oxford University Press, 2006), 104; "At a Meeting of the Head Men of the Upper Creek Nation," 5 April 1763, in *Colonial Records of the State of Georgia*, 9:71–72 (quotations).

9. Peter C. Mancall, Joshua L. Rosenbloom, and Thomas Weiss estimate that the deerskin trade represented about 5 percent of the total production per person among southeastern Indians. That figure seems low, given the amount of time that men dedicated to the hunt. Mancall, Rosenbloom, and Weiss, "Indians and the Economy of Eighteenth-Century Carolina," in *The Atlantic Economy during the Seventeenth and Eighteenth Centuries: Organization, Operation, Practice, and Personnel*, ed. Peter A. Coclanis (Columbia: University of South Carolina Press, 2005), 297–322; "At a Congress Held at the Town of Pensacola," 26 May 1765, Lockey Collection, Public Records Office, London, Colonial Office, 5/582, PKY (quotation); Kathryn E. Holland Braund, *Deerskins and Duffels: The Creek Indian Trade with Anglo-America, 1685–1815* (Lincoln: University of Nebraska, 1993), 69–71; Gregory A. Waselkov, "The Eighteenth-Century Anglo-Indian Trade in Southeastern North America," in *New Faces of the Fur Trade: Selected Papers of the Seventh North American Fur Trade Conference, Halifax, Nova Scotia, 1995*, ed. Jo-Anne Fiske, Susan Sleeper-Smith, and William Wicken (East Lansing: Michigan State University Press, 1998), 193–222; Gregory A. Waselkov, "Seventeenth-Century Trade in the Colonial Southeast," *Southeastern Archaeology* 8, no. 2 (1989): 117–33; Gregory A. Waselkov, "French Colonial Trade in the Upper Creek Country," in *Calumet and Fleur-De-Lys: Archaeology of Indian and French Contact in the Midcontinent*, ed. John A. Walthall and Thomas E. Emerson (Washington, DC: Smithsonian Institution Press, 1992), 35–53.

10. Diego Ortiz Parilla to Marqués de Cruillas, 18 July 1763, Indiferente de Guerra, v. 260.B, 1760–1763, fol. 290, Archivo General de la Nación de México, Mexico City ("They cannot countenance"); George Johnstone and John Stuart to the secretary of state, 12 June 1765, in *Mississippi Provincial Archives: 1763–1766, English Dominion*, ed. Dunbar Rowland (Nashville, TN: Brandon, 1911), 1:187 ("It will be difficult"). There is a voluminous literature on gift giving among Native Americans. For one exploration of the subject in the Southeast, see Joseph M. Hall, *Zamumo's Gifts: Indian-European Exchange in the Colonial Southeast* (Philadelphia: University of Pennsylvania Press, 2009).

11. Thomas Boone to James Wright, 7 March 1764, enclosed in James Wright to the Lords of Trade, 27 March 1764, in *Colonial Records of the State of Georgia*, 28(pt. 2):45–46; Wright to the Lords of Trade, 5 July 1764, in *Colonial Records of the State of Georgia*, 28(pt. 2):81–84; James Grant to the Board of Trade, 30 August 1766, Public Records Office, London, Colonial Office, 5/541, p. 125, PKY; Upper Creeks to Johnstone, 16 May 1766, in *Mississippi Provincial Archives*, 1:529; Gage to Richmond, 26 August 1766, in *Correspondence of General Thomas Gage*, 1:104 (quotation).

12. "Declaraciones del Patron Manuel Caello, y el Capitan Estimaslayche," 15 February 1773, enclosed in Marqués de la Torre to Arriaga, no. 370, 26 February 1773, leg. 1524, PapSD, AGI; Braund, *Deerskins and Duffels*, 148–54, 158–62.

13. In the 1760s, public memory in Havana had it that Indians had fled to Florida to escape from the effects of the conquest. José Martín Félix de Arrate y Acosta, "Llave del Nuevo Mundo," in *Memorias de la Sección de Historia de la Real Sociedad Patriótica de la Habana* (Havana: Las viudas de Arazoza y Soler, 1830), 1:305; Ryan M. Seidemann, "The Bahamian Problem in Florida Archaeology: Oceanographic Perspectives on the Issue of Pre-Columbian Contact," *Florida Anthropologist* 54, no. 1 (2001): 9–23; Richard T. Callaghan, "Comments on the Mainland Origins of the Preceramic Cultures of the Greater Antilles," *Latin American Antiquity* 14, no. 3 (2003): 323–38; Barbara A. Purdy, "American Indians after A.D. 1492: A Case Study of Forced Culture Change," *American Anthropologist* 90, no. 3 (1988): 640–55; John E. Worth, *A History of Southeastern Indians in Cuba, 1513–1823* (Gainesville, FL: 2004), 2–4.

14. John Francis Gemelli Careri, "A Voyage round the World," in *A Collection of Voyages and*

Travels, ed. John Churchill (London: Awnsham and John Churchill, 1704), 4:537, 539. For a price list of goods in seventeenth-century Cuba, see Levi Marrero, *Cuba: Economía y Sociedad* (Madrid: Editorial Playor, 1975), 4:256–62 and 8:82–91.

15. John H. Hann, *Apalachee: The Land between the Rivers* (Gainesville: University Press of Florida, 1988), 15, 20, 137–38, 240; Hall, *Zamumo's Gifts*, 55–74; John W. Griffin, *Fifty Years of Southeastern Archaeology: Selected Works of John W. Griffin*, ed. Patricia W. Griffin (Gainesville: University Press of Florida, 1996), 199–201; John H. Hann, *Missions to the Calusa* (Gainesville: University of Florida Press, 1991), 326–432; John H. Hann, *Indians of Central and South Florida, 1513–1763* (Gainesville: University Press of Florida, 2003), 56–57, 179–86; Worth, *History of Southeastern Indians*, 5–6; Manuel de Montiano to the king, 20 July 1747, PapSD, leg. 866, 534, reel 46, PKY.

16. The first historian to explore systematically relations between Creeks and Cuba was Angel Sanz Tapia. His work was tremendously helpful in tracing the archival record. Sanz Tapia, "Las relaciones entre Cuba y los Indios de la Florida Oriental durante el dominio Ingles (1763–1783)," in *La influencia de España en el Caribe, la Florida, y la Luisiana, 1500–1800*, ed. Antonio Acosta Rodríguez and Juan Marchena Fernández (Madrid: Instituto de Cooperación Iberoamericana, 1983), 281–308; declaration of Manuel López de Gamarra and Juan Lendian, 21 October 1774, leg. 1219, PapC, AGI; Elixio de la Puente to Marqués de la Torre, 6 March 1773, leg. 1524, PapSD, AGI; Bernard Romans, *A Concise Natural History of East and West-Florida* (New York: n.p., 1776), 185–88; William Bartram, *Travels through North and South Carolina, Georgia, East and West Florida, the Cherokee Country . . .* (Philadelphia: James and Johnson, 1791), 227–28. On trade in the Gulf of the St. Lawrence: Laurier Turgeon, "French Fishers, Fur Traders, and Amerindians during the Sixteenth Century: History and Archaeology," *William and Mary Quarterly* 55, no. 4 (1998): 585–610.

17. "Declaraciones del Patron Manuel Caello, y el Capitan Estimaslayche," 15 February 1773, enclosed in Marqués de la Torre to Arriaga, no. 370, 26 February 1773, leg. 1524, PapSD, AGI; Elixio de la Puente to Bucareli, 6 March 1767, enclosed in Bucareli to Arriaga, no. 279, 12 March 1767, leg. 1515, PapSD, AGI ("could be of some importance"); "Declaraz. nes del Patron Fran.co Pelaez y el Yndio Chamilla de Nacion Uchiz," 5 May 1777, leg. 1222, PapC, AGI ("He doesn't understand").

18. Bentura Díaz to Conde de Ricla, 19 January 1764, in "From a Remote Frontier: Letters and Documents Pertaining to San Marcos de Apalache, 1763–1769, during the British Occupation of Florida," *Florida Historical Quarterly* 19, no. 3 (1941): 200 ("a thousand exclamations"); Pierce Acton Sinnot to John Stuart, 2 March 1768, "From a Remote Frontier: Letter and Report Passing between the Commanders at Apalache (St. Marks), Governor Grant at St. Augustine, General Haldimand at Pensacola, John Stuart, Superintendent of Indian Affairs, and General Gage, Commander-In-Chief, at New York, 1768–1769," *Florida Historical Quarterly* 21, no. 2 (1942): 137 ("look very gay" and "rich loud").

19. David Taitt, "Journal of David Taitt's Travels from Pensacola, West Florida to and through the Country of the Upper and Lower Creeks, 1772," in *Travels in the American Colonies*, ed. Newton D. Mereness (New York: Macmillan, 1916), 548–49 ("the sea is very" and "as some of their Women"); certification of Rafael de la Luz, enclosed in Marqués de la Torre to Gálvez, 11 April 1776, PapC, leg. 1221, AGI; Díaz to Conde de Ricla, 19 January 1764, in "From a Remote Frontier," *Florida Historical Quarterly* 19, no. 3 (1941): 200 ("cup of punch").

20. "Declaraciones del Patron Manuel Caello, y el Capitan Estimaslayche," 15 February 1773,

enclosed in Marqués de la Torre to Arriaga, no. 370, 26 February 1773, leg. 1524, PapSD, AGI; Marqués de la Torre to Arriaga, no. 370, 26 February 1773, leg. 1524, PapSD, AGI; and Elixio de la Puente to Marqués de la Torre, 6 March 1773, enclosed in Marqués de la Torre to Arriaga, no. 387, 28 March 1773, leg. 1524, PapSD, AGI (quotations).

21. Elixio de la Puente to Marqués de la Torre, 6 March 1773, enclosed in Marqués de la Torre to Arriaga, no. 387, 28 March 1773, leg. 1524, PapSD, AGI.

22. Marqués de la Torre to Arriaga, no. 625, 1 April 1774, leg. 1524, PapSD, AGI (directive to fishermen); [declaration of Manuel López de Gamarra and Juan Lendian], 21 October 1774, leg. 1219, PapC, AGI (persistence and intimidation); Marqués de la Torre to Arriaga, no. 777, 10 November 1774, leg. 1219, PapC, AGI (stinginess).

23. Braund, *Deerskins and Duffels*, 164–67; Martha Condray Searcy, *The Georgia-Florida Contest in the American Revolution, 1776–1778* (Tuscaloosa: University of Alabama Press, 1985), 12–13, 15, 20–21, 28–30.

24. [Declaración de] Melchor Feliú, 4 March 1763, enclosed in Bucareli to Arriaga, no. 279, reservada, 12 March 1767, leg. 1515, PapSD, AGI ("Captain of Indian Troops"); Fulgencio García de Solís to the king, 8 November 1754, leg. 846, PapSD, reel 17, p. 313, PKY; Alonso Fernández de Heredia to Arriaga, 30 October 1756, leg. 2542B, PapSD, reel 19, p. 214, PKY; "Testimonio de los autos fechos a con.ta de el coronel Don Miguel Román de Castilla y Lugo," 10 November 1761, leg. 17, exp. 10, fol. 157, Marina, AGN, reel 144G, PKY; *South Carolina Gazette*, 12–19 May 1759 ("suspicious"); *South Carolina Gazette*, 14–21 July 1759.

25. "Congress at Pensacola," enclosed in Johnstone and Stuart to the secretary of state, 12 June 1765, in *Mississippi Provincial Archives*, 1:190; "At a Congress held at the Fort of Picolata in the Province of East Florida . . . ," 9 December 1765, Colonial Office 5/548, p. 113, Public Records Office, London, 2:574, PKY (quotations); Stuart to Gage, 24 May 1770, Thomas Gage Papers, American series, reel 140H, PKY.

26. Wright to Hillsborough, 12 December 1771, in *Colonial Records of the State of Georgia*, 28(pt. 2):354 ("of the richest"); "A Talk from the Lower Creeks to John Stuart," 19 September 1772, enclosed in Stuart to Gage, 24 November 1772, Thomas Gage Papers, American series, reel 140H, PKY ("We hope"); Woody Holton, *Forced Founders: Indians, Debtors, Slaves, and the Making of the American Revolution in Virginia* (Chapel Hill: University of North Carolina Press, 1999), 51 ("both the opportunity").

27. Samuel Thomas to Stuart, 10 December 1774, enclosed in Stuart to Gage, 18 January 1775, Thomas Gage Papers, American series, reel 140H, PKY; [declaration of Rafael de la Luz], 2 May 1775, leg. 1220, PapC, AGI (quotation).

28. Marqués de la Torre to Arriaga, no. 880, 4 May 1775, leg. 1524, PapSD, AGI; Marqués de la Torre to Arriaga, no. 954, 28 September 1775, leg. 1220, PapC, AGI (quotation).

29. Allan J. Kuethe and G. Douglas Inglis, "Absolutism and Enlightened Reform: Charles III, the Establishment of the Alcabala, and Commercial Reorganization in Cuba," *Past and Present* 109 (1985): 118–43.

30. Marqués de la Torre to Arriaga, no. 954, 28 September 1775, leg. 1220, PapC, AGI; [declaration of Pedro Yoyasque], 8 January 1783, enclosed in Unzaga to Gálvez, no. 9, 22 January 1783, leg. 1524, PapSD, AGI.

31. [Declaration of Tomas de Noa and of Tibulayche], 16 July 1777, enclosed in Diego José Navarro to Gálvez, no. 7, 20 July 1777, leg. 1290, PapC, AGI; Marrero, *Cuba*, 12:27–28; "Noticias puestas en el Padrón General, conducentes á dar una puntual idea del estado en que se halla la isla de Cuba en el año de 1775," in *Colección de papeles científicos, históricos, políticos y de otros ramos sobre la isla de Cuba*, ed. José Antonio Saco (Paris: d'Aubusson

y Kugelmann, 1858), 1:395; Mowat, *East Florida as a British Province*, 76; John Gerar William de Brahm, *De Brahm's Report of the General Survey in the Southern District of North America*, ed. Louis De Vorsey, Jr. (Columbia: University of South Carolina Press, 1971), 90.

32. Kuethe, *Cuba, 1753–1815*, 44, 49, 82–83; Parcero Torre, *Pérdida de la Habana*, 217–24, 230.

33. "Relacion de los Gastos," 4 March 1773, enclosed in Marqués de la Torre to Arriaga, no. 387, 28 March 1773, leg. 1524, PapSD, AGI.

34. Johnson, *Social Transformation*, 52; Franklin W. Knight, "Origins of Wealth and the Sugar Revolution in Cuba, 1750–1850," *Hispanic American Historical Review* 57, no. 2 (1977): 233, 243; Marrero, *Cuba*, 10:136–38 (sugar production and slave imports). The transformation of Cuba into a sugar island is treated in Manuel Moreno Fraginals, *El Ingenio* (1974; reprint, Barcelona: Editorial Crítica, 2001), 5–86.

35. Julio Le Riverend, *Historia económica de Cuba* (Havana: Editorial Pueblo y Educación, 1974), 66, 111; Marrero, *Cuba*, 12:165.

36. Sherry Johnson, "El Niño, Environmental Crisis, and the Emergence of Alternative Markets in the Hispanic Caribbean, 1760s–70s," *William and Mary Quarterly* 62, no. 3 (2005): 368, 379–96.

37. "To the Royal Danish American Gazette," 6 September 1772, in *The Papers of Alexander Hamilton Digital Edition*, ed. Harold C. Syrett (Charlottesville: University of Virginia Press, 2011) (quotations); Johnson, "El Niño," 387–91.

38. Navarro to Gálvez, no. 802, 16 July 1780, and enclosure, leg. 1524, PapSD, AGI; "Relación de Quinze Yndios Uchises," 30 June 1780, enclosed in Navarro to Gálvez, no. 803, 16 July 1780, leg. 1524, PapSD, AGI.

39. Marrero, *Cuba*, 7:26–28.

40. Le Riverend, *Historia económica de Cuba*, 59–60; Marrero, *Cuba*, 10:257; Kuethe, *Cuba, 1753–1815*, 69–73.

41. On the Spanish Crown's refusal to permit export of aguardiente to Yucatán, see Marrero, *Cuba*, 10:257.

42. Nicolás Joseph Rapún to Marqués de la Torre, no. 803, 15 September 1775, leg. 1152, PapC, AGI; Marqués de la Torre to Arriaga, no. 954, 28 September 1775, leg. 1220, PapC, AGI. On Arriaga: *La política y los politicos en el reinado de Carlos III* (Madrid: Ediciones Rialp, 1962), 88–89.

43. Gálvez to Marqués de la Torre, 25 July 1776, leg. 1524, PapSD, AGI.

44. Marqués de la Torre to Gálvez, no. 1228, 9 October 1776, leg. 1524, PapSD, AGI.

45. "Declaraz.nes del Patron Fran.co Pelaez y el Yndio Chamilla de Nacion Uchiz," 5 May 1777, leg. 1222, PapC, AGI; [declaration of Tomás de Noa and Tibulayche], 16 July 1777, leg. 1290, PapC, AGI; "Declaraciones del Patron Joseph Bermudez y el Cacique Tunapé," 22 December 1777, enclosed in Navarro to Gálvez, no. 167, 15 January 1778, leg. 1524, PapSD, AGI.

46. Light Townsend Cummins, *Spanish Observers and the American Revolution, 1775–1783* (Baton Rouge: Louisiana State University Press, 1991), chap. 6.

47. David McCullough, *1776* (New York: Simon and Schuster, 2005), 115–246; Washington to John Hancock, 12 July 1776, Founders Online, National Archives (http://founders.archives.gov/documents/Washington/03-05-02-0205, ver. 2013-06-26) (quotation); Barnet Schecter, *The Battle for New York: The City at the Heart of the American Revolution* (New York: Walker, 2002), 104–5.

48. Benjamin Franklin to all captains and commanders of armed ships, 10 March 1779, in *The Journals of Captain James Cook on His Voyages of Discovery*, ed. J. C. Beaglehole, vol. 3,

pt. 2, *The Voyage of the* Resolution *and* Discovery, *1776–1780* (Cambridge: Cambridge University Press, 1967), 1535.

EPILOGUE

1. Davida Malo, *Hawaiian Antiquities (Moolelo Hawaii)*, trans. N. B. Emerson (Honolulu: Hawaiian Gazette Co., 1903), 28, 175; James Cook, "Journal of Captain Cook," in *The Journals of Captain James Cook on His Voyages of Discovery*, ed. J. C. Beaglehole, vol. 3, pt. 1, *The Voyage of the* Resolution *and* Discovery, *1776–1780* (Cambridge: Cambridge University Press, 1967), 265 (quotation).
2. Eleanor C. Nordyke, *The Peopling of Hawai'i*, 2nd ed. (Honolulu: University of Hawaii Press, 1989), 17–18; David E. Stannard, "Disease and Infertility: A New Look at the Demographic Collapse of Native Populations in the Wake of Western Contact," *Journal of American Studies* 24, no. 3 (1990): 328–30 (quotations).
3. Thomas Edgar, "Journal," in *Journals of Captain James Cook*, 3(pt. 2):1358.

⁑ ACKNOWLEDGMENTS ⁂

Thanks to Douglas Northrup, Marina Dobronovskaya, Jeff Hass, Uliana Gabara, and Vlodek Gabara for their assistance obtaining documents in Moscow and St. Petersburg; and to Olga Thomason for translating Ivan Solov'ev's report. Thanks also to John Worth for sharing his collection of sources on Creeks in Cuba. G. Douglas Inglis helped me obtain scores of letters from the Archivo General de Indias in Seville. His assistance was unexpected and indispensable, and I am especially appreciative of his generosity. Joshua Haynes contacted libraries and archives around the country and across the Atlantic to obtain the illustrations that appear in this book. I thank him for tackling the job, even while he was occupied finishing his dissertation. I owe much to Peter Wood, who has inspired and encouraged me to study the early American continent since I first met him in 1990. I am grateful to the American Philosophical Society, the Willson Center for Humanities and Arts at the University of Georgia, and the Richard B. Russell Foundation for supporting my research.

Lisa Adams at the Garamond Agency saw early promise in the manuscript and patiently helped me craft a compelling proposal. At W. W. Norton, my fellow northern Californian Tom Mayer—who as a child shared my confusion about the Russian River—understood the need for such a book and enthusiastically agreed to take on the project. He offered clear-sighted editorial advice at every turn.

I am grateful to Paulette Long, as always. She and I have traveled many miles since the Bicentennial in 1976! I thank Rachel Gabara for being my North Star through rough seas and calm waters. This book is dedicated to my two little Giants, Leo and Milo.

INDEX

Page numbers in *italics* refer to figures.
Page numbers beginning with 215 refer to endnotes.